THE SOCIOLOGY OF W. E. B. DU BOIS

The Sociology of W. E. B. Du Bois

Racialized Modernity and the Global Color Line

José Itzigsohn *and* Karida L. Brown

NEW YORK UNIVERSITY PRESS

New York

NEW YORK UNIVERSITY PRESS
New York
www.nyupress.org

An earlier version of chapter 1 was published as José Itzigsohn and Karida Brown, "Sociology and the Theory of Double Consciousness: W. E. B. Du Bois's Phenomenology of Racialized Subjectivity," *Du Bois Review*, 12(2): 231–248. In chapter 1 of this volume, we have developed and expanded the analysis presented in the article.

References to Internet websites (URLs) were accurate at the time of writing. Neither the author nor New York University Press is responsible for URLs that may have expired or changed since the manuscript was prepared.

Library of Congress Cataloging-in-Publication Data
Names: Itzigsohn, José, 1960–   author. | Brown, Karida, 1982–   author.
Title: The sociology of W.E.B. Du Bois : racialized modernity and the global color line /
José Itzigsohn and Karida L. Brown.
Description: New York : New York University Press, [2020] | Includes bibliographical
references and index.
Identifiers: LCCN 2019029128 | ISBN 9781479856770 (cloth) | ISBN 9781479804177
(paperback) | ISBN 9781479842292 (ebook) | ISBN 9781479830961 (ebook)
Subjects: LCSH: Du Bois, W. E. B. (William Edward Burghardt), 1868–1963. |
Sociology—United States—History. | African Americans—Social conditions. |
Race relations—United States—History.
Classification: LCC HM477.U6 I89 2020 | DDC 323.092—dc23
LC record available at https://lccn.loc.gov/2019029128

New York University Press books are printed on acid-free paper, and their binding materials are chosen for strength and durability. We strive to use environmentally responsible suppliers and materials to the greatest extent possible in publishing our books.

Manufactured in the United States of America

10 9 8 7 6 5 4 3 2 1

Also available as an ebook

Frontispiece: W. E. B. Du Bois seated in carved wood Victorian armchair, smiling, December, 1958. Source: W. E. B. Du Bois Papers (MS 312) Special Collections and University Archives, University of Massachusetts Amherst Libraries.

To our graduate students

DU BOIS MY ANCESTOR

Du Bois is not just a man but a rallying cry
For those who—in the academe can't muster a sigh
Those who because of their identity and experiences are aware of
    power
And what it does to those who are lower
As they have lived it through their lives
This is a roar by the one who was quiet
And who has just found their voice—in their own generation
Who are the first-gen of those who CAN call their reflections
    "knowledge"
Before us, the voices of our ancestors were quashed and unheard.
Make no mistake that even now
We would have to struggle to be recognized
They are "me-search" they would say.
They are too "biased" they would say.
"Your life story is not sociology" they would say.
He is a beacon of hope as he stands for all our ancestors who were
    never heard
He is our ancestor—we can point to and say
See he was a sociologist—a scholar denied

—Syeda Quratulain Masood

CONTENTS

Finding Du Bois

We discovered W. E. B. Du Bois at very different points in our careers, and we want to share with you our academic journeys into Du Boisian sociology. Defined in its simplest terms, Du Boisian sociology is a sociological approach that draws from the theoretical and methodological tradition of W. E. B. Du Bois and puts racism and colonialism at the center of the understanding of modernity. In telling how each of us encountered Du Bois, we follow a key Du Boisian insight, which is that lived experience is a basis for reflection about society. In his 1940 book *Dusk of Dawn*, aptly subtitled *An Essay toward an Autobiography of a Race Concept*, Du Bois reflects on his own life to illuminate questions of race and racism. Du Bois, who lived from 1868 to 1963, a period of profound social change that begins with the post–Civil War Reconstruction era and ends with the peak of the American civil rights movement, argues that the value of his life lies not in its details, compelling as they may be, but in its reflection of the broader problem of race during his lifetime.

W. E. B. Du Bois was a seminal figure in American sociology, a major figure in American arts and letters, a prolific scholar, and one of the nation's most influential Black political leaders and organizers for more than half a century. And yet, despite its critical importance, especially for the understanding of the making of the modern world, his work, almost from the start, has been largely ignored by sociologists. To be sure, sociologists knew about his work. After all, when the Department of Sociology of the University of Pennsylvania needed a scholar to conduct research on the city's Black community, they hired Du Bois. Furthermore, the Bureau of Labor Statistics also contracted him to conduct research on African American communities. And some of his contemporaries cited his writings.[1] Yet, he could only find jobs in historically Black institutions, and as the discipline institutionalized in Chicago, Du Bois's work was marginalized. This historical erasure of Du Bois was largely due to prejudice and racism. W. E. B. Du Bois entered a profession that had little to no interest in what a Black person had to say about society.

Like Du Bois, we want to share our own histories, not because they are particularly interesting but because they reflect a problem in the field of sociology—that a study of Du Bois's works is not included in our discipline, despite the fact that he himself was a sociologist. Our experiences were very different, but both of us have this in common: Neither of us discovered Du Bois as part of our training as sociologists.

Karida Brown: Finding Du Bois in My Homes away from Home

I discovered Du Bois in my second year of graduate school, at Brown University, when I was twenty-eight years old. It was at that point that so many doctoral students confront the path that lies ahead of them—that watershed moment when many of us decide whether we will stay in academia or fight the good fight in some other space. During that time I constantly asked myself, What am I doing here? Does any of this even matter? Can I even belong here, in this institution, in this discipline? I, a Black, cis-gender woman, a low-income, first-generation college student, discovered the writings of Du Bois later than I should have, yet fortunately for me at the time in my life when I needed him most. I needed to know that there was room for me and the world in which I lived in the discipline of sociology.

My first encounter with Du Bois occurred when I read *The Souls of Black Folk*, a collection of essays on race published in 1903 that introduced his seminal concept of "double consciousness" and went on to become a classic work of American literature. That book awakened something in my brain that up until that point had lain dormant. In fourteen short essays and what he called a "forethought," Du Bois eloquently gave words to all the intangible meanings of being a Black person in the United States at the turn of the twentieth century. His prose was clear yet lyrical, his arguments subtle yet full of force, and embedded in every sentence was a plain old truth. W. E. B. Du Bois spoke to my own soul. Imagine my surprise when I learned that he too had been a sociologist, and that *The Souls of Black Folk* was one of the early works in the field.

I was surprised because I did not encounter Du Bois in my own department but rather in the Department of Africana Studies. I was surprised because I did not know that people could write so vividly and intimately and still be allowed to call themselves sociologists. I was surprised to realize that *The Souls of Black Folk* was not a mere one-hit wonder but that Du Bois had written, spoken, and curated art, theater, and performances prodigiously, and that there exists a vast body of secondary literature on his life and work. I was pleasantly surprised and even comforted to learn that there was such a thing as a Du Boisian sociology that I could study and incorporate into my scholarly work, and that it had been there all along, hidden in plain sight.

If I were to describe what kind of sociology graduate student I was, I would say that I was at best middling. I came to class, read most of the assigned readings, and wrote cogent enough papers. In my theory courses I read my fair share of the work of white guys we were all supposed to read and cite—Max Weber, Karl Marx, and Émile Durkheim—and to add some "contemporary" flair to the mix, Peter Berger, Thomas Luckmann, Pierre Bourdieu, Michel Foucault, and Bruno Latour. Because I was personally curious about research methods, I took as many courses in that area as I could, not just the required introductory statistics and field methods courses but also courses in event history analysis, legal history, demographic techniques, and geographic information systems. I also took almost every demography course my program had to offer; in fact, I spent two years as a fellow at Brown's Population Studies and Training Center. Nothing that I ever did or said in class was remarkable. And yet, during my years of coursework, I struggled to find meaning in what I was learning. For me, the purpose of earning a PhD was to do something meaningful with it. I needed stakes.

I found those stakes in my "shadow" PhD program at Brown. That is, in the courses I took in Africana studies and comparative literature, in my weekly discussions as a fellow at Brown's Cogut Center for the Humanities, in independent studies with insurgent intellectuals around campus, in conversations with members of my graduate student community, and in every single course, discussion, and program that Professor B. Anthony Bogues offered during my time at Brown, I was repeatedly exposed to the key works of critical theory that helped me develop an intellectual framework to make sense of the world. It was in those spaces that I was introduced to Du Bois's books *Souls of Black Folk*, *Black Reconstruction in America*, and *Darkwater: Voices from within the Veil*, along with seminal texts written by such intellectuals as Sylvia Wynter, Audre Lorde, Stuart Hall, Frantz Fanon, Aimé Cesairé, Hannah Arendt, and Sigmund Freud.

It was also in those spaces that I earned my informal PhD in both the Black Radical Tradition and critical theory. By my fourth year of graduate school, I was coming into my own as an intellectual. I had identified a dissertation project that offered the stakes I had been looking for, I had made friends and found colleagues within the academy, and I had become fluent in a language that gave meaning to the social issues that interested me most. However, I was still unsure about how to transform my newfound intellectual prowess into actual scholarship. Thank God for José. José Itzigsohn was my dissertation chair, and he too shared a deep interest in the sociology of Du Bois. A watershed moment for me occurred when he invited me to cowrite an article on Du Bois's theory of double consciousness—the sensation of forming one's identity by "seeing oneself through the eyes of the other."

It was through a close reading of Du Bois and his contemporaries, including William James, George Herbert Mead, and Charles Horton Cooley, and then engaging in deep discussion about our ideas and putting pen to paper that I began to understand what it meant to publish a journal article as opposed to writing a term paper. We worked on the article for nearly a year, and the resulting piece, titled "Sociology and the Theory of Double Consciousness: W. E. B. Du Bois's Theory of Racialized Subjectivity," was published in the *Du Bois Review* in the fall of 2015. What I didn't know while we were collaborating on the article was that José had been thinking for more than a decade about writing a book about Du Bois's sociological program. From one generous invitation to collaborate on an article came another. This book is the result.

José Itzigsohn: Encountering Du Bois by Chance

I encountered Du Bois much later in my academic career than Karida did, and the incorporation of his work into my sociological practice was longer and more tortuous than hers. I acquired my PhD without reading Du Bois, in fact without even knowing who he was. My first job was as a postdoctoral visiting professor teaching Latin American studies at both Brown and the University of Massachusetts at Amherst. At U Mass Amherst I quickly learned that its main library was named the W. E. B. Du Bois Library. I also realized that several professors and students took pride in the fact that the university housed Du Bois's archives.

All these piqued my curiosity about who Du Bois was. I started reading his works, learning about the man himself, and trying to fill a gap in my education. I was then in my midthirties. It is unsettling to know that had I not taught those two semesters at Amherst, I might have gone through my entire career without knowing of Du Bois's relevance to the discipline of sociology, that is, until the publication in 2016 of Aldon D. Morris's ground-breaking work, *The Scholar Denied: W. E. B. Du Bois and the Birth of Modern Sociology.* However, not all the sociologists who pass through U Mass Amherst become Du Boisian sociologists. Perhaps it was the fact that growing up in Argentina I had already encountered the works of Frantz Fanon in my parents' bookshelves, or that I had had the good fortune of reading C. L. R. James's *Black Jacobins: Toussaint L'Ouverture and the San Domingo Revolution* in a Latin American history course as an undergraduate, or that what initially attracted me to sociology was the Latin American version of dependency theory that made me immediately realize the sociological importance of Du Bois. In any case, my desire to learn about Du Bois's work was further stimulated when I got a tenure-track position at Brown's Sociology Department as part of an effort to establish an ethnic studies program.

My colleague Paget Henry, who has been a source of inspiration during all these years, encouraged me to teach the introduction to ethnic studies course, and it was at that point that I started to teach Du Bois in undergraduate courses. But it took me much longer to incorporate Du Bois into sociology graduate seminars, and even longer to start writing about him. Although from the very beginning I realized that he was a major social theorist, it took me time to understand how to make that argument to sociologists. Eventually, I started to teach a classical sociological theory graduate seminar in our department, but the first years I taught it I did not teach Du Bois. It took me some more time until eventually I started to teach *The Souls of Black Folk* in relation to the work of George Herbert Mead and Alfred Schutz, two classical theorists of the self and subjectivity.

I did not teach the classical sociology seminar the year Karida entered our program, but rather a contemporary theory seminar. As I remember it, in that course we read Cedric Robinson's *Black Marxism: The Making of the Black Radical Tradition*, but we devoted only one week to the whole Black Radical Tradition whereas we devoted several weeks each to a discussion of the works of Jürgen Habermas, Michel Foucault, Pierre Bourdieu, and Bruno Latour. In short, for many years, I reproduced Du Bois's exclusion from sociology. That was how I was trained, and that was how I was training others. These days, I am happy to teach an entire seminar dedicated to reading and discussing Du Bois's work and Du Boisian sociology.

In the beginning, I taught Du Bois simply as a theorist of micro interactions and a theorist of race. It took me time to come to understand him as a global theorist and a critic of racialized modernity, the social system organized around racial differences. Reading his 1935 book *Black Reconstruction*, a history of the Reconstruction era and the role that Black people played in their own emancipation, led me onto that path. I always thought that that book talked not only about the Reconstruction era and the period when it was written but also about contemporary times. Moreover, I believe that if sociologists had read *Black Reconstruction* closely, we might have been spared much of the recent debate about the relationship between race and class. As soon as I read *Black Reconstruction*, I wanted to write an article comparing its sociological relevance to C. L. R James's *Black Jacobins*. It took me years to actually write that article, and I eventually did so only because Paget Henry insisted that I write it for a special issue of the *C. L. R. James Journal*, which he edits.

Although I thought from the beginning that Du Bois should be brought back to sociology, I felt isolated in making that claim. Until recently most sociologists did not recognize him as one of our own, and as one whose work we should know. Except for Paget Henry, I had no one to discuss this issue with. To be sure, other sociologists believed that Du Bois's work had a central place in the field, but I did not know them, and I imagine that they also felt quite isolated. For this reason, meeting Karida was crucial for me. In her I found not only a brilliant student but also someone who shared similar interests—someone with whom I could exchange ideas and from whom I could learn. Meeting Karida, and later on other students who created what might be called a

Du Boisian collective at Brown, broke my intellectual isolation. Now I could consider embarking on the project of thinking and writing about Du Boisian sociology because I had people I could discuss the undertaking with. I don't remember exactly how I came to ask Karida to write our article on double consciousness and sociological theory, but writing that article was such a positive experience that I decided to ask her if she would be interested in writing this book. Coincidentally, the same week we talked about that idea, NYU Press contacted us to ask if we were interested in writing a book about Du Bois's sociology. This is the result.

Towards a Du Boisian Sociology

Writing this book has been a journey of intellectual growth. Both of us share a deep appreciation and respect for Du Bois the scholar activist and a belief in the potential of a Du Boisian sociology to address the problems of the twenty-first century. We started this project believing that we knew his work fairly well. After all, we have read and taught him more than most sociologists have. Yet since we began working on this book, we have read all of Du Bois's books and hundreds of his journal articles, essays, letters, and speeches. What we discovered is that his work is much richer, more complex, and more sophisticated than we initially thought. We have also traveled long distances—from Providence, Rhode Island, to Los Angeles, California, from Montreal, Canada, to Chicago, Illinois—to discuss what we read and to explore the questions that motivate this book: If W. E. B. Du Bois is in fact a founder of the discipline of sociology and one of the most important social theorists, what exactly was his sociology? And what is a contemporary Du Boisian sociology? This book is our answer to these questions.

Introduction

Who's afraid of William Edward Burghardt Du Bois? In the words of leading Du Boisian sociologist Aldon Morris, he was a "scholar denied." He was also a radical activist, and, by the end of his life, a political outcast. Despite his being the founder of American empirical sociology and one of the most important social theorists of both his time and ours, sociologists have ignored him and his work. Today, the American Sociological Association's lifetime scholarly achievement award bears his name: the W. E. B. Du Bois Career of Distinguished Scholarship Award. Yet sociologists barely read his work, and its implications for the discipline today are rarely if ever discussed. This book aims to address these silences. It asks two questions: What was Du Bois's sociology, and what are its implications for the present?

Our first goal is to present and discuss Du Bois's sociological work. The discipline is belatedly starting to acknowledge the fact that Du Bois was one of the founders of sociology. Whereas Marx gave primacy to class, Weber to rationalization and bureaucracy, and Durkheim to solidarity and social order, Du Bois regarded race, racism, and colonialism as central to the construction of the modern world. For Du Bois, race was both the by-product and a central element of the cultural and economic organization of racial and colonial capitalism; it erected an intangible yet very real barrier: the "color line." It is from this premise that Du Bois's entire sociological program emerged. However, he did not just propose a sociology of race. For Du Bois, race was not a subfield of the discipline. Rather, he developed a sociological approach that puts racism and colonialism at the center of sociological analysis, contending that they were the pillars upon which the modern world was constructed. In this way, W. E. B. Du Bois was a theorist of racialized modernity.

We undertook this endeavor because we believe that Du Bois's work is of critical importance to the discipline of sociology, not only to redress the history of the discipline or for intellectual reparations purposes but because his sociology is deeply relevant to the present.

Our second goal is to encourage our readers to join a conversation about developing a contemporary Du Boisian sociology. Du Bois's sociology was, as Morris describes, "a path not taken" by the discipline; we believe it is time for the discipline to take that path. But for that to happen, we must first learn about his work by reading the full scope of his oeuvre. Furthermore, a contemporary Du Boisian sociology would have to go beyond Du Bois and incorporate ideas and issues raised by others, issues and ideas that he did not address or even anticipate. This would be in keeping with a Du Boisian spirit, as he was a self-reflective scholar who wrote extensively about how his ideas and opinions changed and evolved as he encountered new challenges. This book is a guide for those sociologists who want to embark on this journey. And it is an invitation to take part in a conversation about what it means for sociology to take a Du Boisian path in the present day.

A Scholar Activist, an Activist Scholar

The circumstances of one's life are unquestionably important in forging a person's thoughts. We are social creatures, and so are our ways of thinking about the world; that is one of sociology's basic premises. Du Bois consistently brought his personal experiences into his reflections and relied on his biography for his analysis. He wrote profusely about his life and about how his thinking changed along with the circumstances of his life. He wrote two autobiographies, *Dusk of Dawn*, published in 1940, and *The Autobiography of W. E. B. Du Bois*, written when he was in his nineties, published first in Russian in 1962 and only posthumously in English in 1968. There are also autobiographical reflections to be found in *Darkwater* and *The Souls of Black Folk*. In addition, Du Bois's essay "My Evolving Program for Negro Freedom," written in 1944, traces the evolution of his thought and his activism from the 1890s through the 1930s. Thus it is necessary to know something about Du Bois's life in order to understand his sociology. For that reason, we begin by highlighting key moments of his life as a scholar, organizer, and activist that shaped his thought. These highlights, though, cannot replace the reading of the excellent biographical works on his life written by David Levering Lewis.[1]

There are two things about Du Bois's life that are important to emphasize. The first is that he was both a scholar activist and an activist scholar. As Martin Luther King Jr. put it, "It was never possible to know where the scholar Du Bois ended and the organizer Du Bois began."[2] For Du Bois there was no contradiction between these roles. During his lifetime, he was always a scholar, a public intellectual, an activist, and an organizer. His scholarship was dedicated to dismantling the "color line," a term that he used to refer to the centrality of racialization and race in structuring social relations, and his activism drew from and informed his scholarship.

The second point to emphasize is that Du Bois's life and scholarship were, on the one hand, profoundly rooted in the African American experience and at the same time deeply global and decolonial in their aims. Du Bois's thinking and activism were rooted in the experience of American racism. He learned a bit about the color line in Great Barrington, the small town in western Massachusetts where he was born, and a great deal at Fisk University in Nashville, Tennessee, where he began his undergraduate studies in 1885. Much of his activism was focused on achieving political and civil rights and economic opportunity for African Americans in the United States. At the same time, and starting very early on during the time he spent at the University of Berlin (1892–94), he understood that the color line was a global structure. From then on he became a global thinker and a global activist fighting against colonialism and for freedom and equality for all people of color and colonized people around the world.

One example of this is Du Bois's participation in the First Pan-African Conference, held in 1900, where he delivered the conference's collective message to the world, entitled "To the Nations of the World." He went on to organize four Pan-African Congresses between 1919 and 1927, and he was named the international president of the Fifth Pan-African Congress, which met in Manchester, England, in 1945. In addition, because he could not attend the event personally, he sent an address to the All African People Congress that met in 1958 in Accra, capital of the newly independent Ghana. He dedicated the last years of his life to advocating Pan Africanism.

For Du Bois, the color line affected all people of color and all colonized people around the world, and he wrote extensively about past, present, and possible future connections between Africa and Asia. As a scholar and an activist, Du Bois belongs not only to the United States but also to the Africana diaspora and the Global South as a whole.

The details of the life of William Edward Burghardt Du Bois help us understand how he came to develop his worldview. Du Bois was born in 1868, three years after the end of the Civil War, in Great Barrington, Massachusetts. He was raised by his mother, a humble Black woman who worked as a cleaner; his father had left the family when Du Bois was a young child. In his *Autobiography* he remembers a town divided by race but also by class, where the poorest were actually the Irish factory workers. According to Du Bois's recollection, "In Great Barrington there were perhaps twenty-five, certainly not more than fifty, colored folk in a population of five thousand,"[3] with his family being among the oldest inhabitants of the region. After his mother's sudden death during his senior year of high school, through the initiative of prominent white people in Great Barrington, local churches raised money to enable him to go to college. It was there, at Fisk University, in Nashville, Tennessee, a Black college, where Du Bois's racial consciousness was tempered in the fire of the South.

During his time in the South, Du Bois learned that the United States was divided into two worlds, one white and one Black. Through expressed choice, he made his home in the one to which he was ascribed. The experience of encountering the color line is the first and most basic intellectual component of Du Bois's thought and makes him part of the large group of thinkers that constitutes the Black Radical Tradition, a group that also includes, among others, C. L. R. James, Lorraine Hansberry, Frantz Fanon, and Amie Cesairé.

After earning his undergraduate degree from Fisk, he matriculated at Harvard, where he was admitted only as a junior even though he already had a college degree. At Harvard, the philosopher and psychologist William James had a strong influence on Du Bois and was responsible for steering him away from philosophy and toward the social sciences. James's pragmatism represents a second lasting intellectual influence on Du Bois—the first being his lived experience of the color line.[4]

A scholarship he received during his graduate studies led to a year and a half in Berlin. At the time Germany represented the peak of the academic world, and Du Bois remembered with irony how he "derived a certain satisfaction in learning that the University of Berlin did not recognize a degree even from Harvard University, no more than Harvard did from Fisk."[5] At the University of Berlin, he spent time with the Verein für Socialpolitik, a group of scholars who addressed social policy issues. It was in this group's meetings that he became acquainted with the German sociologist Max Weber. Du Bois was particularly influenced by the work of Gustav Schmoller, who advocated an inductive empirical approach to the analysis of social problems.[6] Schmoller's inductive empiricism was a third intellectual influence on Du Bois, and its imprint can be seen in his empirical research program.

It was while studying in Germany that Du Bois realized that the color line was global, place-specific, and rooted in unequal power relations that were the result of European colonial expansion. At that point, however, his criticism of that world was confined to the place of Black people within that global order. His perspective eventually evolved into a full-blown critique of the system itself, not simply his position within it. Over time he developed a perspective that identified colonialism and racism as the structuring elements of historical capitalism. But we are getting ahead of ourselves.

Du Bois received his PhD from Harvard in 1894, making him the first African American to receive a doctorate from that university. He was one of America's best-trained scholars, having studied at two of the world's top universities. Yet, he was only able to secure a job at Wilberforce College in Ohio, teaching Greek and Latin. He proposed developing a sociology course there, but to his disappointment, the college showed no interest in such a course. In 1896, Du Bois was invited by the University of Pennsylvania to conduct a study of the Black community in Philadelphia, an opportunity that he seized immediately. His time in Pennsylvania resulted in *The Philadelphia Negro*, published in 1899, the first empirical urban and community study in American sociology. But Penn invited Du Bois to be only an assistant instructor and did not even offer him an office in the Department of Sociology while he carried out his study, let alone a permanent job.

In 1897, Du Bois accepted a job at Atlanta University, where he led the Atlanta sociology lab until 1910. While at Atlanta, he edited and published a series of annual research reports on Black communities, known as the Atlanta Studies, and conducted other rural and community studies.[7] In fact, he envisioned a hundred years' research program, consisting of ten-year cycles with studies on ten selected topics, with each study to be replicated every decade. At the same time, he published seminal works exploring theories of race. For example, in 1909, he published *John Brown*, his biography of the famous abolitionist. This work represented Du Bois's first attempt to address the study of whiteness, which would become one of his central and unacknowledged contributions to the field of sociology.

As the early twentieth century advanced, Du Bois saw his research funding reduced, a development that he attributed to his feud with Booker T. Washington, which occurred during the early years of the century. This was one of Du Bois's well-known political disputes. At the time, Booker T. Washington was the founder and president of Tuskegee Institute (now Tuskegee University) and the gatekeeper of the philanthropic funds that came from white northerners to southern institutions. In his famous 1895 Atlanta Compromise Speech, Washington urged Blacks in the South to accept the racist political and social order that existed at the time and to concentrate on improving their situation through industrial and vocational training.

Du Bois did not accept this approach. In his opinion, Black people had to demand political and civil rights and access to higher education to develop their own elites who would lead to the uplift of their people, describing these elites as the Talented Tenth. Du Bois included an essay in *The Souls of Black Folk* in which he criticized Washington, an essay that brought their differences into the open. Incidentally, Booker T. Washington's ghost writer was none other than Robert Ezra Park, the founder of the Chicago School of Sociology.

In addition to feuding with Washington, Du Bois found that his attitude toward detached academic research was evolving. At the beginning of his career, influenced by the pragmatists' approach to change that he studied at Harvard and the inductive empiricism that he studied in Berlin, Du Bois believed that by providing scientific evidence on the conditions of the Black community, he could persuade white elites to work toward undoing the racist social order. During his years in Philadelphia and Atlanta, he realized that this was not the case. Du Bois came to understand that no amount of the most well-researched empirical evidence would persuade whites to remove existing racial barriers. As a result, he became increasingly involved in activism and organizing. He was one of the founders of the Niagara Movement, a Black civil rights organization that later merged with the National Association for the Advancement of Colored People (NAACP), a group of which Du Bois was also a founder.

In 1910, he abandoned Atlanta and became the founder and director of the NAACP's new journal, the *Crisis*, which, during his twenty years of leadership, became the most important intellectual journal in the Black community. Du Bois, however, never stopped being a sociologist, and he continued writing sociological works after he left Atlanta. In 1915 he published *The Negro*, the first of three books in which he assessed the history and position of the Africana diaspora in the modern world.[8] In 1920, he published *Darkwater*, a collection of essays interspersed with poetry. Two essays in this volume, "The Souls of White Folk" and "The Hands of Ethiopia," advanced the phenomenological study of whiteness and its relation to colonialism. The essay titled "The Damnation of Women" pointed to his early awareness of the specificity of questions involving gender.

In his 1944 essay "My Evolving Program of Negro Freedom," Du Bois asserts that after leaving Atlanta in 1910, he abandoned Gustav von Schmoller and Max Weber for William James and Josiah Royce.

> I fell back upon my Royce and James and deserted Schmoller and Weber. I saw the action of physical law in the actions of men; but I saw more than that: I saw rhythms and tendencies; coincidences and probabilities; and I saw that, which for want of any other word, I must in accord with the strict tenets of Science, call Chance. I went forward to build a sociology, which I conceived of as the attempt to measure the element of Chance in human conduct. This was the Jamesian pragmatism, applied not simply to ethics, but to all human action, beyond what seemed to me, increasingly, the distinct limits of physical law.[9]

In this book we argue that both James and Schmoller were always part of Du Bois's sociology. The question of the role and scope of agency, the understanding of subjectivity, and the need to gather empirical data were always elements of Du Bois's sociology, elements that took a more or less central place in different situations and at different moments of his life.

It was during his years at the NAACP that Du Bois was involved in an important political confrontation with Marcus Garvey, the Jamaica-born political leader, journalist, and orator. This confrontation was more complex than the one with Booker T. Washington in that it involved different styles of leadership. Garvey was a charismatic leader of the masses; Du Bois was a prudish and sometimes aloof intellectual. Garvey supporters were mostly working class; Du Bois appealed more to the middle class. In the end, their relationship evolved into mutual aggression and bitter recrimination.

While both Garvey and Du Bois embraced Pan-Africanism and Black identity, they did so in very different ways. Garvey advocated Black separatism, the return to Africa, and the development of Black businesses. Du Bois, at that time, advocated integration, education, and civil and political rights for Blacks in the United States. Although he was a Pan-African activist and embraced a connection with the Africana diaspora and people of color around the world, he asserted that the struggle of African Americans was for integration and full equality in the United States. This confrontation is important because, as time passed, Du Bois would come close to some of Garvey's positions, although with different justifications than the ones Garvey used.

By the 1930s, Du Bois's views on how to address the pervasiveness of racism in the United States had shifted yet again. He had become increasingly pessimistic about the possibilities of integration overcoming the depth of racism in the short term. In 1934, Du Bois abandoned his work at the NAACP over political differences regarding its integrationist policy, which he believed was not working. At that point Du Bois was arguing that Black people in America should develop their own cooperative economy. Although this position was close to Garvey's, Du Bois did not argue for this approach on the grounds of Black nationalism, as Garvey did, but rather as a strategy for community survival until such time as Black people could be full citizens and equal members in American society. And Du Bois did not simply advocate the development of Black businesses, as Garvey did, but rather the development of a cooperative economy, a belief that reflected his socialist leanings.

After leaving the NAACP, Du Bois returned to Atlanta University, where he served as chairman of the Department of Sociology from 1934 to 1944. It is important for sociologists to note this fact, given that many argue that Du Bois left the discipline when he first left Atlanta in 1910. At Atlanta University, he started a publication called *Phylon*, an interdisciplinary journal on issues of race and culture that is still being published today. He also tried to revive his community studies research program by involving the Black land-grant colleges in a broad program of empirical research. He hoped that this research program would generate information that would help address the question of Black unemployment and, in particular, help lead to the development of a self-supporting community economy, which was the focus of his efforts. His forced retirement from Atlanta University in 1944 prevented this program from coming to fruition.

During his second tenure at Atlanta University, Du Bois also published important books that reflect the broad scope of his work. *Black Reconstruction*, published in 1935, showcases his encounter with the ideas of Karl Marx. Marxism was the fourth and final important intellectual tradition that influenced Du Bois's thinking, along with the Black Radical Tradition, James's pragmatism, and Schmoller's inductive empiricism. But Du Bois incorporates Marxism in a creative way and in his own terms. In *Black Reconstruction*, he developed an analysis of the intersection of class and race in the American social structure in the nineteenth century, and he argued that the enslaved Black people, rather than the North or the abolitionists, were the actors of their own emancipation. Furthermore, Du Bois presents a theory of the racial state that views the end of Reconstruction as a result of a convergence of class and racial interests between the northern bourgeoisie and the southern white elites and poor that reconstituted the white ruling bloc. The difference between the early and late Du Bois is the incorporation of Marx's ideas and the critique of racial and colonial capitalism as a historical system.

His 1940 book, *Dusk of Dawn*, analyzes the place of race in the modern world through an examination of his own life history. This book is an early example of what today we call auto-ethnography, and it shows how lived experience can be used for theoretical analysis. *Dusk* advances the phenomenological study of the Black and white experience and puts it in the historical context of Du Bois's life—prefiguring C. Wright Mills's argument that the sociological imagination aims to put biography in the context of history and social structure.

In 1944, Du Bois was forcefully retired from Atlanta University, as his institutional support within the university disappeared. After his dismissal from Atlanta, Du Bois returned to the NAACP and focused his work on promoting Pan Africanism, long a personal passion. During these years, he published two important books in which he developed his anticolonial thinking. *Color and Democracy*, published in 1945, presents an analysis of colonialism at the end of World War II and urges the architects of the new international order to address the colonial question. The book also presents an analysis of the intersection of class, race, and the state in the colonial order. Perhaps more importantly, his 1947 work, *The World and Africa*, situates the history of Africa and the slave trade within a global relational world history. In this book, Du Bois elaborates on the idea that the exploitation of racialized and colonial labor was a core element that structured the capitalist world system. These books present Du Bois's theoretical analysis of the racial and colonial character of historical capitalism in its most developed form.

Pan-Africanism was a constant in Du Bois's thinking, but his understanding of the concept also changed over the years. In his early Pan-African work, Du Bois expressed his belief that Black Americans would lead their African brethren into the modern world, much as the Talented Tenth would lead the African American masses. In his later years, however, he came to believe that it was the African anticolonial movement that would lead the Africana diaspora. His understanding of the movement's goal also changed. Rather than pursuing a belief in uplifting Africa and the Africana diaspora into Western modernity, Du Bois started to seek answers to the questions of how to build independent nations within the historical institutions of African societies that promoted a collectivist orientation. In his late years, Du Bois became convinced that Western models of development did not provide a path forward for newly independent African nations.

In the post–World War II years, Du Bois was also an activist for world peace and against nuclear weapons. His activism included a run for the US Senate in 1950 in New York on the ticket of the American Labor Party. A difficult event in his late life was his indictment and federal trial in 1951 for his activities as chair of the Peace Information Center. He was acquitted of all charges, but the course of the trial affected him. He expected the Talented Tenth to come to his defense. Instead, he found that given the fears aroused by the Red Scare, many of his friends and colleagues in the struggle for civil rights distanced themselves from him. His disappointment about this turn of events comes through clearly in his writings. In fact, Du Bois's left turn, which ultimately led him to join the Communist Party—his last act before permanently leaving the United States—distanced him from the established civil rights organizations and their leadership.

Despite his acquittal, Du Bois's passport was revoked, and he was not allowed to travel abroad until 1958, a situation that forced him to decline many invitations to speak at international gatherings. Du Bois was invited to address the 1955 Bandung conference in Indonesia, whose purpose represented Du Bois's ideal of African and Asian cooperation, but he could not attend that event. He also could not attend the 1957 ceremonies marking Ghana's independence, to which he was invited by Kwame Nkrumah, the leader of Ghana's independence movement and a strong proponent of Pan-Africanism. On that occasion Du Bois wrote to Nkrumah, calling upon the new African states to build a socialism based on communal African practices. When the United States government finally returned Du Bois's passport to him in 1958, he traveled to the Soviet Union and to China. In both countries he was received by their top leaders—then Nikita Khrushchev and Mao Zedong.

The invitations to address the Bandung conference and attend the celebration of Ghana's independence, along with the fact that he was received by the heads of states of world powers, point to the stature that Du Bois had toward the end of his life as a Pan-Africanist and anticolonial thinker and activist. This is important to note because people sometimes remember him only for his writings on the Talented Tenth or on double consciousness, and the global and anticolonial dimensions of Du Bois's thinking and activism are missed. He was a man of the Global South.

Toward the end of his life, Du Bois embraced socialism and focused his activism on Pan-Africanism and anticolonial solidarity. The latter was particularly the case after his 1951 trial, when he perceived that important segments of the Black elites in the United States had abandoned him. But his support for socialism was always rooted in the experience of the Africana diaspora and colonized people. The color line was at the root of Du Bois's understanding of modernity, but his thinking on how to undo it evolved. He had always understood the color line as global, but in his early years he was a pragmatist who believed that science could show whites the errors of their ways and that Black elites could uplift the masses. Over time, he came to understand the color line as intrinsic to colonial and racial capitalism, and he thought that decolonization, African-centered development, and socialism were the ways to undo it.

In 1961 Nkrumah invited Du Bois to travel to Ghana to direct the writing of the Encyclopedia Africana. At the age of ninety-three, Du Bois decided to accept the invitation and moved to Ghana to undertake a new project. He died there, a Ghanaian citizen, in 1963. There he received a state funeral. Paradoxically, it was Du Bois and not Garvey who ended his days in Africa. As Martin Luther King Jr. remarked, Du Bois "died in exile, praised sparingly and in many circles ignored. But he was an exile only to the land of his birth. He died at home in Africa among his cherished ancestors, and he was ignored by a pathetically ignorant America but not by history."[10]

Du Bois was a unique individual who produced a monumental oeuvre, more than most people can even imagine. Yet it is important to note that he did not work alone. He was a mentor, a teacher, a collaborator, and an organizer, a person deeply embedded in intellectual and activist networks. At Atlanta, as Aldon Morris and Earl Wright II have shown, he created a school, working with others such as Monroe Work, Richard R. Wright, George Haynes, and Mary Ovington. As an organizer of the Atlanta conferences, he invited and conversed with leading scholars of his time, among them Franz Boaz and Jane Addams. He also conversed with such leading Black feminists as Ida B. Wells and Anna Julia Cooper, from whom he undoubtedly learned, although probably not enough. As a civil rights and Pan-African activist, Du Bois was in the center of the organizing networks of important international gatherings. Toward the end of his life, his friendships with Kwame Nkrumah and George Padmore[11] were central in shaping his vision of a Pan-African socialism.

Du Bois's was a fascinating life that encompassed the whole world— from Great Barrington, Massachusetts, to Accra, Ghana, from Atlanta, Georgia, to Berlin, Germany, from New York City to Beijing, China. As a thinker and an organizer, he participated in some of the most important political debates of his time in not only the United States but the whole world. His writing was prolific and his oeuvre is immense. Yet at the same time, he was always embedded in networks of intellectual exchange and collaboration.

Du Bois's Critical Sociology

While Du Bois developed the first sociology school, his contributions were not appreciated by the discipline. As sociologist Aldon Morris points out, Du Bois's sociology represented "a path not taken."[12] More than a century after his early work, scholars continue to argue that Du Bois's contribution to the emergence of American sociology should be recognized by the discipline. Two scholars in particular have led this charge. Morris in *The Scholar Denied* details how Du Bois built a school of empirical scientific sociology in Atlanta well before the Chicago School built a sociology based on community and urban studies, and how the gatekeepers of the discipline intentionally excluded Du Bois and his research from the mainstream.[13] Earl Wright II, in his 2016 book, *The First American School of Sociology: W. E. B. Du Bois and the Atlanta Sociological Laboratory*, describes the depth and scope of the pioneering research that Du Bois and his collaborators conducted to study Black life through the Atlanta University Studies.[14] This book shows how the Atlanta School pioneered empirical research methods that later on became part of the mainstream tools of sociology. A third relevant work is Reiland Rabaka's *Against Epistemic Apartheid: W. E. B. Du Bois and the Disciplinary Decadence of Sociology*, published in 2010.[15] Rabaka is not a sociologist and his book has not made inroads in the discipline, yet it is important because it presents a detailed analysis of Du Bois's early empirical sociological work.

With few exceptions, however, previous sociological studies of Du Bois have focused on his urban and community studies conducted between 1896 and 1910, particularly *The Philadelphia Negro* and, recently, the Atlanta University Studies. In fact, at the beginning of his career Du Bois carried out systematic community studies on the Black population in America, and making use of these studies, he came to propose a unique methodological approach that combined history, statistical analysis, and sociological interpretation. This approach was different from the one developed at Chicago two decades later in that it placed the social actions of individuals and communities within their historical context, emphasized the structural constraints created by the color line, and paid attention to the agency of Black people.

But from the very beginning Du Bois was a social theorist as much as a ground-breaking empirical sociologist. He was the first social theorist to analyze the historical and social construction of race, its interaction with economic inequality and social class, the phenomenology of racialized lived experience, and the working of the racial state, a political institution in which race is the organizing principle. While Du Bois's thinking was based on his experience as a Black person in the United States, his understanding of race and racialization, meaning the ongoing process of making race, was global. Du Bois saw racialization and colonialism as global processes that constructed a historical system of exploitation, oppression, and dispossession of people of color. At the same time, he always emphasized that racialized people had the possibility of agency to try to take control of their lives and their communities, in spite of the constraints imposed by the racist societies in which they lived.

The first sentence of a recent book by the sociologists Mustafa Emirbayer and Matthew Desmond, titled *The Racial Order*, asserts that "there has never been a comprehensive and systematic theory of race."[16] Unlike most contemporary sociologists, these authors have read Du Bois extensively and cite a wide range of his works. They rightly credit him with developing many research lines on race, but conclude that he was not consistent and systematic in his theorizing. Contrary to Emirbayer and Desmond, we argue that Du Bois did in fact develop a theoretical perspective that put racialization, colonialism, and coloniality at the center of the understanding of modernity and sociological theorizing.[17] Furthermore, while Emirbayer and Desmond offer a theory of race that can be extended to different social fields, such as gender, ethnicity, or class, Du Bois's theorizing is rooted in history and context, and arose through the analysis of a particular historical social formation—racialized modernity.[18]

Key Concepts

It is important to emphasize that Du Bois's sociology was not a sociology of race but a critique of racialized modernity.[19] To fully grasp his original sociological approach, it is necessary to understand how he used key theoretical concepts. This section introduces the main concepts that build Du Bois's theoretical frame. To help the reader, the glossary at the end of the book presents short descriptions of these concepts and their use throughout the book.

Racialized Modernity

Modernity is a vague concept used to refer to our contemporary historical period. Different scholars define modernity by reference to various social processes, including the growth of urbanization and industrialization, the rise of bureaucracy, the application of science and technology to production and everyday life, the deepening of the division of labor, and the spread of secularization and democracy. Modernity is seen as a positive phenomenon, usually linked to ideas of progress and civilization and to the image of a successful present or a desirable future. This teleological vision of a historical trajectory lies behind Marx's historical laws of motion of capitalism, Durkheim's transition from mechanical to organic solidarity, Weber's rise of bureaucracy and rationality, and all the late-nineteenth- and early-twentieth-century historical development models. It also lies behind Talcott Parsons's pattern variables and the post–World War II modernization theory.

But modernity was always tied to colonialism. And the progressive vision of modernity occludes this fact. For Du Bois, what stood at the center of his time was the color line that produced a global racial division. The defining characteristics of modernity for Du Bois were colonialism and the creation of race, the invention of whiteness, and the global denial of humanity and multiple forms of exclusion, oppression, exploitation, and dispossession constructed along racial lines. Hence we describe his sociology as a critique of racialized modernity. Du Bois reflects in his autobiography,

> Had it not been for the race problem early thrust upon me and enveloping me, I should have probably been an unquestioning worshiper at the shrine of the established social order and of the economic development into which I was born. But just that part of this order which seemed to most of my fellows nearest perfection, seemed to me the most inequitable

and wrong; and starting from that critique, I gradually, as the years went by, found other things to question in my environment.[20]

Modernity, for Du Bois, is racialized. And his sociology sought to analyze, criticize, and ultimately undo this historical construct. But as Du Bois notes, his understanding of the modern world changed with time and with the events of his own struggle against racism. At the beginning of his scholarly and activist career, Du Bois accepted the notions of progress that sustained the existing social order but questioned the position of people of color within it. Over the years, he became a critic of racial and colonial capitalism as a whole. As he puts it in his posthumously published autobiography, "At first, however, my criticism was confined to the relation of my people to the world movement. I was not questioning the world movement in itself. What the white world was doing, its goals and ideals, I had not doubted were quite right. What was wrong was that I and people like me and thousands of others who might have my ability and aspiration, were refused permission to be a part of this world."[21]

From the beginning Du Bois saw the color line as global and tied to the emergence of the Atlantic slave trade. But at the beginning of his career as a scholar and an activist, he believed in the possibility of persuading American and European white elites of the error of their ways. Du Bois believed that presenting scientific data demonstrating that racial barriers explained the stunted progress of the Black masses would persuade the white elites to remove racial barriers. Then it was up to the Talented Tenth, the elite of the Black population, to uplift the masses. This was his Talented Tenth theory. It was an elitist theory in that it accepted the cultural backwardness of the Black masses and put the elites in the role—and the duty—of uplifting their people. The early Du Bois was an elitist, and for this he has been justifiably criticized.

At the same time, from the very beginning Du Bois asserted that Black people had the capacity for agency. He also insisted that the gaps between whites and Blacks could be closed, something that was strongly denied by the racism prevalent among sociologists at the time, either in its popular biological version or in the culturalist version that was more accepted among social scientists.[22] Finally, it is important to point out that Du Bois's Talented Tenth was not a big-money philanthropic elite but instead an educated elite of teachers, professors, religious leaders, and small-business owners, a petite bourgeoisie of sorts. Ultimately, the Talented Tenth theory was Du Bois's early attempt at figuring out how to deracialize modernity.

Over time Du Bois realized that he could not persuade the white elites through the presentation of scientific data and rational arguments, as he came to realize that racism and colonialism were pillars of capitalism, an understanding he developed through his original incorporation of the work of Karl Marx. He understood capitalism as a historical system based on the global production of commodities for markets through the exploitation of labor. But unlike Marx, who began his theorization of capitalism from the perspective of the European factory worker, Du Bois looked at capitalism from the perspective of racialized and colonized workers. Whereas Marx tried to show that exploitation worked through the exchange of equivalent amounts of labor without coercion, for Du Bois, coercion and oppression were permanent features of the experience of racialized and colonial labor and of racialized modernity.

Racialized Subjectivity and Agency

Racialized modernity generated for Du Bois a particular kind of subjectivity. By "subjectivity" we mean the forms and patterns of understanding, thinking, and feeling about the self, other people, and the world we live in.[23] Du Bois's phenomenology analyzed the construction of the self and of racialized subjects' modes of understanding. His best-known articulation of the phenomenology of racialized subjectivity is the theory of double consciousness.[24] Mainstream theories affirm that the self and subjectivity are built through social interaction, communication, and mutual recognition. Du Bois's theory of double consciousness analyzes how the veil—Du Bois's metaphor to describe the work of the color line in the process of self-formation—interrupts interactions, communication, and recognition among people who inhabit social spaces organized around the color line, a fact that early theorists of the self, such as William James, George Herbert Mead, and Charles Horton Cooley, failed to see.

Racialized subjectivities and selves are formed in specific oppressive social locations. But Du Bois insisted on the possibilities of agency for both the racialized and the colonized. In "Sociology Hesitant," an unpublished essay written in late 1904 or early 1905, Du Bois argues that sociology's goal is to determine the scope of law and chance in human action. For Du Bois, chance refers to the ability of people to make undetermined choices and affect the reality in which they live. Du Bois set his argument for chance against the prevalent approaches of his time, such as Comte's, which postulated sociology as the study of an abstractly conceived society, or Spencer's, which took a deterministic position in the study of human action.

Du Bois borrowed the language of chance from William James. James argued for the recognition of the role of chance, which for him meant the presence of meaningful alternative courses of action, and against the idea that human actions were fully determined. James did not negate causation or constraints; he acknowledged that actions were taken in contexts—contexts formed by external constraints and by the individual's views—and he argued that once actions were taken they became definite and part of a new constraining context. But James argued that at any particular point, alternatives existed and therefore moral action was meaningful.[25] For the pragmatists, the self was socially constructed but retained the possibility of making choices and generating social alternatives.

While Du Bois's contention that people can affect the reality in which they live was articulated in the language of pragmatism, that belief emerged from his own experience fighting the color line and asserting the humanity of racialized people. Du Bois's take on human agency was rooted in the Black Radical Tradition. Furthermore, he saw human action as taking place in the context of a world structured around colonialism and the color line, something the pragmatists were oblivious to.

Du Bois referred to the constraints to action as the realm of law. Law refers to the historically created institutions that regulate social practices and limit the ability of individuals to make choices. Du Bois refers to two types of law-like regularities, which he refers to as two rhythms—one that he likens to physical law, external to human action, and another that emerges as the result of planned human activity and can change as a result of such activity. In "Sociology Hesitant," he gives as an example the functioning of a women's club, and he also mentions human customs, laws, patterns of trade, and the organization of government. That is, the limits to human action are the result of the institutionalization of repeated contingent human action. The color line was the product of historical contingencies and agencies.

For Du Bois, the multiple forms of individual and collective action of the racialized could challenge the color line and the conditions of the lives of racialized and colonized people. All through his life Du Bois rooted the struggle for recognition of the humanity of racialized and colonized people and for a more humane society in the cultural resilience and creativity of people of color. He did so early in his life in the final chapter of *The Souls of Black Folk*, in which he links the assertion of Black humanity to the sorrow songs, and late in his life in his 1957 response to Kwame Nkrumah's invitation to attend the ceremony marking Ghana's independence, in which he argues that the new independent African countries should build political and social orders based on African communitarian traditions rather than on Western modernity.

The Color Line

The color line—the division of people according to racial classifications—stands, then, at the center of Du Bois's understanding of modernity and subjectivity. But his understanding of the color line changed over the course of his life and career. Du Bois was the first sociologist to propose a social constructionist approach to the analysis of race. This approach is rooted in the analysis of historical processes of labor exploitation, cultural classifications, and social exclusions. Race is both a category of oppression and exclusion and a form of group identification. Du Bois struggled all his life to dismantle the first but also to define and build the second. As Nahum Chandler points out, the question of group constitution and construction was one of Du Bois's central concerns.[26] And an important concern of Du Bois's theoretical work was to consider the materials with which African Americans and the Africana diaspora are to construct their identity.

Du Bois's first attempt to theorize race is elaborated in "The Conservation of Races," his presentation to the American Negro Academy in 1897, in which he argues that world history is the history of groups, not individuals, and not of any group but of racial groups. He asks, What is a race? and then responds, "It is a vast family of human beings, generally of common blood and language, always of common history, traditions and impulses, who are both voluntarily and involuntarily striving to-gether for the accomplishment of certain more or less vividly conceived ideals of life."[27] In this definition, Du Bois alludes to common blood, a reference to biological lineages and ancestry. But he refers also to lan-guage, common history, and traditions, and gives history and traditions a greater weight than common blood. The former is always the basis of racial formation, while the latter is only generally so. These two themes continue to be present in his discussion. Later in the text he asserts, "What is the real distinction between these nations? Is it the physical dif-ferences of blood, color and cranial measurements? Certainly, we must all acknowledge that physical differences play a great part, and that, with wide exceptions and qualifications, these eight great races of to-day follow the cleavage of physical race distinctions."[28] These references to blood and physical differences have created some debate concerning whether at this point he had broken with the dominant biological un-derstanding of race. While Du Bois makes concessions to the biological common sense of his time, it is clear that he thinks that the more rel-evant and important differences are the product of social history.[29] He asserts, "But while race differences have followed mainly physical race lines, yet no mere physical distinctions would really define or explain the deeper differences—the cohesiveness and continuity of these groups. The deeper differences are spiritual, psychical, differences—undoubtedly based on the physical, but infinitely transcending them."[30] Philosopher Kwame Anthony Appiah notes that in "Conservation," Du Bois equates race to a Herderian notion of peoplehood: a group of common history and of common destiny. Du Bois emphasizes the common striving of racial groups and their contributions to human history as groups.[31]

Shortly after the presentation and publication of "Conservation," Du Bois published "The Study of Negro Problems," a key text for under-standing his sociological thinking.[32] In this essay, Du Bois argues that empirical community studies should include four elements: historical analysis, statistical description, sociological interpretation, and the an-thropological measurement of bodies. As in "The Conservation of Races," Du Bois is preoccupied with the dominant biological language of race of his time. But rather than accept this language, his goal is to undermine it by using the same methods as "scientific" racism. This Du Bois does in the Atlanta study of 1906, which directly confronts the question of measurement of physical differences and concludes that there are no physical differences between people ascribed to different races.[33]

As time passed, this concern with demonstrating the absence of physical differences faded. Already in *The Negro*, published in 1915, Du Bois asserts that there are no physical differences between the races, that there is no one homogenous Black or white race, and that there are many physical differences within each race. This is a formulation that he would return to repeatedly in his writings, always emphasizing that differences between social groups are the product of sociohistorical processes, not biological or essential cultural differences.

Du Bois argues that race, in the sense of groups separated by the color line, was the result of historical processes of social exclusion. His understanding of these processes also changed over time. When he wrote *The Philadelphia Negro*, Du Bois believed that racism was the product of ignorance and that science could enlighten white elites to undo racial barriers. In *John Brown*, published in 1909, he argues that prejudice is the result of the rise of a wrong interpretation of Darwin's theories.[34] In *The Negro*, published in 1915, he attributes the pervasiveness of prejudice to the slave trade, the historical process of transforming human beings into chattel. But in *Black Reconstruction* and *The World and Africa*, texts written in the 1930s and 1940s, after Du Bois's engagement with Marx's theories, discourses of racism and racial inequalities are described as resulting from the need to justify a global system of exploitation and dispossession of people of color, based on colonialism.

In *Dusk of Dawn*, we encounter his mature understanding of race. He reiterates that internal diversity within groups and the mixing of populations render any scientific definition of race invalid. He asserts, "Thus it is easy to see that scientific definition of race is impossible; it is easy to prove that physical characteristics are not so inherited as to make it possible to divide the world into races . . . [A]ll this has nothing to do with the plain fact that throughout the world today organized groups of men by monopoly of economic and physical power, legal enactment and intellectual training are limiting with determination and unflagging zeal the development of other groups."[35] Addressing the question of how then one could know who is Black, he answers, "I recognize it quite easily and with full legal sanction; the Black man is a person who must ride 'Jim Crow' in Georgia."[36] Furthering his conceptualization of race, he elaborates, "Perhaps it is wrong to speak of it at all as 'a concept' rather than as a group of contradictory forces, facts and tendencies."[37] For the mature Du Bois, race is a product of institutionalized power. Racialization and racism were the product of a system of global colonial exploitation, but they also became constitutive and structuring elements of modernity, not just its by-product.

As Du Bois moved away from his early ideas of common fate and group striving, he began to identify common history and self-making action as the bases for group formation. Despite the violent history of the Africana diaspora, despite slavery and exploitation, Du Bois always emphasized the capacity for resistance and agency. He went to great lengths to describe the ways Black people have built their own lives and institutions behind the color line. From his earliest works, Du Bois was concerned with showing the liveliness of Black communities and organizations despite the hostile and dire conditions in which they lived. This goal informs his work in *The Philadelphia Negro* and the Atlanta Studies, and is also clearly present in *The Negro*, in which Du Bois details the ways Black enslaved people opposed slavery and the progress the freed people made through their own actions during Reconstruction, a topic to which he returns in detail in *Black Reconstruction*.

Du Bois developed a social constructionist understanding of race informed by historical processes that institutionalized racial differences and privileged the power and action of the dominant white group. He regarded these historical processes as global and inherent to historical capitalism, but not definitive: group formation among the racialized, including organizing communities and creating shared cultural meanings, was a way of resisting oppression and potentially building emancipatory collective action.

Du Bois was also the first sociologist to develop the study of whiteness as lived experience. In his writings, he recognizes that the veil affects not only the racialized but also the racially dominant group. If the lived experience of the racialized is characterized by double consciousness, the lived experience of the racializing is characterized by ignorance and bad faith. Du Bois shows that racial discourses and understandings became part of the natural attitude of whites. His analysis of white subjectivity reveals how it constructs social inequality and furthers racial and colonial capitalism.

Undoing the Color Line

As a scholar, an activist, and an activist scholar, Du Bois was committed to eliminating the color line, and dedicated much of his life's efforts to that goal. His activism, though, was informed by his evolving sociological understanding of the color line and racialized modernity.[38] The young Du Bois believed that as a result of centuries of slavery, Black people were not ready to function efficiently in society—and by "efficiency" he meant the ability of people and groups to adapt to the social order and thrive within it. Much like the early white sociological thinkers, Du Bois believed that there was a cultural gap between the Black masses and the white mainstream. Yet unlike the white mainstream thinkers of his time, Du Bois believed that it was possible to close that gap.[39] Furthermore, he believed that the uplifting of the Black masses was the task of Black people themselves, specifically the Black elites, the Talented Tenth.

The early Du Bois believed that with the right leadership and access to education, the Black population would be able to become an efficient social group.[40] In *The Philadelphia Negro* Du Bois analyzes the internal class structure of the Black community and describes an elite composed of educators, clergy, small merchants, and some professionals. This relatively small group of educated, middle-class individuals, the Talented Tenth, plays an outsized role in Du Bois's initial thinking. Du Bois's early writings combined an early statement of modernization theory (uplifting through the action of the Talented Tenth) with an early statement of incorporation theory (the Black masses adapting to the expectations of the white mainstream and working efficiently within it).

The young Du Bois, in writing *The Philadelphia Negro* and conducting the Atlanta Studies, believed in the possibility of persuading white elites to abandon racism. He viewed their racism as a product of faulty knowledge and information: If they would understand the predicament of African Americans, they would let the Talented Tenth do the work of uplifting the group. His early writings often mention the importance of the encounter between the Black and white elites. If the white elites were acquainted with the Black elites, he believed, they would realize that by ending the barriers to progress, Black people would become just as efficient as whites.[41] Yet, in *Dusk of Dawn* he asserts that this approach was fruitless. He realized that there was no audience for his scientific findings, that no matter how much evidence he could provide, whites would not change their minds.

As Du Bois explains in "My Evolving Program for Negro Freedom," his understanding of the process of change evolved. During his time in Atlanta he realized the importance of political activism to achieve civil and political rights. His description of the masses also changed. Already in his biography of John Brown he emphasizes how the Black masses have changed themselves.[42] In this stage of his political and sociological evolution, he puts a stronger emphasis on the actions of organizations and the masses. Thus, in *The Negro* he asserts that since Emancipation, despite dire expectations and predictions from the white community, the Black masses amassed wealth and education through hard work and self-organization in churches and mutual aid societies. Anticipating his analysis in *Black Reconstruction*, Du Bois praises the work of the Black political leaders in the Reconstruction period in promoting widespread educational and economic opportunities.

In the 1930s Du Bois's views on how to address the pervasiveness of racism evolved yet again. He had become increasingly pessimistic about the possibilities of overcoming the depth of racism in the short term. In 1934, Du Bois abandoned his work at the NAACP over political differences regarding its integrationist policy, which he believed was not working. Du Bois's new approach to understanding and fighting racism comes through in his writings. In *Black Reconstruction*, he coins the term the "psychological wage" of whiteness, what we may today call "white privilege"—that is, the benefits that being white confers in everyday life and in the construction of self-esteem, and that make whites invest in protecting racial inequality. In *Dusk of Dawn*, Du Bois notes the resilience of whites' irrational beliefs and habitus of domination. At this point Du Bois also emphasizes the role of the masses in their own emancipation. This comes across clearly in *Black Reconstruction*, in which he shows how runaway enslaved people won the Civil War and forced the North to emancipate them; in *Dusk of Dawn*, he advocates for the development of a Black-owned cooperative economy to withstand racism. He still believed that the educated elites had a role to play in Black emancipation, but it was an accompanying role, not the leading role that he imagined in "The Talented Tenth."[43]

Du Bois always understood the color line as global, but in his early Pan-African work, he stated his belief that Black Americans would lead their African brethren into the modern world, much as the Talented Tenth would lead the African American masses. In his late years, however, Du Bois came to believe that it was the African anticolonial movement that would lead the Africana diaspora. He came to understand the color line as intrinsic to colonial and racial capitalism, and he thought that decolonization, African-centered development, and socialism were the way to erase it.

This Book

We have written this book so that young sociologists will not have to go through the same experiences of belatedly discovering Du Bois as we did. We write it so that sociologists who did not study his work in graduate school will have a tool with which to start becoming familiar with it. And we write it so that the discipline of sociology will not be able to continue to deny or ignore the full scope of Du Bois's work or his relevance as a social theorist. In this book we build upon the work of the legion of Du Boisian scholars who have worked to redress this erasure. Our contribution to this long tradition of scholarship on Du Bois is to define his sociological program and explore what a Du Boisian sociology could be in the twenty-first century. However, three elements of tension run through this book.

First is the tension throughout the text between Du Bois's voice and our own. This tension exists because we were intentionally generous with the use of extended quotations. By doing this, we sought to have Du Bois's eloquent and powerful voice come through in the text to convey a point, bolster an argument, or locate his thinking at a particular moment in history. Du Bois's voice has for so long been suppressed and his work understudied that we thought it important to make sure that his voice can be heard clearly in this work. To do so, we drew from sources that are less often cited, with the intent of leaving a trail of references for a reader to follow up on.

There is also a tension regarding the use of biography. We struggled to strike the right balance between theoretical analysis and information about Du Bois's own life. Several works deal with his biography, notably the two volumes by historian David Levering Lewis, who won Pulitzer Prizes for both works. Many other books explore specific aspects of Du Bois's life and help illuminate how his life and his thought were intertwined because of his position on the color line. While not wanting to duplicate these efforts, we realized that ignoring his life story would impoverish the text by failing to consider the context through which his sociology emerged—that as a Black person he moved in the upper echelon of the white world during the nineteenth and twentieth centuries. Therefore, we chose to bring his life into our analysis by way of biographical montage. We draw from key moments in his life to set the scene for where he was both spatially and intellectually at the time.[44]

Finally, we struggled with the tension among articulating the contours, complexities, and contributions of W. E. B. Du Bois the man, Du Bois's sociology, and a contemporary Du Boisian sociology. Although we are admirers of Du Bois, we did not want to present him as infallible. Although Du Bois achieved many extraordinary things during his lifetime, he was not a man without faults. Further, Du Bois's personal life, while interesting, was not our primary concern. Our goal was to focus on Du Bois's sociology—that is, the sociological works carried out by Du Bois himself. Defining Du Bois's sociology is a main goal of this book. But we have another goal. We want to explore, along with you, the reader, the potentiality of Du Bois's sociology in this contemporary moment.

We believe that acknowledging the full extent of Du Bois's theoretical and empirical contributions can help us rethink the discipline as it currently exists. Our goal is to provide the building blocks for the construction of a contemporary Du Boisian sociology, reflecting on what it would mean for sociology at the beginning of the twenty-first century to take that seldom-traveled path of learning from Du Bois's sociology. Developing a contemporary Du Boisian sociology, however, is not a task for an isolated scholar or even two scholars working together. This book aims to generate a lively conversation as to what exactly is Du Boisian sociology and why it is of critical importance that we understand its roots and significance, a conversation in which we hope many people will participate. Our hope is that the reader will come to realize the potential of a Du Boisian sociology, something that we of this generation must make and remake, based on our life and times.

1

Double Consciousness

The Phenomenology of Racialized Subjectivity

Double consciousness is the pillar of Du Bois's analysis of subjectivity, that is, the culturally and historically situated understandings of self and other, and the meanings that construct the world in which we live. The best-known articulation of double consciousness is found in the first essay in *Souls*, titled "Of Our Spiritual Strivings," although Du Bois initially introduced the concept in an essay titled "Strivings of Negro People," published in 1897 in the *Atlantic*. In these essays Du Bois poses the question that animates his exploration of the lived experience of Black people: "How does it feel to be a problem?" In answering this question Du Bois develops a phenomenological analysis of Black subjectivity; that is, he sets out to describe how Black people experience the world and themselves in everyday life.[1] The sociological importance of the theory of double consciousness is barely acknowledged.[2] Yet Charles Lemert, one of the few sociologists who recognizes its importance, asserts, "Du Bois's double-self concept deserved a prominent place in the lineage of self theorists which, from James and Baldwin through Cooley to Mead to the symbolic interactionists, has been one of sociology's proudest traditions."[3]

But the theory of double consciousness does not simply deserve a place in a lineage of the early sociology of the self. The theory is central to the analysis of subjectivity under racialized modernity, and it addresses an important "ontological myopia" in the work of other classical theorists of the self and subjectivity.[4] The theory points to something that other theorists of the self and identity who were Du Bois's contemporaries, such as William James, Charles Horton Cooley, and George Herbert Mead, did not comprehend: the significance of the color line as the central social structure organizing lived experiences under racialized modernity. As a result of his personal encounter with the color line, Du Bois is able to analyze racialized subjectivity in ways that his contemporaries, and many of our contemporaries, cannot. The theory of double consciousness points to the epistemological importance of lived experience for social theory.

Double Consciousness

Double consciousness describes the subjectivity of racialized subjects. In one of his most famous and often cited passages, Du Bois asserts that Black people in America are

> a sort of seventh son, born with a veil, and gifted with second-sight in this American world,—a world which yields him no true self-consciousness, but only lets him see himself through the revelation of the other world. It is a peculiar sensation, this double-consciousness, this sense of always looking at one's self through the eyes of others, of measuring one's soul by the tape of a world that looks on in amused contempt and pity. One ever feels his two-ness,—an American, a Negro; two souls, two thoughts, two unreconciled strivings; two warring ideals in one dark body.[5]

In this short but significant paragraph, Du Bois introduces the three elements of the theory of double consciousness: the veil, twoness, and second sight. The veil—i.e., the color line—structures the subjectivity of racialized modernity. The social world is seen and experienced differently on either side of the color line. The veil works as a one-way mirror: Whites project their own constructions of Blacks onto the veil and see their projections reflected on it. They have the power to define themselves and others, and for them, the racialized subject is invisible. On the other hand, the projections of whites onto the veil become realities that Black subjects have to contend with in their self-formation.

The internal processing of the external gaze gives rise to the second element of Du Bois's theory: the sense of twoness. Twoness means that in the process of self-formation, the racialized subject must account for the views of two different social worlds—the Black world, constructed behind the veil, and the white world, which dehumanizes Blacks through lack of recognition of their humanity. The third element of the theory of double consciousness is second sight. A world in which the racialized can "only see himself through the revelation of the other world" forces Black people to wrestle with constant dehumanization but, on the other hand, allows them to glance into the white world. This may in some cases neutralize the mirroring effects of the veil. And indeed, Du Bois relied on his second sight to develop an analysis of white subjectivity and lived experience.[6]

Du Bois's phenomenological account of racialized subjectivity is present throughout his work, but it is most developed in *The Souls of Black Folk* and in *Dusk of Dawn*.[7] *Souls* is a text that most sociologists do not embrace.[8] Few are aware that Max Weber wanted to get the work translated and published in German. Charles Lemert suggests that *Souls* is a canonical work in the discipline, and views its rejection as an example of how work that comes from behind the veil is rendered invisible.[9] We agree that *Souls* should be read and discussed as a classical text in the discipline, a text that inaugurates the phenomenological study of Black subjectivity, that is, the analysis of the basic structures of Black consciousness and experiences.

Du Bois's analysis of double consciousness is rooted in his reflections on the life of African Americans, particularly in the South, and in his own lived experience. Autobiographical reflections are at the core of his theorizing. In "Of Our Spiritual Strivings," the first essay of *The Souls of Black Folk*, he tells of a moment in which he understands that he is different. It is a moment in his boyhood when a girl refuses his card while playing a group childhood game. Du Bois does not return to this particular moment in *Dusk of Dawn* or in his posthumous *Autobiography*, but those texts make it clear that when he was growing up in Great Barrington, Massachusetts, a predominantly white community of middle- and working-class families, he understood the difference the color line makes. And in *Souls* he asserts that this difference is built on what he describes as "a thousand and one little actions." Still, if it is in his growing up in New England that Du Bois learns that he is different, it is only when he goes south to study at Fisk that he fully comprehends the exclusionary work of the color line.

His experiences studying at Fisk and later on teaching in Atlanta are front and center in the essays in *Souls*. Some of the essays, including "Of the Black Belt" and "Of the Quest of the Golden Fleece," are descriptions of the social and economic structure of the South and the place and predicament of African Americans within it. Sociologists should recognize these as early examples of community studies. Other essays in the book, such as "Of the Meaning of Progress" and "Of the Coming of John," are analyses of the lived experience and subjectivity of Blacks in the South around the turn of the twentieth century. We should pay close attention to these essays, which focus on Du Bois's analysis of the lifeworld of Black people. In the first one, "Of the Meaning of Progress," he recalls his experience teaching school in rural Tennessee, describes the hopes of the people he teaches, and shows how those hopes were crushed by the color line. In "Of the Coming of John," Du Bois returns to the question of the lifeworld inhabited by rural Blacks in the South, to the hopes and attempts related to leaving it behind, and to the disciplinary forms and effects of the color line.

One essay in particular reflects the development of Du Bois's thought and political activism at the turn of the twentieth century: his essay titled "Of Mr. Booker T. Washington and Others." In this essay, he airs his political differences with Booker T. Washington, who was the most influential power broker between the white elite class and the Black serving institutions of the time.[10] Du Bois's disagreement with Washington was central to his development as an intellectual and political leader. In particular, his differences with Washington regarding the importance of accessing higher liberal education and demanding political rights led Du Bois to become a founder of the Niagara Movement, and later the NAACP.

Whereas few sociologists embrace *Souls*, *Dusk of Dawn* is almost entirely ignored by the discipline. Upon the republication of *Souls* on its fiftieth anniversary, Du Bois stated that he thought about updating the book but decided not to so do because the work reflected his thoughts in 1903 and he hoped that other works would reflect his evolving thought. This is indeed what *Dusk* accomplishes.

While neither *Souls* nor *Dusk* was intended as a scholarly text, these two books' analysis of racialization and self-formation makes them key texts for sociological theory. *Dusk* is organized as an autobiography, but Du Bois explains that his life "is a digressive illustration and exemplification of what race has meant in the world in the nineteenth and twentieth centuries," adding that the "peculiar racial situations and problems could best be explained in the life and history of one who has lived them. My living gains its importance from the problems and not the problems from me."[11]

In *Dusk* Du Bois takes us through his life and tells us how his understanding of what race is and how it works changed as a result of his encounters with the color line as a scholar and as an organizer. Even more than *Souls*, *Dusk* underscores the centrality of lived experience in Du Bois's analytical approach. There we learn how his time in Germany led him to understand race as a global phenomenon, not just an American one, and to attend to the presence of local differences within the global construction of the color line. As he explains, when he was young he thought that the color line was particular to the United States, but his years studying in Germany led him to realize that racialization was a global phenomenon and that "the majority of mankind has struggled through this inner spiritual slavery."[12] Already at the beginning of the second essay in *Souls,* titled "Of the Dawn of Freedom," he states, "The problem of the twentieth century is the problem of the color line, the relation of the darker to the lighter races of men in Asia and Africa, in America and the islands of the sea."[13] As sociologist Katrina Quisumbing King shows, many people are aware of the first part of the phrase—the color line as the central problem of the twentieth century—but not of its continuation—that is to say, Du Bois's understanding of the color line as a global phenomenon. Du Bois was the first sociologist to develop a historical and social constructionist understanding of race.[14]

Du Bois's autobiographical reflections in *Dusk* help him to develop a phenomenological analysis of the lived experience of racialized people, and to link lived experiences to a broader analysis of the intersections of class, race, and colonialism. His aim in this book and others was not so much to give an account of his life and worldviews relating to the color line as to theorize from his own experience as a Black person living behind the veil. He introduces the book thusly:

> My life had its significance and its only deep significance because it was part of a Problem; but that problem was, as I continue to think, the central problem of the greatest of the world's democracies and so the Problem of the future world. The problem of the future world is the charting, by means of intelligent reason, of a path not simply through the resis-

tances of physical force, but through the vaster and far more intricate jungle of ideas conditioned on unconscious and subconscious reflexes of living things; on blind unreason and often irresistible urges of sensitive matter; of which the concept of race is today one of the most unyielding and threatening. I seem to see a way of elucidating the inner meaning and significance of that race problem by explaining it in terms of the one human life that I know best.[15]

This focus on lived experience and its link to global structures of oppression, exploitation, and exclusion is a central element of Du Bois's sociology and something that differentiates it from the sociologies of his, and our, contemporaries.

Du Bois relies on his second sight to develop an analysis of the lived experience of whiteness. The phenomenology of whiteness, an inquiry into the meaning and experience of being socially constructed as white, was a subject of Du Bois's analyses throughout his life. He first explored this in his biography of John Brown, and further developed it in "The Souls of White Folk" and "The Hands of Ethiopia," two essays in *Darkwater*. He also dedicates a full chapter to this topic in *Dusk*, and returns to it, in a global context, in his analysis of the subjectivity of the colonialist in *The World and Africa*.

For Du Bois, whiteness confers material privilege as the result of the exploitation of workers of color and the appropriation of colonial resources, and it also grants social and symbolic privilege, as a result of the power to define the social world and the many little and large forms of social recognition attached to this power in everyday life. In *Black Reconstruction* Du Bois refers to these forms of privilege as the psychological wage of whiteness. The power of whites to impose a definition of who they and others are is the basis for racialization and double consciousness.[16]

To better understand the uniqueness and importance of Du Bois's theory of double consciousness, it is useful to contrast it with the work of his contemporaries who were theorizing about subjectivity and the self. Classical as well as contemporary theorists affirm that subjectivity and the self are constructed and reconstructed through continuing social interaction. At the core of social interaction are the acts of communication and mutual recognition between individuals in society.

William James, Du Bois's mentor and friend at Harvard, was one of the first American theorists of the self and subjectivity. James was a professor of philosophy and psychology and one of the founders of the philosophical approach known as pragmatism. In his book *The Principles of Psychology*, James divided the self between the "I" (the self as knower) and the empirical self, or "me" (the self as known, the accumulated experiences that constitute the self).[17] He further divided the "me" into four components: the material self (our material existence, our bodies, our families, our possessions), the spiritual self (our states of consciousness and feelings), the pure ego, and, most important in this context, the social self. The social self emerges through interaction and mutual recognition between people and from the internalization of the images that others have of us.

As mutual recognition is central to the formation of the self, lack thereof has a devastating impact on the formation of the self. Of this condition James wrote,

> No more fiendish punishment could be devised, were such a thing physically possible, than that one should be turned loose in society and remain absolutely unnoticed by all the members thereof. If no one turned round when we entered, answered when we spoke or minded what we did, but if every person we met "cut us dead" and acted as if we were non-existing things, a kind of rage and impotent despair would ere long well up in us, from which the cruelest bodily tortures would be a relief; for those would make us feel that, however bad might be our plight, we had not sunk to such a depth as to be unworthy of attention at all.[18]

Recognition is so crucial to one's own subjective understanding that we may develop as many social selves as there are individuals that recognize us.[19] In James's formulation, this splitting divides us into several selves, which may at times adopt group positions that are misaligned with one another. Du Bois reformulates this splitting of the selves into the concept of "twoness."

Although James's work was highly influential in theorizing the self as a social construct, the most important classical sociological theorist of the self is George Herbert Mead. Mead and Du Bois had parallel careers. Both studied at Harvard and in Germany. Both were influenced by James's pragmatism and his emphasis on the creative possibilities of human action. But they came to understand these possibilities in very different terms. Mead, like James, was a pragmatist who believed in the possibilities of progress through human creativity and adaptation. In their opinion, social interaction and communication in the solving of social problems was the way in which progress took place.

For Mead, what characterizes the self is that "it is an object to itself."[20] That is, the self emerges through the process of social interaction as a result of the ability of individuals to reflect on themselves and their actions by taking the position of other individuals or the community as a whole. In other words, the self develops from internalizing the view that others have of us. This is a two-stage process. First, children internalize the viewpoints of specific individuals who are close to them, such as their parents. As they grow up, they learn to take in the views of larger groups, and finally they are able to internalize the views of society in general, which Mead describes as the "general other."

Mead uses the metaphor of "the game" to describe this process. We learn to play a game by internalizing its rules. Once we do that, we can fulfill any role in the game because we know what is expected from us. In internalizing the positions of one's community toward different aspects of cooperation and interaction, the self "reflects the unity and structure of the social process as a whole."[21] According to Mead, only when a person "takes the attitudes of the organized social group to which he belongs . . . does he develop a complete self."[22] He emphasizes the mind's ability to symbolize, that is, to attach shared meanings to signs beyond the specific situation in which they are found. This ability to symbolize characterizes human communication and allows individuals to understand the viewpoints and take the position of their community.

Furthermore, Mead, like James, realized that lack of recognition can hamper the development of the self. If a person is denied recognition, Mead wrote, "if others could not take his attitude in some sense, he could not have appreciation in emotional terms, he could not be the very self he is trying to be."[23] This, he asserts, is especially the case in caste societies, in which the lack of communication and the absence of common attitudes "cut down the possibility of the full development of the self."[24] In discussing caste society, Mead makes brief references to India and to

Europe's Middle Ages, yet he does not extend this thinking to explore how the American racialized social system affects self-formation.

For Mead, communication allows individuals to recognize and come to understand new people they encounter, and in this way allows individuals to expand the boundaries of the society in which they live. Communication and recognition are also the base for democracy, as those elements allow people to acknowledge the rights of others. Pragmatist thinkers such as James and Mead believed in perfecting democracy in America through interaction, creativity, and adaptation. Yet the veil prevented them from seeing those who were excluded from recognition and were precluded from full participation in the broad processes of societal communication and therefore from American democracy. In contrast, Du Bois's encounter with the color line allowed him to see and understand the limits to recognition, communication, and democratic participation. Du Bois's social position and lived experience as a Black man allowed him to build on the pragmatist tradition and to transcend it in his theorizing and analysis, which we examine in the coming sections of this chapter.

Charles Horton Cooley was another early theorist of subjectivity. A sociology professor at the University of Michigan in the early twentieth century, he is mostly remembered for his concept of the "looking-glass self," which theorizes that individuals learn who they are by viewing themselves through the imagined eyes of others.[25] Cooley's work on the self does not figure as centrally in sociology as Mead's, but it is relevant here because he intuits the effects of lack of recognition on racialized subjects. Only through communication and recognition can people imagine how they are seen by others. Like James, Cooley emphasized that recognition is a human need. He argued that people need "fellowship and that appreciation by others which gives his self social corroboration and support."[26] But Cooley realized that such support was not universally received. Reflecting on the predicament of Black people and immigrants in early twentieth-century America, he asserted, "The immigrant has for the most part been treated purely as a source of labor, with little or no regard to the fact that he is a human being, with a self like the rest of us. . . . The negro question includes a similar situation. There is no understanding it without realizing the kind of self-feeling a race must have who, in a land where men are supposed to be equal, find themselves marked with indelible inferiority."[27] Unfortunately, while Cooley intuits the effect of lack of recognition on the self-formation of racially excluded people, he does not develop this point.

The work of Alfred Schutz also contributes to our understanding of the effects of lack of communication and interaction in the construction of intersubjectivity. Schutz was an Austrian refugee from Nazism who taught philosophy and sociology at the New School for Social Research in New York City, where he also worked in finance. Schutz's contribution was to adapt the philosophical work of Edmund Husserl to develop a sociological phenomenology of subjectivity and consciousness. In his phenomenological description of the social world, Schutz distinguishes between consociates, those with whom we share a common social space and with whom we interact, and contemporaries, those who live in our times but, because they are distant, we do not encounter in everyday life.[28] We become familiar with our consociates and test our ideas about them through interaction. Yet as we distance ourselves from our everyday experiences, the world becomes more opaque to us.

One can find in Schutz's analysis of contemporaries a parallel with relationships, or lack thereof, across the veil. Schutz argued that we have no communication or interaction with our distant contemporaries. We come to understand our contemporaries only through ideas about them that we are exposed to in our everyday life. In the same way, those who live behind the veil are invisible to whites, who can think of them only within the rubric of their existing ideas. Schutz's analysis of consociates and contemporaries, however, does not address power relations and exclusionary dynamics such as those involved in racialization. The world behind the veil is not the distant world of contemporaries; it is an adjacent world that whites do not see. As the sociologist Anne Rawls points out, "While Black and White appear to occupy the same world geographically, they rarely occupy the same interactional space."[29] The presence of the veil explains why, despite living in adjacent social worlds, whites think about Blacks only through their racialized preconceptions about them.

The theory of double consciousness illuminates the blind spot in the early theorists of subjectivity: their lack of attention to the limits to communication and mutual recognition under racialized modernity. The classical theorists of the self were aware of the negative effects of lack of recognition but devoted little attention to the millions of Black Americans who lived under this condition. James and Mead wrote eloquently about the predicament of people who do not receive social recognition, but they did not explore what this might have meant in the lives of Black people living near them, and how that experience affects their theories. Cooley acknowledged the consequences of racial exclusion for self-formation, but this issue was a minor point in his large body of work. Schutz, who understood the effects of lack of interaction on our understanding of the world, was also blind to the presence of the veil.

The theory of double consciousness brings the lack of recognition for the racially excluded subject to the fore, and posits that the veil creates different subjectivities on different sides of the color line. The key to the lived experience of the Black subject is double consciousness. The key to the lived experience of the white subject is ignorance of the humanity of those who live behind the veil. Furthermore, Du Bois argued that white subjects fiercely defended their ignorance when challenged about their role in creating and maintaining racial classifications and racial inequality.

Du Bois's ability to theorize these different subjectivities emerged from his own encounter with racialization. In *Dusk*, he states, "Had it not been for the race problem early thrust upon me and enveloping me, I should have probably been an unquestioning worshiper at the shrine of the social order and economic development into which I was born."[30] It was the concrete and everyday experience of racialization, from the awkward silences that his sheer presence often generated to blatant acts of exclusion, discrimination, and racial violence that he encountered in various public and professional spaces, that led Du Bois to critique racialized modernity. His experiences as a racialized subject and as an activist and organizer against racism allowed him to understand the relationship among power relations, exclusionary dynamics, and the formation of racialized subjectivities and identities. Theorizing from experience and linking the micro analysis of subjectivity and the macro analysis of racial and colonial capitalism are distinct characteristics of Du Bois's sociology.

The Phenomenology of Black Subjectivity

Du Bois's phenomenology posits three elements as structuring the understanding of the self and the world of racialized subjects. The first is the presence of the veil. Du Bois uses the metaphor of the veil to describe how the color line appears in the everyday experience of racialized people in racialized modernity. The effect of the veil in the racialized subject's consciousness is a feeling of twoness on the one hand and the emergence of second sight on the other. Du Bois uses different analytical and narrative strategies—quasi-ethnographic analysis of Black lives, auto-ethnography, and fiction—to illustrate the work of double consciousness.

Of the Veil

The main point of the theory of double consciousness is that the presence of the veil prevents the full recognition of the humanity of racially excluded groups. The veil structures the everyday experiences, self-formation, and perception of the world for people living on both sides of it. The invisibility of those who live behind the veil means that there is no process of mutual recognition or true communication between the racializing and the racialized subjects.

In *Dusk*, Du Bois shows that no matter how clearly, articulately, or sincerely the people living behind the veil present themselves, the white world either does not hear or completely misrecognizes what they try to convey. Invoking Plato's *Allegory of the Cave*, Du Bois describes life behind the veil as being cut off from the dominant world of whites:

> It is as though one, looking out from a dark cave in a side of an impending mountain, sees the world passing and speaks to it; speaks courteously and persuasively, showing them how these entombed souls are hindered in their natural movement, expression, and development; and how their loosening from prison would be a matter not simply of courtesy, sympathy, and help to them, but aid to all the world. One talks on evenly and logically in this way, but notices that the passing throng does not even turn its head, or if it does, glances curiously and walks on. It gradually

penetrates the minds of the prisoners that the people passing by do not hear; that some thick sheet of invisible but horribly tangible plate glass is between them and the world.³¹

At the heart of the matter, Du Bois is preoccupied with how the veil distorts Black subjects to the extent that their humanity becomes unrecognizable to others. Confronted with the systematic ignorance on the part of the world outside the cave, "the people within may become hysterical. They scream and hurl themselves against the barriers, hardly realizing in their bewilderment that they are screaming in a vacuum and unheard and that their antics may actually seem funny to those outside looking in."³² This excerpt highlights how lack of recognition affects the lives of Black people. This state of despair, however, is a symptom of living in the racist American society, not an ontological state of being. As Shawn Michelle Smith argues, Du Bois "describes the struggle of a healthy mind forced to confront and inhabit a perverse world; pathology finally resides not in an African American brain but in the American social body."³³

The analysis of double consciousness in both *Souls* and *Dusk* emphasizes the oppressive character of the racialized world and its consequences for people living behind the veil and simultaneously highlights how Black subjects strive to shape their world. Du Bois's depiction of the racialized world is one characterized by oppression and suffering but also by dignity, self-assertion, and creativity.

Of Twoness

Du Bois introduces the concept of twoness as the feeling of being both American and Black. In *Souls*, he describes this as a person having "two souls, two thoughts, two unreconciled strivings; two warring ideals in one dark body." Racialized subjects do not have the option, as Mead would suggest, of taking the position of the whole community; instead, subjectivity and self-formation are affected by the two conflicting worlds to which they belong: on the one hand the world of the dominant group that denies their humanity and on the other their own community, which is a source of support and a space of agency. Between these two worlds is a constant tension between the oppressiveness of the veil and the agency and creative practices of the racialized population. In *Dusk,* Du Bois describes the world behind the veil as an overbearing one:

> I lived in an environment which I came to call the White world. I was not an American; I was not a man; I was by long education and continual compulsion and daily reminder, a colored man to a White world; and that White world often existed primarily, so far as I was concerned, to see with sleepless vigilance that I was kept within bounds. All this made me limited in physical movement and provincial in thought and dream. I could not stir, I could not act, I could not live, without taking into careful account the reaction of my White environing world.[34]

Yet, although seemingly all-consuming, the white world does not fully determine the lived experience of the racialized subject. Du Bois also reminds us that the "Negro American has for his environment not only the surrounding white world but also, and touching him usually more completely and compellingly, is the environment furnished by his own colored group."[35] In *Souls,* Du Bois identifies religion and the church as the primary sites of such world building.[36] In the essay "Of the Faith of the Fathers," he asserts that the Black church is "the social center of Negro life in the United States, and the most characteristic expression of African character."[37] The church is identified as the hub of Black communities: "Various organizations meet here—the church proper, the Sunday-school, two or three insurance societies, women's societies, secret societies, and mass meetings of various kinds. Entertainments, suppers, and lectures are held beside the five or six regular weekly religious services."[38] Du Bois also emphasizes the centrality of music in the everyday experience of Black subjects: "The Music of Negro religion is that plaintive rhythmic melody, with its touching minor cadences, which, despite caricature and defilement, still remains the most original and beautiful expression of human life and longing yet born on American soil. Sprung from the African forests, where its counterpart can still be heard, it was adapted, changed, and intensified by the tragic soul-life of the slave, until, under the stress of law and whip, it became the one true expression of a people's sorrow, despair, and hope."[39]
These passages reveal a rich cultural and social world behind the veil, a world invisible to the dominant world.

For Du Bois, twoness characterizes self-formation and subjectivity behind the veil, but he recognizes that twoness can lead to different responses to the veil. He articulates this point in his essay on Booker T. Washington in *Souls*. In a short paragraph in that essay, Du Bois proposes a typology of three modes in which racialized groups typically manage living behind the veil. As he states, "But when to earth and brute is added an environment of men and ideas, then the attitude of the imprisoned group may take three main forms, a feeling of revolt and revenge, an attempt to adjust all thought and action to the will of the greater groups or finally a determined effort at self-realization and self-development despite environing opinion."[40]

One response to the veil is self-assertion despite the oppressive context. Du Bois cites the example of the establishment of the Black Episcopal Church in Philadelphia and New York as examples of this. Du Bois's thoughts and actions aligned most with this choice, and during his life he advocated various ways to travel this path: from his early belief in science and the Talented Tenth during his Atlanta years through his activism for civil rights during his time with the NAACP to his advocacy of Black self-organization during his second term as a faculty member at Atlanta University to Pan-African socialism at the end of his life. Nonetheless, he realized that there were other responses to the veil, including rebellion (such as the Haitian Revolution) and attempts at assimilation. It is clear from his scathing critique that he believed that Booker T. Washington had unabashedly adopted the third path. For Du Bois, embarking upon a project of assimilation without full recognition was a losing proposition for Black people because such an approach denied them the possibility of full acceptance and self-consciousness from the start.

Du Bois returned to considerations of responses to the veil in *Dusk*, where he analyzes the ways in which educated young Blacks deal with twoness. He argues that the responses range between two poles. Those who "avoid every appearance of segregation" eschew contact with Black organizations and try to join the world of whites in an attempt at assimilation.[41] At the other pole is a group that "prides himself on living with 'his people'" and seeks to distance themselves from whites whenever possible.[42]

For Du Bois, each response has a cost. The first group must deal with rejection from the white world because the "thick plate glass" of the veil keeps them from truly assimilating into mainstream society.[43] The second group lives in an isolated cultural world. Du Bois argues that neither group ultimately obtains recognition or participates in the communication process to define social reality across the veil. Between these two extremes are "all sorts of interracial patterns, and all of them theoretically follow the idea that Blacks must only submit to segregation 'when forced.'"[44] The result, he says, is a "crystallization of the culture elements among colored people into their own groups for social and cultural contact."[45]

In *Dusk* Du Bois also returns to the topic of Black self-assertion and the possibilities of agency in the world behind the veil. There he discusses different cultural, social, and political initiatives, in addition to the church, that take place beyond the veil. He points to movements to advance literature and art, he describes demands for improved healthcare for Blacks, and he proposes establishing consumer cooperatives to put the purchasing power of the Black population at the service of community economic development. These initiatives embody the constant striving of African Americans for recognition and for shaping their selves and their world—in other words, for full emancipation and equality.

Of Second Sight

Second sight is the potential ability of the racially excluded to see the world beyond the veil. In *Souls*, Du Bois describes the experience of living behind the veil as living in "a world which yields him no true self-consciousness, but only lets him see himself through the revelation of the other."[46] For Du Bois, second sight emerges in Black people's consciousness as the awareness of their invisibility, and the world beyond the veil gradually becomes apparent to Black subjects. What is important is not only the abject condition of invisibility but also the "gift" of awareness that is granted through this second sight. Thus the veil has a doubling effect. It creates a barrier of recognition between the Black and white worlds, and it leads the Black person to misrecognize his or her own self. Yet, turning the screw on Plato's allegory, while the prisoners in the cave have a distorted view of themselves, they also have the possibility of glimpsing the world beyond the veil.

The racially excluded have no choice but to see themselves through the eyes of the dominant subjects. This situation allows them to, at least partially, suspend the optics of the veil and see other possibilities of organizing the world. In his analysis of Black subjectivity, Du Bois points to different ways in which this ability may emerge and develop. We can see this process in the essay "Of the Meaning of Progress," in *Souls*, in which Du Bois describes his experience teaching in a poor rural Black community in Tennessee during one of the summers at Fisk. He describes the community in which he taught as having a "half awakened common consciousness." Specifically, he writes,

> There was among us but a half-awakened common consciousness, sprung from common joy and grief, at burial, birth, or wedding; from a common hardship in poverty, poor land, and low wages; and, above all, from the sight of the Veil that hung between us and Opportunity. All this caused us to think some thoughts together; but these, when ripe for speech, were spoken in various languages.
>
> Those whose eyes twenty-five and more years before had seen "the glory of the coming of the Lord," saw in every present hindrance or help a dark fatalism bound to bring all things right in His own good time. The mass of those to whom slavery was a dim recollection of childhood found the world a puzzling thing: it asked little of them, and they answered with little, and yet it ridiculed their offering. Such a paradox they could not understand, and therefore sank into listless indifference, or shiftlessness, or reckless bravado.
>
> There were, however, some—such as Josie, Jim, and Ben—to whom War, Hell, and Slavery were but childhood tales, whose young appetites had been whetted to an edge by school and story and half-awakened thought. Ill could they be content, born without and beyond the World. And their weak wings beat against their barriers,—barriers of caste, of youth, of life; at last, in dangerous moments, against everything that opposed even a whim.[47]

The distortions of the veil lead to different degrees of awakening of second sight. The veil distorts everybody's view of the world and the self, but it does so in different ways, "as spoken in various languages" in Du Bois's compelling description. Josie, Jim, and Ben had ambitions to transcend their predicament. Others expected little from the world. But in all cases, the veil stands between the people whom Du Bois is writing about, including Du Bois himself, and the world of opportunity that they are able to glimpse, though in different ways.

The analysis of the emergence of second sight is most developed in "Of the Coming of John." Telling the story from the perspective of a faculty member at a fictional college, Du Bois poetically depicts the changes in John's second sight through the use of narrative fiction. Growing up as a young man in the Jim Crow South, Black John is completely uncritical of his condition and unaware of his place in the world. The white people in his town viewed him as "good natured," but were dismayed when his mother decided to send young Black John away to college. White John was off to Princeton at the same time. Although Black John and White John grew up together and were even playmates, they were seldom thought of in the same mind. As Du Bois writes, "And yet it was singular that few thought of two Johns,—for the black folk thought of one John, and he was black; and the white folk thought of another John, and he was white. And neither world thought on the other world's thought save with a vague unrest."[48]

Black John goes to college, but his lackadaisical attitude and indifferent performance lead the faculty to suspend him for a term. The suspension produces in him a grave seriousness, and he returns to college with a new vision of the world. Upon his return, he receives the "gift" of second sight: "He had left his queer thought-world and come back to a world of motion and men. He looked now for the first time sharply about him, and wondered how he had seen so little before. He grew slowly to feel almost for the first time the Veil that lay between him and the white world; he first noticed now the oppression that had not seemed oppression before."[49] Black John's access to education and his encounter with the white world prompt the emergence of second sight—a startling yet gradual revelation that allows him to see the structures of his racialized environment and the ways in which he is situated and constrained in and around the veil.

Later in the essay Black John and white John encounter each other at an opera house in New York City, an encounter in which Black John is made to give up his seat at the behest of white John. This enrages Black John and makes him attend to his "destiny," which is to go back and uplift the Negro in his home town of Altamaha, Georgia, after seven long years of being away. The ride home is unpleasant because, as always, he has to sit in the Jim Crow car, but this time, thanks to his second sight, he is acutely aware of the situation.

The return home portrays the transformation of Black John's understanding of the world. Yet Du Bois explains that with this new second sight, Black John is disjointed and finds it difficult to navigate comfortably within the white and Black worlds. Upon his return, Blacks thought that he was aloof, and whites thought that he was uppity. The mayor warned Black John about infecting his Black pupils with his notions of equality and making them discontented and unhappy.

Both essays end in tragedy, demonstrating the unique dilemma of racialized subjectivity. Running through them is both the faint likelihood that things will be different and the overwhelming presence of the veil. Although second sight gives the Black subject the possibility of understanding the world constructed around the veil, it does not change their subordinate position.

In *Souls*, second sight emerged only in those who possessed an internal desire to learn—in going away to college for Black John and through learning in his small classroom for select students in "Of the Meaning of Progress." While Du Bois always held higher education and the role of people with higher education in high esteem, over time he developed a more nuanced understanding of the role of knowledge.

Initially he thought that addressing the veil was merely a matter of scientific inquiry and evidence: "The Negro problem was in my mind a matter of systematic investigation and intelligent understanding. The world was thinking wrong about race, because it did not know."[50] But the practice of academic science helped Du Bois understand that this was not the answer to racialization and racism, an awareness articulated in powerful language: "Two considerations thereafter broke in upon my work and eventually disrupted it: first, one could not be a calm, cool, and detached scientist while Negroes were lynched, murdered and starved; and secondly, there was no such definite demand for a scientific work of the sort that I was doing."[51]

Although he conveyed his ideas using the language of scientific inquiry, which enjoyed considerable legitimacy, the power of the veil to hide and distort was stronger than the clearest voices coming from behind it. This led Du Bois down the path of political activism, first at the Niagara Movement, the NAACP, and the directorship of the *Crisis*, and then through tireless advocacy of organizations that focused on self-development, self-preservation, and the struggle for equality. Whereas in *Souls* second sight emerges as a result of access to education, in *Dusk* Du Bois describes how his encounters with the daily practices of racialization, from little slights on the playground when he was but a young child to living through the 1905 Atlanta race riots, made him question the world around him and how resisting the veil expanded his second sight.

The Phenomenology of White Subjectivity

Second sight provides a sober look at the racialized world. Whereas the racially excluded are invisible to the dominant group, the former can develop an understanding of the latter. Encountering the veil allows for the development of a critical perspective on the white world. Du Bois used this ability to see life on the other side of the veil to pioneer the study of whiteness and develop a critique of white subjectivity. Du Bois argues that whites have the power to define the social world and, in this way, they are able to deny the humanity of the racialized and reproduce their own privilege in all its forms: material, social, and symbolic.

In *Dusk*, Du Bois devotes an entire chapter to the study of the natural attitude of whites through conversations with two imaginary white friends, a vivid example of his use of fictional narrative for sociological theorizing and analysis. In these imagined conversations, Du Bois makes two points. The first concerns the relationship of whites to Blacks. Here Du Bois notes the tension between the power of whites to define social reality and their inability to see the social world in its entirety. In his first imaginary dialogue, Du Bois emphasizes the purposeful ignorance of white people and their inability to fully recognize the humanity of other people. In explaining the white subject's basic understanding of the world, Du Bois writes, "His thesis is simple: the world is composed of Race superimposed on Race; classes superimposed on classes."[52] White people presuppose themselves to be superior and do not acknowledge that they are active participants in domination or oppression. This allows white people to rationalize the racial order of society, as they see it, and take pity on (or show contempt for) Blacks.

As we have seen, Mead notes that caste systems prevent individuals from internalizing the full social processes in which they participate. This is the situation Du Bois describes. Whites cannot take the position of the whole community because they do not see or recognize the humanity of part of the community in which they live. As a result, the racializing subjects do not see their own position as oppressors within the system of racialization. The white subjects can understand their place in the racialized world and their role in maintaining racial inequality only if they transcend their positionality as socially white. If the corollary of the veil for the racialized is the devastating anguish of not being recognized, for the racializing it is living in constant and persistent denial. As Judith Blau and Eric Brown put it in their 2008 essay "Du Bois and Diasporic Identity," "Blacks bear the burden of Twoness but whites are deluded by how they position themselves in their invented hierarchy."[53]

The second point Du Bois makes in his analysis of white subjectivity involves the relationship of white subjects to their own ideas of justice. Du Bois points to the tension between white people's ideals of justice and their blindness to their own position in relation to the veil. For this part of the analysis, Du Bois launches into another dialogue with an imaginary white friend: "He represents the way in which my environing white group distorts and frustrates itself even as it strives toward Justice and all because of me. In other words, because of the Negro problem."[54] Du Bois argues that the white subject lives with a perpetual contradiction between aspirations for justice and a good society and the need to justify the unjust order of white supremacy. He describes the different cultural codes that inform the world of whiteness, cultural codes that emphasize contradictory norms. He points to a Christian cultural code that emphasizes peace, goodwill, and especially the golden rule—"do unto others as you would have others do unto you"—but this contrasts with a coexisting "White Man" cultural code built on war, hate, suspicion, exploitation, and empire (Du Bois also defines "Gentleman" and "American" cultural codes). These codes are internally coherent, but they contradict one another. The contradiction is based on the fact of race. White subjects cannot live up to their ideals of justice because of their role in perpetuating a racialized world. When this contradiction must be resolved, the white subject almost invariably forgets the golden rule and chooses racial oppression, justifying it as the defense of civilization. This is how a nation that rests upon a foundation of land theft, genocide, slavery, and segregation can take pride in its ideals of freedom, liberty, and equality. Du Bois argued that those occupying the subject position of whiteness had to rely not on science, truth, and rational action but instead on acrobatic logics and irrational sleights of hand to reconcile the fundamental contradictions between their ideals and their actions.

The blindness of whites to their role in maintaining racial oppression leads them to renege on their stated ideals of justice and defend racial exclusion and inequality. In his dialogues in *Dusk*, Du Bois argues that the carefully cultivated ignorance produced by the veil is the result of white positionality. But he argues that when their ignorance is challenged, whites mobilize all their cognitive resources to defend it. When Du Bois confronts his friends with facts that contradict their views of the racialized world, they reject them and actively defend their ignorance, a point that Du Bois develops further in his analysis of the subjectivity of the colonizer. The white subject strives for justice, but abandons this striving as soon as a connection is made between injustice and the positionality of the white subject.

Du Bois explains the blindness and self-justification of whites in terms of both economic interest and habitus. Whites have economic interests to defend. Du Bois argues that colonialism and the exploitation of racialized people worldwide are central to the construction of the white natural attitude. But economic interest does not fully explain racialized modernity. As Du Bois writes, "The present attitude and action of the white world is not based solely upon rational, deliberate intent. It is a matter of conditioned reflexes, of long followed habits, customs and folkways, of subconscious trains of reasoning and unconscious nervous reflexes."[55] The defense of ignorance is rooted in what sociologists Eduardo Bonilla Silva, Carla Goar, and David Embrick call a white habitus, that is, the constructed and deeply internalized racialized views, tastes, and emotions of white people.[56] The defense of ignorance is in part the defense of material privilege, but it is also the defense of social and symbolic privilege, that is, of the habits and customs of social recognition that white subjects derive from their power to define the social world. Du Bois argues in *Black Reconstruction* that whites engage in the defense of the psychological privilege they derive from their social position in the racial order. Subjectivity constructs social structure as much as social structure constructs subjectivity.

Yet just as Du Bois allowed for a diversity of Black forms of subjectivity—that is, for different responses to the predicament of double consciousness—he also recognized the possibility of alternative forms of subjectivity within whiteness. His first treatment of white subjectivity, in his 1909 biography *John Brown*, elaborates this point. Nahum Chandler argues that Du Bois looks at John Brown from the perspective of the experience of African Americans, that is, the experience of double consciousness, arguing that it was John Brown's second sight that allowed him to pierce the veil and see the humanity of enslaved Black people.[57] In his analysis of John Brown's subjectivity, Du Bois is probing the possibility for transcending whiteness, for being what today we would describe as a race traitor.

Du Bois documents how John Brown's views evolved from merely opposing slavery to dedicating his life to its abolition. Du Bois roots John Brown's ability to transcend the blindness of his positionality and see the humanity of Black people—the life behind the veil that is typically inaccessible to the dominant group—in his understanding of religious scripture. It was John Brown's attachment to the golden rule that led him first to Kansas to fight against the expansion of slavery and then to the raid on Harpers Ferry that cost him his life.[58]

A key point of *John Brown* is the presence of an alternative white subjectivity, one that rejects racialization and the social order that originates and sustains it. In 1909, when he wrote *John Brown*, Du Bois thought that this form of alternative white subjectivity was becoming widespread in the late nineteenth century but was pushed aside by the rise of an erroneous interpretation of Darwin's theories. The racist understanding of humanity derived from the dominant interpretation of Social Darwinism, which displaced other constructions of white subjectivity that advocated for equality. Du Bois would later change his mind about the possibility of an alternative white subjectivity. By the mid-1930s, when he wrote *Black Reconstruction*, Du Bois was highly skeptical of the possibility of dissident whiteness.

Indeed, in his analysis of white labor and the labor movements in the second chapter of *Black Reconstruction*, Du Bois describes white abolitionism as a small and not very effective fringe movement. This is the point at which he advocates self-segregation and the construction of a cooperative economy for the survival of the Black community until the day in which the racist social order could be undone. Yet in his posthumously published autobiography, written at the end of his life, Du Bois puts forward the possibility of common action across racial lines based on embracing socialism and anticolonial solidarity.[59] In *John Brown* and in his late autobiography, Du Bois points to the possibilities of whites transcending their own positionality, but he emphasizes that this possibility is conditioned on whites choosing their ideals over their race and rebelling against the social order that sustains their privilege.

The Hypothesis of Law and the Assumption of Chance

Du Bois's phenomenology analyzes the basic elements of the modes of perception, understanding, and feeling—to paraphrase Sherry Ortner's definition of subjectivity—of racialized and racializing subjects. Du Bois points out that these modes of seeing and situating oneself in the world are conditioned by the veil. At the same time, Du Bois always emphasized the possibility of human agency. The question of agency, the possibilities open to humans to take action to shape their lives and their world, was central to Du Bois's work. In "Sociology Hesitant," an unpublished essay written in late 1904 or early 1905, Du Bois argues that sociology's goal was to determine the scope of law and chance in human action. He asks why sociologists do not openly "state the Hypothesis of Law and the Assumption of Chance, and seek to determine by study and measurement the limits of each."[60] In defining sociology in this way, Du Bois argued against dominant approaches of his time, approaches, such as Comte's, that regarded sociology as the study of an abstractly conceived society, or others, such as Spencer's, that took a deterministic position in the study of human action.[61]

For Du Bois chance refers to the ability of people to make undetermined choices. As he writes, "Behind Chance we place free human wills capable of undetermined choices, frankly acknowledging that in both these cases we front the humanly inexplicable."[62] Du Bois borrowed the language of chance from William James.[63] For James, and the pragmatists, individuals acted within established social constraints but retained the ability to make choices and generate social alternatives. This was the point of James's critique of determinism. Similarly, Du Bois affirmed that Black people have the agency to make choices and shape the reality in which they live.

While Du Bois asserts that there is a space for free will in human action, he is mindful of the constraints that people encounter. For him law refers to the historical and structural limits to the ability of individuals to make meaningful choices. He finds the constraints to agency "in the rhythm in birth and death rates and the distribution by sex; it is found further in human customs and laws, the form of government, the laws of trade, and even in charity and ethics."[64] Birth and death rates he likens to physical law, external to human action, but customs, laws, and government he regards as the result of the crystallization of historical human agency. For Du Bois, the multiple forms of individual and collective action of the racialized had the potential to challenge the color line. The ability of the racialized and the colonized to imagine change is rooted in their second sight, the element of double consciousness that allows them to see beyond their dehumanizing present.

Dusk is in part a narrative about the emergence and evolution of Du Bois's second sight and his changing understanding of race and racism. It also describes Du Bois's experience of organizing and working to achieve large-scale social change. In Du Bois's life this effort was expressed in his activism and organizing in support of civil and political rights at the NAACP in the early twentieth century, in his advocacy of an autonomous Black cooperative community economy in the 1930s and 1940s, and in his participation in the Pan-African movement and anticolonial advocacy throughout his life. It was also expressed in his writings and academic activities, which were never separated from his efforts to seek emancipation and equality. Du Bois always emphasized the importance of building community institutions for asserting agency behind the veil. This is expressed in his analyses of the role of Black organizations in building and sustaining communities in *Souls*, *Dusk*, and other of his writings.

But Du Bois's experience also taught him that the agency of the racialized had an additional dimension: the relentless fight for dignity and the assertion of humanity even under the most adverse conditions. Du Bois rooted this struggle for the recognition of the humanity of the racialized in the cultural resilience and creativity of people of color. He did

so early in his life in the final chapter of *Souls*, where he links the assertion of Black humanity to the sorrow songs, the music created by Black
enslaved people that is a testament to their ability to endure and affirm
their humanity under the most horrifying conditions. And late in his
life, in a 1957 letter to Kwame Nkrumah, the first president of independent Ghana, he argued that the newly independent African countries
should build political and social structures based on African communitarian traditions rather than on Western modernity.[65] For Du Bois,
subjectivity is where people find the energy and the ideas to assert their
humanity. For Du Bois, agency refers to the possibility of macro social
change but also to the world-making and self-affirming actions of racialized communities.

Human agency, however, is not solely the action of the oppressed,
and is expressed not only for the sake of change. As our discussion of
Du Bois's analysis of whiteness reveals, white people mobilize to defend
their privilege. Some of the constraints to the agency of the oppressed are
the historical crystallizations of their oppressors' actions. For Du Bois,
the color line, the main constraining social structure of racialized modernity, was the result of white agency, and it was maintained through
the construction of white subjectivity. Indeed, in *Dusk* Du Bois argues
that the goal of science is "to explore and measure the scope of chance
and unreason in human action, which does not yield to argument but
changes slowly and with difficulty after long study and careful development."[66] That is, chance—human free will—is not only emancipatory.
Chance is also at the root of colonialism and racism, which are historical
structural forces but also very much the product of human action.

The theme of sociology being the science that aims to determine the
scope of law and chance is recurrent in Du Bois's work. He recasts this
question in his 1947 book, *The World and Africa: An Inquiry into the
Part Which Africa Has Played in World History*, in the context of exploring what the future economic order will bring: the tensions between
the technical and managerial constraints imposed by industrial production on the one hand and democratic decision making over economic
priorities on the other. And the tension between law and chance is also
explored in his posthumous *Autobiography of W. E. B. Du Bois*. In that
book, in which he laments the failure to restart his empirical research
program during his second tenure at Atlanta in the late 1930s and early

1940s, he stated, "The opportunity was surrendered and the whole sci-ence of sociology has suffered. I even had projected a path of scientific approach: I was going to plot out beside the world of physical law, a sci-ence of sociology which measured the limits of chance in human action. If this field proved narrow or non-existent, world law was proven. If not, the resultant 'chance' was what men had always regarded as 'free will.'"[67] The tension between human free will as a force for change and the his-torical social structures that constrain human agency stood at the center of Du Bois's sociology. And Du Bois refused to offer an a priori solution to this tension. His sociology was one that left this question open, to be answered through empirical research.

Du Bois asks us to be hesitant when analyzing concrete forms of human action.[68] He calls upon us to consider specific situations from both the perspective of chance and the perspective of law before propos-ing an explanation. And while he asserted his belief in the potential of human agency, he argued that the relationship between law and chance varied in different historical periods and different geographic locations and that the analyst must examine the options available to specific actors in specific times and places.

To understand the uniqueness of Du Bois's approach to human agency, it is useful to contrast that approach, much as we did with his theory of double consciousness, to the work of other theorists who have addressed these questions. One such theorist was sociologist Erving Goffman, who was a graduate of the University of Chicago and was in some ways influenced by the work of Mead and symbolic interaction-ism. Goffman was a theorist of the micro interactional order. In his works he discusses how people act to present themselves to others and establish who they are in their social milieus.

In his first book, *The Presentation of Self in Everyday Life*, Goffman analyzes how people manage the external impressions they make in their encounters with others.[69] In *Asylums*, he describes how total insti-tutions, that is, institutions that have total control over the subject, affect the construction of self of the people who are confined in them.[70] And in *Stigma*, Goffman analyzes how people manage identities that carry negative social connotations.[71] One might find in Goffman's works, particularly in *Asylums* and *Stigma*, another take on Du Bois's opening question in *Souls*: "How does it feel to be a problem?" Goffman shows how individuals deal with oppressive institutions or with labels that stigmatize them, and how they have a measure of agency to present who they are vis-à-vis others.

Yet the works of Du Bois and Goffman, despite their shared interest in the experiences of people who suffer from a negative social definition of their selves, are very different from each other. For one thing, Goffman, unlike Du Bois, is interested not in phenomenology—the analysis of the basic structures of experience and perception—but rather in the strategies individuals use to manage their self and identity when they encounter stigma or institutions that deny their autonomy. In this there is a parallel with Du Bois's analysis in *Dusk*, or in the *Souls* essay on Booker T. Washington, of the strategies Black people use to deal with a racist world. But whereas Goffman presents an analysis of how individuals who are thrown into dehumanizing institutions deal with them—an analysis that perhaps more sociologists should take on—Goffman does not analyze the historical and global structures of oppression that created those institutions. On the other hand, for Du Bois "the problem" he alludes to is a historically concrete one of unequal power relations that result in the systemic oppression of Black people. In addition, Goffman offers no analysis of agency, either for macro social change or for the assertion of humanity, beyond his analysis of the strategies individuals use to manage their identities.

A second important contrast is with the work of the French sociologist Pierre Bourdieu, which has had enormous influence on contemporary social theory and sociological analysis. Bourdieu's theory of practice asserts that society is remade through the actions of people who internalize their social position into their understandings and social practices—"habitus," in Bourdieu's language.[72] Individuals internalize cultural expectations and dispositions related to their social position into what Bourdieu calls a class habitus that guides their everyday actions and interactions. According to Bourdieu, people in their everyday lives engage in different fields that constitute different areas of social action. Each field has its own rules, currencies, and rewards. Although individuals have the ability to act strategically to improve their position within those fields, Bourdieu's emphasis on the power of habitus leads him to see human action as reproducing the structures of fields. People may act to change or assert their position within social fields but not to change the fields themselves.

Subjectivity for Bourdieu is determined by the internalization of social position and symbolic violence. This is the imposition on subordinates of the dominant ideas about who they are and their social positions. There is a parallel here with Du Bois's analysis of action within the veil, but the self-asserting and meaning-making agency that Du Bois sees behind the veil is absent in Bourdieu's theorization. Bourdieu's theory of agency is focused mostly on social reproduction. Change, to the extent that it happens, results from tensions between different fields of action. In Du Bois's analysis, on the other hand, the reproduction of racialized modernity was to a large extent the result of the purposeful actions of the powerful, and the response was the organized action of the oppressed.

Like Bourdieu, although at an earlier time, Du Bois shows the importance of habits and customs in reproducing the social system. He also showed how marginalized individuals can buy into the system's ideology. But there is in Du Bois an emphasis on the possibilities of agency, both for macro change and for asserting humanity, that is absent in Bourdieu. This emphasis comes from the fact that Du Bois theorized from his own experience as a Black person asserting his humanity in his everyday life, something common to the Black Radical Tradition that mainstream theorists do not share.

The third contrast we propose is with the work of William Sewell Jr. Sewell is a historian and an emeritus professor of history and political science at the University of Chicago. But his work, particularly his book *Logics of History: Social Theory and Social Transformation*, has been very influential in social theory debates across the social sciences.[73] Sewell proposes an understanding of agency that is closer to that of Du Bois.

Sewell postulates that "a capacity for agency—for desiring, for forming intentions, and for acting creatively—is inherent in all humans."[74] But this general capacity for agency is exercised within specific historical contexts. These contexts determine the prevailing cultural schemas that people use to make sense of their experiences. They also determine differential access to resources for different groups of people. For Sewell, historically specific forms of agency are produced by the prevailing cultural discourses, the available resources, and the varying access that different social groups have to these resources.

But Sewell cautions us not to take too structural a vision of agency. He affirms the fact that different societies are comprised of different social structures in which different resources and cultural schemas can be exported or transposed across settings. In this he is not different from Bourdieu. But Sewell argues that different cultural schemas can help people articulate different visions of the social order and that there is always a measure of unpredictability in the accumulation of resources. The tensions produced by the intersection of different social structures, the possibility of articulating new cultural schemas, and the window of opportunity to redistribute the accumulation of resources generate opportunities for agency and change.

Sewell proposes a vision of agency that is rooted in historical structures but is much more open to change and less determined by those structures than Bourdieu's theory allows. For Sewell structure is limiting, but it also enables new possibilities. Sewell, like Du Bois, emphasizes the inherent ability of humans for agency and to see and articulate new ways to organize social life. Where they differ is that Du Bois applies his understanding of agency to the analysis of a particular historical system—racial and colonial capitalism—and puts the question of recognition and humanity at the center of his understanding of agency. Sewell's general theorizing of agency does not preclude considering these issues, but he does not emphasize them.

Du Bois formulated an understanding of agency that is unique in its emphasis on the human capacity for action and in its focus on both macro change and the demand of recognition across the color line. Du Bois's assertion of the possibility of agency is in part a result of his roots in pragmatism and its emphasis on the human ability to shape the social world. Pragmatism provided Du Bois with a language to speak about his concerns. And if he was attracted to the pragmatists' assertion of free will and the indeterminacy of action, it was because that understanding related to his own experience.

But his experience was also the root of the main differences between Du Bois's analysis of agency and pragmatism. Du Bois's emphasis on agency is rooted in his theorizing from his own experience as a Black subject in America and in the world struggling to assert humanity and identity, to achieve political and social rights, and to fight racism and colonialism. He was born just three years after the end of the United States Civil War. Although he was born into freedom, he was nonetheless born into a world shaped by racial caste, prejudice, discrimination, and racial violence. During his long life he experienced major events that reshaped the global color line, including two world wars and the various independence movements across Africa and Asia. As a result, he saw agency as taking place in a historically concrete social system—racial and colonial capitalism—that has very specific dynamics of exclusion that were central to Du Bois's life and analysis but that pragmatists were oblivious to.[75] Theorizing from personal experience and from political praxis and emphasizing the struggle to assert humanity and dignity in everyday life, even when major change seems unachievable, are characteristic of Du Bois's sociology and his understanding of agency.

A Contemporary Du Boisian Sociology of Racialized Subjectivity

To complete our discussion of racialized subjectivity and agency, it is necessary to address the methodological and analytical challenges these concepts pose to the contemporary practice of sociology. Du Bois's theory of double consciousness and his hesitant sociology emerge from his reflections on his own experiences. His articulation of double consciousness in *Souls* starts with a moment in which he understands that he is different—the well-known story in which a girl, a newcomer to the local school, rejects his visiting card—the moment when Du Bois tells us he first experienced the color line. The development of this point in *Dusk* is based on autobiographical reflections. He does not return to the visiting-card story. But he tells us how his experience studying and living in the South allowed him to truly see and understand the predicament of Black people in the United States. He states, "The three years at Fisk were years of growth and development. I learned new things about the world. My knowledge of the race problem became more definite. I saw discrimination in ways of which I had never dreamed . . . [T]he public disdain and even insult in race contact on the street continually took my breath; I came in contact for the first time with a sort of violence that I had never realized in New England."[76] And he explains how studying in Germany taught him that the color line is a global structure and

that racialization works differently in different places. Du Bois's autobiographical reflections consistently link his life to the larger historical
events in which it unfolded.

Dusk portrays Du Bois's exploration of the scope of law and chance in
his own life, through his ever-evolving program for freedom and equality for all people of color—spanning from a belief that science and truth
alone would dismantle the color line to organizing various multiracial
and Black-only organizations and coalitions. In that book, Du Bois discusses his own efforts and struggles in challenging the color line, among
them his participation in the foundation of the Niagara Movement and
the NAACP, his organizing of Pan-African conferences, and his advocacy for a Black cooperative economy. Frequently these efforts did not
achieve their goals, but they nonetheless involved building community
and affecting the larger society in which Du Bois lived. Thus the first
two methodological aspects of a Du Boisian analysis of subjectivity and
agency are the centrality of theorizing from lived experience and the
continuous linking between subjectivity and the larger context of racialized modernity.

Du Bois also draws his analysis of subjectivity and agency from his
observations of his encounters with Black communities. His recollec-
tions of his time as a schoolteacher in rural Tennessee, reflected in "The
Meaning of Progress," are as close as Du Bois ever comes to contemporary ethnography. However, the goal of Du Bois's phenomenology is
different from that of most contemporary urban and community ethnography. The latter focuses on the behavior and choices of poor and
marginalized populations. Often these ethnographies try to explain why
the poor, particularly poor people of color, engage in behaviors that
do not correspond to the norms of the white middle class. By contrast,
critical ethnographies often try to humanize the poor and contextual-
ize their behavior within their institutional and structural constraints.
Du Bois was perhaps the first to take this approach: Several chapters in
The Philadelphia Negro are devoted to the social problems of the Black
community, including the chapters "The Negro Criminal" and "Alcoholism and Pauperism." Du Bois understands that poverty and exclusion
may lead to self-destructive behavior. For example, in "The Meaning
of Progress," he describes some young people as lacking ambition and
sinking into what he describes as "listless indifference, or shiftlessness,

or reckless bravado."[77] But he clearly attributes the social problems of the Black community to racism and racial exclusion, as will become clear in our discussion of his urban and community studies, a facet of Du Bois's sociology that we address at length in chapter 3.

The goal of Du Bois's phenomenology, however, is different. It is to analyze subjectivity and identity under racialized modernity.[78] His analysis of double consciousness asks his audience not to explain the social problems of the poor but rather to reflect on the experience of dealing with racism, or living under the color line, or, as Du Bois puts it, "*How does it feel to be a problem?*" Du Bois makes it clear that a person cannot escape this question through social mobility. Josie, in "The Meaning of Progress," aspired to go beyond the limits of her rural world, and John, in "The Coming of John," succeeded in graduating from college. Yet for both of them the encounter with the veil was tragic. The veil weighs on both those without ambition and those with ambition, on those who accept their circumstances and those who try to change them. This was also the case with Du Bois himself, who was constrained by the veil throughout his life. Education and social mobility are not enough to enable a Black person to escape the veil as long as the racist system is in place. The analysis of racial subjectivity is intended to describe the lived experience of exclusion and to construct a critique of the social order that perpetuates the color line.

The discussion as to the place of lived experience in sociological analysis refers us to the question of the standpoint from which Du Bois thinks, writes, and acts. Throughout this book, we argue that Du Boisian sociology takes the standpoint of the racially oppressed. Du Bois asserted, "Only the man himself can speak for himself. We say: Put yourself in his place; but after all we know that no human soul can thus change itself. The voice of the oppressed alone can tell the real meaning of oppression and, though the voice be tremulous, excited and even incoherent, it must be listened to if the world would learn and know."[79]

Du Bois tells us that the oppressed can speak, and although their voice may not be loud or clear, we need to make the effort to listen and understand it. But as he shows in his essay on Booker T. Washington in *Souls* and in his discussion of the responses of the Black elites to the veil in *Dusk*, the oppressed do not necessarily share a common outlook on the world. Furthermore, as intersectional analysis shows, subjectivities develop in complex and contradictory social positions. People living behind the veil understand their predicament in different ways.[80]

And yet, as Du Bois's own trajectory shows, the experience of racial exclusion was central for the development of his critical perspective on racialized modernity. Taking the standpoint of the racially excluded means starting our reflections from their historical predicament and experience, rather than approaching the subject from a position of abstract and universal neutrality. It means accounting for experiences of exclusion and the encounters with the specific historical structures that generate those experiences. Taking the standpoint of the racialized and the colonized allows Du Bois to see and reflect on experiences and structures that are not perceived from the perspective of abstract universalism. Abstract universalism is, in fact, the standpoint of the dominant, and as Du Bois argues, this standpoint is characterized by a carefully cultivated ignorance toward the humanity and life on the other side of the veil.

It is tempting to think about double consciousness and the veil as universal and generalizable concepts that apply to other situations of oppression and exclusion. Thus, we can think of the world as divided by multiple veils, with people located on different sides of different veils. This approach would argue that individuals occupy different positionalities according to the different social categories to which they belong and that each of these social positions could be affected by the dynamics of different veils.

We argue against using concepts in such an ahistorical way. Du Bois develops the analysis of the veil in the context of the experience of Black people in the South in the early twentieth century, and he applies it to the experience of African Americans in the United States in general. Later, in *Dusk* (and, as we will show, in *The World and Africa*), he links the idea of double consciousness to the analysis of colonial subjectivity and the idea of empire. There are also powerful parallels between Du Bois's and Frantz Fanon's analysis of Black subjectivity that point to how the analysis of the veil applies to colonial situations.[81] But double consciousness and the veil are not automatically generalizable concepts. In applying them, we need to take into account concrete historical forms of domination.

A key point of a Du Boisian methodology, then, is the historical embeddedness of sociological analysis. Du Bois offers us concepts and theories that are situated in concrete historical and social contexts, i.e., racial slavery, white supremacy, forced segregation and exclusion, and institutionalized inequality Those concepts and theories are generalizable only through an examination of whether and how they fit other historically situated social contexts and may have to be readapted to apply to different situations. As we will show, this is a major difference between Du Boisian sociology and the mainstream approach that originated in Chicago. A contemporary Du Boisian sociology will explore and contrast how different forms of racialization are experienced in concrete historical situations.

Du Bois's phenomenology is central to a contemporary Du Boisian sociology. It provides an analytical approach for conducting analyses of the lived experiences of people on both sides of the veil without unduly pathologizing individual groups or proposing essentializing cultural explanations. It also provides an analytical framework that allows for the examination of subjectivity and agency within the broader contexts of racialized modernity. In that sense, a Du Boisian phenomenology entails a particular kind of research method, one in which the researcher invites people to reflect upon and describe how their lived experience was constructed through their encounters with racialization.[82]

But a present-day Du Boisian sociology should go beyond Du Bois's analysis by embracing an intersectional perspective on the study of subjectivity and agency, looking at how different intersections of race, coloniality, gender, sexuality, and class affect the construction of self and agency. A contemporary Du Boisian sociology must pay attention to local and intersectional differences in lived experience but also reflect on the possibilities of bridging those differences to build coalitions and alliances to struggle to undo all forms of exclusion and oppression—always keeping in mind that for Du Bois the goal of knowledge was to undo the color line. This expansion of Du Boisian analysis beyond the work of Du Bois is consistent with his practice of self-reflexivity and his constant incorporation of new ideas and practices when confronting new situations or the limits of his previous understandings.

2

Racial and Colonial Capitalism

In October of 1945 the Fifth Pan-African Congress met in Manchester, England. The purpose of the congress was to articulate and advance an anticolonial agenda for the post–World War II period. Du Bois attended the meeting and was named the congress's international president.

This honorary title was not the result of his leading role in organizing the meeting. Other leaders from the emerging African liberation movements, such as Kwame Nkrumah[1] and George Padmore,[2] played a larger role in making the meeting take place. The title accorded Du Bois, however, was a recognition of his trajectory as a Pan-Africanist intellectual and organizer. In 1945 Du Bois was seventy-seven years old and renowned worldwide for his work against colonialism and for Pan-Africanism, an ideology grounded in the belief that people of African descent, both in the continent and in the diaspora, share a common history and fate. Du Bois lived in an era in which empire and colonialism stood at the center of the world's political, economic, and cultural organization, and in his sociology, empire and colonialism are central categories of analysis.[3] For him the color line was a global historical structure that affected all aspects of life under racial and colonial capitalism.

The best-known articulation of the global character of the color line can be found in the essay "Of the Dawn of Freedom" in *Souls*, in which Du Bois states, "The problem of the twentieth century is the problem of the color-line, the relation of the darker to the lighter races of men in Asia and Africa, in America and the islands of the sea."[4] Scholars often focus on the first part of the statement—about the color line being the century's problem—and overlook the more global understanding of race and racialization that the remark offers.[5] Du Bois leaves no doubt about this point. The next sentence in that essay starts with, "It was a phase of this problem that caused the Civil War."[6] From the very beginning, Du Bois embedded American racial history in a larger global history of colonial and racial relations.

Du Bois's early insights about colonialism, articulated in such essays as "The Present Outlook for the Dark Races of Mankind,"[7] published in 1900, lacked a systemic analysis of the link among racism, colonialism, and capitalism.[8] Yet as early as his 1915 essay "The African Origins of War"[9] and in two of his essays in *Darkwater*—"The Souls of White Folk" and "The Hands of Ethiopia"[10]—Du Bois clearly links war to colonialism, racism, and whiteness as a category of social classification that structures lived experience.

Colonialism and empire also stood at the center of Du Bois's organizing practices. In 1900 he participated in the Pan-African Conference that met in London, and though only thirty-three at the time, he was the one who wrote the conference's "Address to the Nations of the World." It is in this address that he first asserts that the problem of the century is the problem of the color line.[11] Between 1919 and 1927, Du Bois organized four Pan-African congresses. In addition to attending the fifth one, he was also invited to address the Bandung Conference, held in 1955, an event that established the foundations for the Non-Aligned Movement.[12] Although he could not attend because the US government denied him a passport after his 1951 trial, he sent a statement to be read at the conference.[13]

Du Bois was also invited to attend the All African People's Congress, held in Accra in April of 1958. He was unable to attend for health reasons, but his second wife, Shirley Graham—a Pan-African intellectual and activist in her own right—delivered a message from Du Bois to that meeting. Du Bois would die in Ghana in 1963 as a Ghanaian citizen by choice, the culmination of a life of thinking deeply about the destiny of Africa and the Africana diaspora and fighting colonialism and the color line. As the Reverend Martin Luther King Jr. asserted in his 1968 speech honoring Du Bois, "He died at home in Africa among his cherished ancestors, and he was ignored by a pathetically ignorant America but not by history."[14]

The global color line and colonialism were clearly central elements of Du Bois's understanding of the modern world, and he put both racism and colonialism at the center of his critique of racialized modernity. Three of his books published in the 1930s and 1940s best articulate his analysis of historical capitalism: *Black Reconstruction*, *The World and Africa*, and *Color and Democracy*. These books ground Du Bois's global sociology in the interconnection of transnational economic, political, and cultural processes, the centrality of slavery in the emergence of historical capitalism, and the colonial and racial character of contemporary capitalism. With few exceptions, however, sociologists have ignored these books, perhaps because they consider them insufficiently "sociological." *Black Reconstruction* is viewed as a work of history, while *Color and Democracy* and *The World and Africa* are generally regarded as nonacademic works written to influence public debates. Yet, as renowned political theorist and professor of Black studies Cedric Robinson described it, *Black Reconstruction* is "not simply a historical work, but history subjected to theory."[15] The same can be said of *Color and Democracy* and *The World and Africa*. *Black Reconstruction* places the southern slave economy in its transnational context. In this work Du Bois argues that the enslaved people in the South were part of the global proletariat and central to the most important global commodity chains of the nineteenth century. *Color and Democracy*, published in 1945, was an indictment of colonialism and a call for decolonization as part of the post–World War II world. *The World and Africa*, published in 1947, was the third and most fully realized of Du Bois's attempts to bring Africa and the African diaspora into the center of modern world history.[16]

These two later books might be considered "public sociology," but they are nonetheless informed by and structured around Du Bois's theoretical understanding of capitalism.[17] In these works, Du Bois develops theoretical analyses of the colonial and racial character of historical capitalism, informed by his encounter with the work of Karl Marx in the late 1920s. This chapter discusses Du Bois's global and historical sociology, focusing on his original understanding of Marx's thought, his analysis of capitalism, the global veil, the intersections of race, class, and gender, and the racial state. These dimensions of Du Bois's sociology are mostly unrecognized by the discipline, and yet they are central to the construction of a contemporary Du Boisian sociology.

Du Bois's Encounter with Marx

In his 1944 essay, "My Evolving Program for Negro Freedom," Du Bois affirms that it was through the writings of Karl Marx that he most fully understood the economic foundations of human history. In fact, Du Bois's earlier work had already considered the importance of the economy. He first encountered economic and institutional analysis while studying at Harvard and in Germany in the early 1890s. In *The Philadelphia Negro*, he places lack of economic opportunities at the center of his analysis of the predicament of the Black community. In that book, Du Bois emphasized the structural constraints that drastically limited the mobility of African Americans, and analyzed the internal class stratification of the Black community, a recurrent topic in his writings.

This early form of stratification analysis later became central to American sociology, although Du Bois goes beyond later analyses of stratification in that he addressed the political role of the Black elite. But it was only as the result of his encounter with the work of Karl Marx that Du Bois fully incorporated into his work both class analysis—the analysis of the formation of class collective actors and class struggle—and the systemic analysis of historical capitalism.

In *Dusk* Du Bois asserts, "I believed and still believe that Karl Marx was one of the greatest men of modern time and that he puts his finger squarely upon our difficulties when he said that economic foundations, the way that men earn their living, are the determining factors in the development of civilization, in literature, religion, and the basic pattern of culture. And this conviction I had to express or spiritually die."[18]

Yet Du Bois does not simply adopt Marx's analytical framework. Rather, he merges Marx's ideas with his own analysis of the central role of the color line in structuring modernity. He incorporates Marx's ideas into his thinking in a creative and highly heterodox—vis-à-vis other Marxists—way. In his 1971 "Lectures on the Black Jacobins," C. L. R. James, the famous Trinidadian anticolonial writer and activist, describes the difference between his and Du Bois's use of Marxism thusly: "He examined what was taking place, mastered all the events and mastered all the writings and so forth that were significant for the revolution, and from that he drew what were the Marxist conclusions. He didn't bring the Marxist conclusions to apply to the material as I was able to do in Britain and in France in 1938. Du Bois used the material and saw that only the Marxist analysis could fit."[19]

Du Bois's approach extends and differs from Marx's in four fundamental ways. First, Du Bois analyzes capitalism as a global system structured around colonialism and racialization. For Marx, primitive accumulation—that is, the expropriation and displacement of the peasantry and the extraction of colonial wealth through the use of coerced labor—constitutes a historical precondition for the emergence of capitalism, a particular moment in history rather than an ongoing process. His comments on imperialism in India indicate that for him, colonialism, despite its cruelty, had the progressive historical role of dissolving precapitalist structures and replacing them with capitalist social relations. The spread of capitalist social relations was destined to create a global working class that faced similar life conditions and a similar predicament.

Du Bois, on the other hand, argues that colonialism and racism are structuring elements of historical capitalism. For Du Bois, as opposed to Marx, the process of accumulation based on the coerced labor of workers of color and the extraction of resources from the colonies is not just a moment of primitive accumulation but is constitutive of racial and historical capitalism. Slavery and the plantation economy were the historical base upon which the industrial economy of the nineteenth century was built. But the Industrial Revolution did not eliminate either forced labor or colonial dispossession. Rather, it was contemporaneous with a new period of colonial expansion and the exacerbation of global racism.[20] In Du Bois's view, there is no possible equalization of the conditions of workers worldwide because historical capitalism as a global system is structured on the racial and colonial differences between workers.[21]

The second aspect in which Du Bois goes beyond Marx is in his analysis of race and subjectivity. Marx assumed that the proletariat would become conscious of its common class interests and become a class for itself, a historical actor destined to bring down capitalism. For Du Bois, however, the global color line shapes subjectivity and the self, and the lived experience of class groups is racialized. As we have shown, Du Bois explains how the consciousness of racially excluded groups is constructed as a result of their encounter with the veil. Du Bois also analyzed the lived experience and forms of consciousness of whites, showing that they are blind to life and humanity behind the veil and to their own position of domination.[22] Du Bois extends his analysis to address the fragmented nature in which the colonial world appears to the colonizer. Du Bois points out how the colonizer is blind to the brutality involved in the production of the colonial commodities they enjoy.

The third way in which Du Bois departs from Marx's analytical frame follows from the previous two. That is the point that class, for Du Bois, always intersects with colonialism and the global color line. Du Bois emphasizes the racialization of the class structure and how race fractures class interests and hinders collective action. For example, in *Black Reconstruction* he shows how the white working class in the American South was central both to the maintenance of slavery and to the ending of the Reconstruction period, and in *Color and Democracy* he asserts that the European working classes were the backbone of colonialism. At the same time, he argues that resistance to racist and colonial exploitation takes place along racial and anticolonial lines. For Du Bois, class struggle is always racialized.

The fourth difference between Marx's and Du Bois's approaches has to do with the analysis of political power and the state. For Marx, the state represents the political power of the dominant classes. Du Bois, however, took his analysis in a different direction. He regards the state and global power as racialized class power in which the dominant strata are both class groups and racial groups. For example, in *Black Reconstruction* he argues that the end of Reconstruction brought about the reunification of the white bourgeoisie and the white poor as a dominant bloc whose combined power led to the rebuilding of southern white political power. And in *Color and Democracy* he argues that the colonial state was based on the class alliance between fractions of the European colonial bourgeoisie and the white working class.

Du Bois arrives at Marxism through his disenchantment with liberal pragmatism, but he merges Marx's thought with his own previous analysis of the centrality of the color line in structuring modernity. Hence, he is not constrained by Marxist categories of analysis. Marx begins his analysis of capitalism from the perspective of the free factory worker. By contrast, Du Bois begins his analysis of historical capitalism from the perspective of the enslaved and the colonial laborer. The central point of his analysis is that capitalism is a global social formation based on colonial relations and the exploitation of racialized labor.

Racial and Colonial Capitalism

Du Bois writes *The World and Africa* to tell the story of a continent that has been erased from history. In this book, he puts African history in the context of large regional and global processes. Du Bois argues that throughout history the peoples of Africa were part of political, cultural, and economic developments in Europe and Asia.[23] In his analysis Du Bois makes two key methodological points. The first is the centrality of history in his sociology. For Du Bois, it is impossible to understand the present without understanding its historical construction; his sociological thinking is rooted in history. Second, he asserts the importance of what today we call relational analysis. Du Bois's analysis shows how different African political, economic, and cultural institutions were the product of long histories of contact, trade, conflict, and cultural exchange between peoples. Thus, for example, while he emphasizes the Africanness of Egypt and its role in the development of European culture, he also shows how the Egyptian society and politics were also the product of long histories of contact and change as a result of Egypt standing at the crossroads of different political and cultural regions in both Africa and Asia.

Du Bois argues that social relations and structures of power in precapitalist Africa were more fluid than they became under racialized modernity. Prior to this historical epoch, there was not a clear, stable, world-hierarchical structure. Nor was there a stable scheme of classification of peoples. That changed with European expansion and the emergence of racial and colonial capitalism. It is in this analysis of Africa in the context of world history that Du Bois argues that slavery and colonialism were central to the rise of Europe-centered capitalism: "This then was the history of the slave trade, of that extraordinary movement which made investment in human flesh the first experiment in organized modern capitalism; which made the system possible."[24] Du Bois asserts the centrality of Black labor in the emergence of modernity:

> The Negro race has been the foundation upon which the capitalist system has been reared, the Industrial Revolution carried through, and imperial colonialism established. If we confine ourselves to America we can-

not forget that America was built on Africa. From being a mere stopping place between Europe and Asia or a chance treasure house of gold, America became through African labor the center of the sugar empire and the cotton kingdom and an integral part of that world industry and trade which caused the Industrial Revolution and the reign of capitalism.[25]

Du Bois's assertion reveals that Black people are the first modern subject. Race is the first social construction of modernity, an imagined but violently real social construction. In Du Bois's historical and relational account, capitalism was always a global and racialized social formation that would not have existed as we know it without slavery, colonialism, and racism. If for Marx capitalism emerges with the rise of wage workers in factories, for Du Bois it emerges with the rise of slavery in colonial plantations.

Du Bois addresses recurring arguments—made in his time and ours—that colonialism is not central to European capitalism. He shows the evolution of different forms of colonial capital accumulation and the emergence of different class segments driving the accumulation process. But he argues that although the particular groups that benefit from colonialism changed, the extraction of wealth and profit from the colonies remained central for capital accumulation. As he asserts in *Color and Democracy*,

Much has been said, for instance, of the fact that colonies do not pay the mother country, in the sense that usually the direct payments of the mother country to the colony exceeds [sic] the money returns of the colony to the country which owns it. This is true today, although in the sixteenth century it was not true. In the fifteenth and sixteenth centuries, the object of colonial territory was the direct return in gold, silver, jewels, and luxuries. Why, then, does the mother country today not only wish to retain the colonies but also is willing to fight expensive wars for such retention and for increasing the colonial area?

The answer to this question has often been that raw material in colonial regions is of such value that countries must control it in order to retain their "place in the sun." This was true in the eighteenth century, when cotton, sugar, tobacco, were the monopolies of empires owning colonies which raised these materials. But here again this was once true but is not universally true today. It has been shown recently that only 3 per cent of the more valuable raw materials of the world are in colonial areas. Still empires want colonies. The answer to all this seeming paradox is the fact that colonies are today areas for the investment of capital in which the investor can make a rate of profit far beyond that which comes to him from domestic ventures.[26]

Du Bois asserts that one characteristic of racial and colonial capitalism is widespread economic inequality between its regions, with the colonized parts of the world enduring extended poverty. The wealth of Europe, for Du Bois, is intrinsically linked to the poverty of the colonies. "Colonies are the slums of the world," he asserts. "They are today the places of greatest concentration of poverty, disease, and ignorance of what the human mind has come to know."[27] And he adds, "Extreme poverty in colonies was a main cause of wealth and luxury in Europe."[28] Marxist theories of imperialism recognize the role of colonialism in shaping peripheral economies. Yet Du Bois's argument differs from them in that he does not see imperialism as a stage in the development of capitalism but instead sees capitalism as a global colonial system from the start, one that takes different shapes at different times. The forms of using racialized and colonial labor change, but capital accumulation is predicated on the continuous racialization of global labor and the exploitation of colonial workers.

Whereas Marx emphasizes that capitalism is based on wage labor and the free extraction of surplus labor, Du Bois argues that racial and colonial capitalism is based on different coercive forms of extracting profits. These different views are the result of a third methodological point of Du Bois's global and historical sociology: the standpoint from which one looks at social and historical changes. Du Bois looks at capitalism from its margins, from the perspective of the colonized, enslaved, and racially excluded workers. This standpoint allows Du Bois to provide a richer account of the development and functioning of historical capitalism, an account that ends up modifying and enriching the Marxist analytical frame.

For Du Bois racialization is a fundamental yet changing structure of global power. Referring to England's opposition to the slave trade in the nineteenth century, Du Bois argues, "Eventually, Negro slavery and the slave trade were abandoned in favor of colonial imperialism, and the England which in the eighteenth century established modern slavery in America on a vast scale, appeared in the nineteenth century as the official emancipator of slaves and founder of a method of control of human labor and material which proved more profitable than slavery."[29] England's turn against the slave trade did not mean the end of colonialism and racism. The forms of exploitation and coercion of racialized and colonial labor changed through history, but did not disappear.

Another characteristic of racial and colonial capitalism is its inherent and constant violence. Violence is the outcome of dispossession, the result of the attempt to control the colonies and subdue rebellion, and also the outcome of competition between colonial powers for colonies or spheres of influence. Of the consequences of dispossession, Du Bois asserted, "The colonial system caused ten times more deaths than actual wars. In the first twenty five years of the nineteenth century famines in India starved a million men, and famine was bound up with exploitation. Widespread monopoly of land to deprive all men of primary sources of support was carried out either through direct ownership or indirect mortgage and exorbitant interest. Disease could not be checked: tuberculosis in the mines of South Africa, syphilis in all colonial regions, cholera, leprosy, malaria."[30] Violence was also used openly for the purpose of control. Writing in 1947, Du Bois is as explicit as one can be in his description and condemnation of colonial violence: "There was no Nazi atrocity—concentration camps, wholesale maiming and murder, defilement of women or ghastly blasphemy of childhood—which the Christian civilization of Europe had not long been practicing against colored folk in all parts of the world in the name of and for the defense of a Superior Race born to rule the world."[31] The violence of the colonial system, though, was not only directed towards the colonized. Colonial competition was, for Du Bois, the cause of the two world wars of the twentieth century. As he states, "But imperialism does not stop there; it not only promotes civil war, strife and jealousy within the colony, but it is, as we have seen, a main cause of struggles between powers to possess colonies."[32]

In *Color and Democracy*, Du Bois lists a large number of conflicts that took place between 1792 and 1939 and attributes them to six factors:

rivalry for colonies, spheres of influence, colonial conquest, internal-group conquest, colonial revolts, and strife within colonies. He recognizes that it is very difficult to establish the causes of specific conflicts but maintains that the dynamic of colonialism is one that leads to permanent violence and conflict. This violence affects the colonizer and the colonized differently. As he asserts, "Many persons naturally will dissent from cataloguing several of these wars as colonial or caused by the strife for colonies. Strict interpretation might reduce the list, but with the greatest logical reduction we nevertheless have a formidable array of wars which took place in an era dominated largely by organized pacifism, but, as the event proved, pacifism designed 'for white people only.'"[33] Racial and colonial capitalism was, then, for Du Bois, a system based on structural and actual violence against the colonized and a system that generated war between colonial powers.

In *Color and Democracy*, Du Bois also reveals prescience about the emerging postcolonial world, pointing to the weight of debt and the political limits of peripheral countries within a neocolonial power structure. He writes, "So long as the chief business of free nations today is to tax and starve their peoples so as to pay their debts to the empires, and so long as these imperial debts do not always represent actual hire of real wealth so much as speculation, legal claims and threats of aggression, just so long world politics will be bedeviled by hunger and hate."[34] This statement anticipates the neoliberal globalization of the late twentieth and early twenty-first centuries. In this vein, Du Bois warns the newly independent states that following the Western path of development will lead to new forms of oppression. In a letter to the All African Peoples' Congress that met in Accra in 1958, Du asserts that the West

> offers a compromise, but one of which you must beware: She offers to let some of your smarter and less scrupulous leaders become fellow capitalists with the white exploiters, if in turn they induce the nation's masses to pay the awful cost. This has happened in the West Indies and in South America. This may yet happen in the Middle East and Eastern Asia. Strive against it with every fiber of your bodies and souls. A body of local private capitalists, even if they are black, can never free Africa; they will simply sell it into new slavery to old masters overseas.[35]

And in *Color and Democracy* he anticipates how racial minorities in developed capitalist countries will be excluded in the newly emerging neocolonial order.

> Beyond the colonies and the free nations which are not free, is the plight of the minorities in the midst of both the great and minor nations. There are the Jews of Europe, the Negroes of the United States, the Indians of the Americas and many other smaller groups elsewhere. They form often little nations within nations, who are encysted and kept from participation in the full citizenship of their native lands.[36]

One of the absences in Du Bois's work is an examination of the predicament of indigenous peoples and a full analysis of settler colonialism. Although he insists throughout his work that colonialism and empire affected the world as a whole, his worldview is one that emphasizes the exploitation of workers of color and is silent concerning the experience of dispossession of indigenous people. The Black experience in the United States, the Africana diaspora, and Africa are the main perspectives from which Du Bois looked at the world. Yet in *Color and Democracy* he asserts, "The Indians of the Americas are for the most part disfranchised, landless, poverty-stricken, and illiterate, and are achieving a degree of freedom only as by the death of individuality they become integrated into the blood and culture of the whites."[37]

Du Bois decries this policy of forced assimilation and cultural disappearance. In both *The World and Africa* and *Color and Democracy: Colonies and Peace*, he argues that one of the worst consequences of colonialism is the destruction of the culture of colonized people.

The Global Veil

Racial and colonial capitalism relies on racial classification and the veil. Du Bois argues that the racial categories and differences that organize our world are the product of the global colonial system of organizing labor. Racial classifications as we know them were created when Europeans marked specific groups of people for slavery or forced labor.

Du Bois acknowledges that physical differences were recognized before European expansion, but these differences did not organize social relations. In his writings Du Bois mentions different racial types and refers to different physical types, but he maintains that there are no pure types and that there is no relation between physical type and culture or development. In *Color and Democracy*, he asserts that there is "no African race and no one Negro type. Africa has as great a physical and cultural variety as Europe or Asia."[38]

Du Bois argues that racism and race are the product of the European need to legitimize the system of colonial exploitation and displacement, yet at the same time they are social forces that structure lived experience and social relations within historical capitalism. The category of whiteness emerged to refer to the dominant peoples in historical capitalism. As Du Bois asserts in *Color and Democracy*,

> It is the habit of men, and must be if they remain rational beings, to find reasons, and comforting reasons, for lines of action which they adopt from varying motives. First of all, religion rationalized slavery as a method of saving souls, but this bade fair to interfere with profit and investment and soon was changed by the new science to a doctrine of natural human inferiority on the part of the majority of mankind, making them forever inferior and subservient to the ruling nations of the world.[39]

Du Bois develops similar ideas in *The World and Africa*. Elaborating on the idea that both the theory and the science of race emerged with slavery and capitalism, he asserts,

> In order to establish the righteousness of this point of view, science and religion, government and industry, were wheeled into line. The word "Negro" was used for the first time in the world's history to tie color to race and blackness to slavery and degradation. The white race was pictured as "pure" and superior; the black race as dirty, stupid, and inevitably inferior; the yellow race as sharing, in deception and cowardice, much of this color inferiority; while mixture of races was considered the prime cause of degradation and failure in civilization. Everything great, everything fine, everything really successful in human culture was white.[40]

For Du Bois, racial thinking did not disappear when slavery formally ended, and its roots endured in modern Europe and America. He argues, "The slave trade; that modern change from regarding wealth as being for the benefit of human beings, to that of regarding human beings as wealth. This utter reversal of attitude which marked the day of a new barter in human flesh did not die with the slave but persists and dominates the thought of Europe today and during the fatal era when Europe by force ruled mankind."[41] The dominant ways of seeing and classifying human beings are a direct product of slavery and colonial capitalism and inform and structure how we think about and understand the world. In order to maintain their cultural and political hegemony, the dominant white ruling classes developed forms of "scientific" knowledge designed to transform historical inequalities and injustices into natural law.

> Ability, self-assertion, resentment, among colonial peoples must be represented as irrational efforts of "agitators"—folk trying to attain that for which they were not by nature fitted. To prove the unfitness of most human beings for self-rule and self-expression, every device of science was used: evolution was made to prove that Negroes and Asiatics were less developed human beings than whites; history was so written as to make all civilization the development of white people; economics was so taught as to make all wealth due mainly to the technical accomplishment of white folks supplemented only by the brute toil of colored peoples; brain weights and intelligence tests were used and distorted to prove the superiority of white folk.[42]

Writing *Black Reconstruction* and *The World and Africa* was Du Bois's way of challenging these colonial forms of knowledge. In this way, Du Bois's work prefigures contemporary postcolonial and decolonial analyses.

Broadening his early analysis of the veil, which he began in *Souls*, Du Bois links the phenomenology of lived experience to the global historical processes of capitalist expansion, colonialism, and racialization.[43] Du Bois relies on his analysis of double consciousness to reflect on the lived experience of colonized people and the world of white people from a global perspective. In *The World and Africa* and *Color and Democracy*, Du Bois underscores the constant opposition and resistance of colonized people to racism and colonialism. He argues that the colonial powers tried to represent the colonized as docile and colonialism as civilization, in keeping with the "white man's burden," but Du Bois emphasizes the fact that from the very beginning, the colonized people rebelled against colonial oppression. As he asserts, "Almost unnoticed, certainly unlistened to, there came from the colonial world reiterated protest, prayers, and appeals against the suppression of human beings, against the exclusion of the majority of mankind from the vaunted progress of the world."[44]

Du Bois lists numerous rebellions of enslaved people that occurred between the sixteenth and the nineteenth centuries and argues that while these are often portrayed as unconnected events, they in fact convey a consistent resistance to colonialism: "The slave revolts were the beginnings of the revolutionary struggle for the uplift of the laboring masses in the modern world. They have been minimized in extent because of the propaganda in favor of slavery and the feeling that the knowledge of slave revolt would hurt the system."[45] Du Bois does not deny the differences between or the specificities of these rebellions, but he emphasizes the common thread that unifies them all—the opposition to a system that denies the humanity of people of color.[46]

One of Du Bois's major contributions in *Black Reconstruction* is the analysis of the lived experience of the rebelling enslaved people. By analyzing the subjectivity of the enslaved Du Bois addresses the lived experience of emancipation. Thus, talking about the effects of Lincoln's Emancipation Proclamation, Du Bois asserts that enslaved people understood it and reacted to it on the basis of their religious beliefs: "The Proclamation made four and a half million laborers willing almost in mass to sacrifice their last drop of blood for their new-found country. It sent them into transports of joy and sacrifice. It changed their pessimism and despair into boundless faith. It was the coming of the lord."[47]

This is a point noted by C. L. R. James in a series of lectures on *The Black Jacobins* that he delivered in 1971. James compares his book to *Black Reconstruction* and emphasizes Du Bois's descriptions of the ideas and feelings of the enslaved people as they joined the fight for their emancipation. As James writes, "Du Bois is poetic and dealing there with psychological matters, which in reality are a contribution to an understanding of what took place. The blacks who entered, this is what they entered with in their mind."[48] The analysis of concrete forms of historical subjectivities helps Du Bois to address the notorious problem in Marxist theory of the link among structural analysis, the emergence of class consciousness, and the formation of collective actors. For Du Bois, as later for British Marxist historian E. P. Thompson, the formation of collective actors is rooted in communities, traditions, and everyday lives.[49] But unlike Thompson, who studied the emergence of the English working-class communities and identities, for Du Bois, collective Black identities in the American South were based on the lived experience of slavery and racism rather than class.

Du Bois further proposes that rebellion of enslaved Black people was key to determining the course and outcome of the Civil War, particularly when enslaved people ran away from plantations to join the northern armies. He argues that at the beginning of the war the enslaved were passive, as they did not know how the war would unfold and what they could expect from the northern armies. Yet, as these armies advanced into southern territories, enslaved people began running away from the plantations, an action Du Bois describes as a general strike: "This was not merely the desire to stop work. It was a strike on a wide basis against the conditions of work. It was a general strike that involved in the end perhaps a half million people. They wanted to stop the economy of the plantation system, and to do that they left the plantations."[50]

Du Bois asserts that this strike won the war for the North, as the running away of the formerly enslaved helped undo the southern economy and provided soldiers to a northern army that was challenged by white resistance to the draft. As he states,

> It was not the Abolitionists alone who freed the slaves. The Abolitionists never had a real majority of the people of the United States back of them. Freedom for the slave was the logical result of a crazy attempt to wage war in the midst of four million black slaves. . . . Yet, these slaves had enormous power in their hands. Simply by stopping work, they could threaten the Confederacy with starvation. By walking into the Federal camps, they showed to doubting Northerners the easy possibility of using them as workers and as servants, as farmers, and as spies, and finally, as fighting soldiers. . . . It was the fugitive slave who made the slaveholders face the alternative of surrendering to the North, or to the Negroes.[51]

On the other hand, as Black labor rebelled against slavery, white labor became the backbone of the racist social order. In *Black Reconstruction* Du Bois argues that a white racial subjectivity was key to explaining both the reluctance of white workers to support abolitionism and the failure of Reconstruction. Du Bois states that racial division led to the emergence of a caste psychology that is central to contemporary capitalism. This caste psychology forms the base of what he calls the "psychological wage" of whiteness. White workers received public recognition and deference while Blacks were subjected to public humiliation.

> It must be remembered that the white group of laborers, while they received a low wage, were compensated in part by a sort of public and psychological wage. They were given public deference and titles of courtesy because they were white. . . . On the other hand, in the same way, the Negro was subject to public insult; was afraid of mobs; was liable to the jibes of children and the unreasoning fears of white women; and was compelled almost continuously to submit to various badges of inferiority.[52]

Racial difference and inequalities may have originated in the need to exploit labor, but they were perpetuated and constantly reproduced through social interaction and the construction of racial subjectivity. The resulting social system is one in which race trumps class in the assignment of social status, the formation of identities, and the development of collective action. Ultimately, the lived experience of being the favored segment of the working class is structured around the veil, the not-seeing of the predicament of the other.

Colonialism affected the European labor movement in the same way in which racism affected the white working class in the United States. Du Bois shows how the global veil leads to blindness in the dominant groups just as his analysis of the veil and whiteness in the United States pointed to the blindness of whites towards the existence of life, humanity, and resistance behind the veil. He asserts, "Because of colonialism, Socialists have long been unable to be true to their principles. The questions of Egypt and India, Kenya and Palestine, made it impossible for Ramsey MacDonald, Lord Olivier, Sidney Webb and many others to follow out their Socialist principles."[53]

Despite the colonizers' belief that they are promoting civilization, the colonized rebelled from the first moment in defense of their lifeworlds, their work, their dignity, and their humanity. The colonizer is unable to see this because the inherent violence of colonialism is kept hidden. As Du Bois contends, "If in the end the colony is kept at work, made to pay interest, and turns out materials at low cost, few persons at home are going to ask how this was accomplished; and the men who bring this to pass, no matter at what cost or by what disreputable means, stand to receive wealth and honor. Under this veil, cheating, lying, murder, and rape, force, deception, bribery, and destruction, become methods of achieving imperial power, with few questions asked."[54]

An original contribution of Du Bois is the analysis of how the world appears fragmented to the population of colonial metropolises. This analysis parallels Marx's analysis of commodity fetishism. For Marx, this concept referred to the fact that workers encounter the commodity as an entity independent and separate from them, hiding the fact that the commodity is the product of the worker's labor. Du Bois's analysis, on the other hand, focuses on how colonial commodities, used for conspicuous consumption in Europe and America, hide the brutality of the exploitation, destruction, and displacement that were required to create them:[55]

> Because of the stretch in time and space between the deed and the result, between the work and the product, it is not only usually impossible for the worker to know the consumer; or the investor, the source of his profit, but also it is often made impossible by law to inquire into the facts. Moral judgment of the industrial process is therefore difficult, and the crime is more often a matter of ignorance rather than of deliberate murder and theft; but ignorance is a colossal crime in itself.[56]

Indeed, in assessing the ignorance of the consumers of colonial commodities, Du Bois imagines a British upper-middle-class woman playing the piano—one of the marks of European civilization—in her home and asks to what extent such a person is responsible for the crimes of colonialism:

> It will in all probability not occur to her that she has any responsibility whatsoever, and that may well be true. Equally, it may be true that

her income is the result of starvation, theft, and murder; that it involves ignorance, disease, and crime on the part of thousands; that the system which sustains the security, leisure, and comfort she enjoys is based on the suppression, exploitation, and slavery of the majority of mankind. Yet just because she does not know this, just because she could get the facts only after research and investigation—made difficult by laws that forbid the revealing of ownership of property, source of income, and methods of business—she is content to remain in ignorance of the source of her wealth and its cost in human toil and suffering.[57]

For Du Bois, as for Walter Benjamin, the marks of civilization are also marks of barbarism.[58] Du Bois, however, links Benjamin's famous condemnation of European culture to its colonial and racist context. The illusion of civilization and legitimate wealth is sustained only through willful ignorance as to the origin of the material sources of that wealth. The originality of Du Bois's sociology is that it combines the analysis of both the colonial and racialized economic structures of historical capitalism and the coloniality of the cultural categories that structure social life and knowledge formation—and does so in a historical, relational, and nondeterministic way.[59]

Intersectionalities

The veil and the color line are central to the analysis of another aspect of historical capitalism in which Du Bois modifies and extends Marx's analysis: the intersectionalities that characterize the lived experience and identities of different segments of the working class. In *Black Reconstruction*, the intersection of class and race is a central aspect of Du Bois's analysis. The first three chapters focus on the classes central to the slave-based economy: the Black Worker, the White Worker, and the Planters.[60] In his analysis of these different classes, Du Bois shows how the institution of slavery created deep racial fault lines that traversed class lines.

The first chapter of *Black Reconstruction* analyzes the position and experiences of the Black workers, that is, the enslaved. Du Bois, like C. L. R. James in *Black Jacobins*, considers the enslaved worker of the southern plantations an integral part of global commodity chains linking the southern and northern United States, emerging European manufacturing regions, Africa, and the Caribbean. In this respect, the enslaved people of the American South were part of a global proletariat, but their experience as part of that group was determined by their status as slaves, their lack of freedom, and the lack of recognition of their humanity.

The second chapter of *Black Reconstruction* examines the white worker. The chapter shows how white labor in the North detached itself from the fight against slavery. Immigrant workers in the North were often initially opposed to slavery but soon came to regard Black enslaved people as competitors. For the northern working class, the detachment from the Black emancipatory struggle is accompanied by a perception of the enslaved that denies their humanity. Therefore, Du Bois argues, two labor movements emerged: one centered on the emancipation of Black enslaved people and another centered on improving the working conditions of the white immigrant working class. Due to the potential of labor-market competition between white workers and freed slaves, these two movements never converged.[61] This tension may have been grounded in labor-market competition but was experienced as racial animosity. In Du Bois's words,

> These two movements might easily have cooperated . . . but the trouble was that black and white laborers were competing for the same jobs, just of course as all laborers always are. The immediate competition became open and visible because of racial lines and racial philosophy. . . . This situation, too, made extraordinary reaction, led by the ignorant mob and fomented by authority and privilege; abolitionists were attacked and their meeting places burned; women suffragists were hooted, laws were proposed making the kidnaping of Negroes easier and disfranchising Negro voters.[62]

In the same way that the northern working class detached itself from the struggle against slavery, in the South the white poor identified with their whiteness rather than with the enslaved, with whom they may have shared a common class interest. The white poor in the South provided the labor power necessary to control the enslaved and avoid slave rebellions. Du Bois argues that in the South, "Slavery bred in the poor white a dislike of Negro toil of all sorts. He never regarded himself as a laborer, or as part of any labor movement. If he had any ambition at all it was to become a planter and to own 'niggers.' To these Negroes he transferred all the dislike and hatred which he had for the whole slave system. The result was that the system was held stable and intact by poor whites."[63]

Class is central to Du Bois's analysis, but in ways that are very different from Marx's. The Marxist framework could not account for the class structure of the United States (or the class structure of racial and colonial capitalism in general). Du Bois modifies Marx's class analysis by introducing the analysis of the intersections of race and class, and the fractures that these intersections create along class lines. In doing so he creates a theoretical understanding of capitalism that goes far beyond Marx's framework and the later additions by European Marxist theorists. For Du Bois, race and racism are constitutive of historical class relations and identities. As he writes,

> The theory of laboring class unity rests upon the assumption that laborers, despite internal jealousies, will unite because of their opposition to exploitation by the capitalists. . . . Most persons do not realize how far this failed to work in the South, and it failed to work because the theory of race was supplemented by a carefully planned and slowly evolved method which drove such a wedge between the white and black workers that there probably are not today in the world two groups of workers with practically identical interests who hate and fear each other so deeply and persistently.[64]

Moving beyond the United States, Du Bois also addresses the intersection of race and class in his analysis of the politics of colonial metropolises. In *Color and Democracy*, he argues that colonialism was based on the support of the white working class for the colonial system: "Organized labor in the United States and Europe has seldom actively opposed imperialism or championed democracy among colonial peoples, even when this slave labor was in direct competition with their own. The Social-Democratic party of prewar Germany once openly declared that the wages and working-conditions which it asked for white labor did not include any such demand for yellow labor."[65]

In reflecting on the likely politics of European unions and labor parties after the end of World War II, Du Bois argues that the possibility of addressing the demands of the working class depended on the continuous extraction of profits from the colonies and predicts that labor parties will thus support colonialism. He asserts,

> When, for instance, during and after this war the working people of Britain, The Netherlands, France, and Belgium, in particular, are going to demand certain costly social improvements from their governments—the prevention of unemployment, a rising standard of living, health insurance, increased education of children—the large cost of these improvements must be met by increased public taxation, falling with greater weight than ever heretofore upon the rich. This means that the temptation to recoup and balance the financial burden of increased taxation by investment in colonies, where social services are at their lowest and standards of living below the requirements of civilization, is going to increase decidedly; and the disposition of parties on the left, liberal parties, and philanthropy to press for colonial improvements will tend to be silenced by the bribe of vastly increased help by government to better conditions. The working people of the civilized world may thus be largely induced to put their political power behind imperialism, and democracy in Europe and America will continue to impede and nullify democracy in Asia and Africa.[66]

These predictions proved correct. European and American labor did not support the postwar anticolonial struggles, nor the realization of a more egalitarian world order. Racism and coloniality trumped class interest. Colonial powers, whether reluctantly or by force, ultimately gave up their colonies, but, as we have seen, Du Bois intuited how new forms of neocolonialism, such as financial indebtedness and the political limits imposed on newly independent countries, could perpetuate racialized global inequalities. To what extent the standard of living of the Global North, particularly that of its elites and labor aristocracies, depends on the continuation of neocolonial policies is an empirical question. But the continuation of mechanisms of neocolonial exploitation and extraction highlights the fact that these activities remain profitable for sectors within the core countries of the world system.

Du Bois also presented an incipient analysis of the intersections of race and gender. This has been a source of controversy in the assessment of both his politics and his scholarship. On the one hand, Du Bois was aware of the importance of addressing gender issues in the struggle for emancipation. In his essay "The Damnation of Women," he asserted, "The uplift of women is, next to the problem of the color line and the peace movement, our greatest modern cause. When, now, two of these movements—women and color—combine in one, the combination has deep meaning."[67] Yet he articulated his position from what political theorist Joy James describes as a masculinist worldview, that is, a worldview that centers male normativity. James criticizes Du Bois for his relationship to women activists and scholars who were his contemporaries and for the ambivalence of his representations of women. James summarizes this tension by arguing, "It is disingenuous to minimize Du Bois' significant contributions towards women's equality. It would also be deceptive to ignore his problematic literary representations of and political relationships with influential African American women activists."[68] And later on, she adds, "Profeminism permitted Du Bois to include women in democratic struggles; paternalism allowed him to naturalize the male intellectual."[69] This same tension is present in Du Bois's sociological analysis of race and gender. Du Bois was ahead of male scholars and public intellectuals of his time in his analysis of gender issues and advocacy of women's rights. But his analysis of the intersection of race and gender was characterized by serious limitations and was not a central element of his writings.

Du Bois's essay "The Damnation of Women" presents a critique of women's oppression and gender roles. For him the predicament of women derives from the tension between motherhood and independent work. The source of this tension is the subordination of women in the household. As he states, "The world wants healthy babies and intelligent workers. Today we refuse to allow the combination and force thousands of intelligent workers to go childless at a horrible expenditure of moral force, or we damn them if they break our idiotic conventions. Only at the sacrifice of intelligence and the chance to do their best work can the majority of modern women bear children."[70] Du Bois describes the conventions on women and work prevalent in his time as idiotic and states clearly that women have a right to economic independence and to decide on their own about motherhood. But he does not break with the conventions that equated womanhood and motherhood.

The predicament he describes is that of all women, but Du Bois goes on to argue that race, as well as class, makes a difference when it comes to the experience of women. Du Bois argues that the experience of African American women is unique, as they bear the brunt of both exploitation and the legacy of slavery; furthermore, they suffer under the combined weight of gender and racial violence.[71] Du Bois is eloquent in his condemnation of the violence to be found at the intersection of racism and patriarchy, stating, "I shall forgive the white South much in its final judgment day: I shall forgive its slavery, for slavery is a world-old habit; I shall forgive its fighting for a well-lost cause, and for remembering that struggle with tender tears; I shall forgive its so-called 'pride of race,' the passion of its hot blood, and even its dear, old, laughable strutting and posing; but one thing I shall never forgive, neither in this world nor the world to come: its wanton and continued and persistent insulting of the black womanhood which it sought and seeks to prostitute to its lust."[72] Du Bois also emphasizes the agency of African American women: Despite the suffering, exploitation, and violence they have endured, they led the struggle for emancipation and were the main agents of community institution building: "Black women (and women whose grandmothers were black) are today furnishing our teachers; they are the main pillars of those social settlements which we call churches; and they have with small doubt raised three-fourths of our church property."[73]

In Du Bois's analysis class is also deeply related with race and gender. Du Bois recognizes that African American women have always worked and were not expected to stay at home. The consequence of this historical predicament was threefold: "The economic independence of black women is increased, the breaking up of Negro families must be more frequent, and the number of illegitimate children is decreased more slowly."[74] For economic reasons, Black women had to work and, in many cases, earned more than Black men. This, combined with existing ideas about gender roles, led to the breakup of poor and working-class Black families. Du Bois makes clear that this is the result of economic conditions rather than racial differences and points to similar trends that have been observed among white groups in similar situations.

Ever since the publication of the Moynihan report in 1965, the structure of the Black family has been a recurrent theme in studies that discuss the "pathologies" of poor Black families and neighborhoods.[75] This was not the case for Du Bois. In his opinion, the work of women reflected their strength and independence. Furthermore, Du Bois argued that the Black family presented a model for how the needs of working-class families would be addressed in the future. Du Bois develops this point in "The Freedom of Womanhood," a chapter of his 1924 book *The Gift of Black Folk*. In that chapter, Du Bois argues that Black women, in working for a living and finding ways to care for the family, are showing all women the way forward. He states, "In our modern industrial organization the work of women is being found as valuable as that of men. They are consequently being taken from the home and put into industry and the rapidity by which this process is going on is only kept back by the problem of the child; and more and more the community is taking charge of the education of children for this reason. In America the work of Negro women has not only pre-figured this development but it has had a direct influence upon it."[76] For Du Bois the labor of Black working-class women and the ways of organizing their families pointed towards the future organization of the modern industrial system. And he emphasizes the right of women to economic and personal development, asserting, "The future woman must have a life work and economic independence. She must have knowledge. She must have the right to motherhood at her own discretion."[77]

In considering Du Bois's sociological work one can paraphrase Joy James's summary of his gender politics. On the one hand, it would be a mistake to deny his contribution to an early analysis of the intersectionality of race, class, and gender. On the other hand, it would also be a mistake to exaggerate his contribution, or to place him at the center of the development of gender intersectional analysis. To be sure, Du Bois considered gender issues more than most other male scholars and public intellectuals of his time. He was certainly ahead of both his contemporary American sociologists and the discipline's founding fathers (and many contemporary sociologists as well). But the analysis of gender was not as integral to his writings as such issues as the color line, empire, colonialism, and class, and he did not embed his analysis of gender intersectionality within his broader analysis of global racial capitalism.

More important, Black women intellectuals and activists had already introduced work on gender intersectionality. Du Bois was familiar with this work although he fails to properly and fully acknowledge it. In "The Damnation of Women" he cites Anna Julia Cooper's famous statement that only when Black women achieve emancipation will all Black people achieve emancipation.[78] But although Du Bois quotes Cooper, he does not mention her by name. Rather, he attributes her famous phrase to some-one he describes as "one of our women."[79] Similarly, while Du Bois was familiar with Ida B. Wells's work on lynching, he does not credit her in his writings.[80]

Acknowledging the work of Cooper and Wells would not only have been an act of justice and recognition; it would have improved Du Bois's work. His analysis of gender intersectionality addresses women's work outside the home, but he does not address the work of women at home. Anna Julia Cooper's essay "What Are We Worth?"—part of her book *A Voice from the South*—develops an early analysis of reproductive work as creating value. Cooper does not articulate her analysis in those terms, but that is what she does.[81]

Addressing Cooper's argument could have helped Du Bois construct a more sophisticated analysis of women's work inside and outside the home and a more sophisticated critique of gender roles. Instead, his analysis of gender roles remains limited by his equating womanhood with mother-hood. Cooper's work could also have helped Du Bois to criticize the pro-ductivist ethos of racial and colonial capitalism that is so central to the many forms of racial and colonial violence he describes in his work. Simi-larly, had Du Bois addressed the work of Ida B. Wells, he could have devel-oped a more sophisticated analysis of the intersection of racial and gender violence.

Despite its important limitations, Du Bois's sociology recognized the centrality of the study of the intersectionalities of race, class, and gender. Furthermore, his refusal to identify the structure of the Black family as a pathology remains highly relevant to contemporary debates. Therefore, it would be a natural extension of his work to include a full analysis of race, class, and gender intersectionality in a contemporary Du Boisian sociology.

The Racial State and the Limits of Democracy

An important contribution of Du Bois's sociology was his analysis of the racial state and the racial limits of democracy. Starting his analysis of democracy from the perspective of the Black worker, Du Bois develops an analysis of the class and racial character of the state. For Du Bois, the state is not just Marx's class-dominated state, although he does identify the state as a locus of class power. For Du Bois the state is a racial state, and the politics of class is racial politics.[82] In other words, in a racist society, class power is intrinsically racial. In *Black Reconstruction*, Du Bois describes the end of Reconstruction as the reestablishment of white power and political control of the state.[83]

The racial character of the state, in turn, limits the possibilities for democracy. In *Black Reconstruction*, Du Bois asserts that the fate of the emancipated slaves stood at the center of the possibility of establishing democracy in the United States after the Civil War. For him, the possibility of a thorough democratization of American politics depended on the economic empowerment of the emancipated Black laborers. As he asserts,

> The true significance of slavery in the United States to the whole social development of America, lay in the ultimate relation of slaves to democracy. What were to be the limits of democratic control in the United States? If all labor, black as well as white, became free, were given schools and the right to vote, what control could or should be set to the power and action of these laborers? Was the rule of the mass of Americans to be unlimited, and the right to rule extended to all men, regardless of race and color, or if not, what power of dictatorship would rule, and how would property and privilege be protected?
>
> This was the great and primary question, which was in the minds of the men who wrote the Constitution of the United States and continued in the minds of thinkers down through the slavery controversy. It still remains with the world as the problem of democracy expands and touches all races and nations.[84]

In his analysis of the politics of the newly freed Black population under Reconstruction, Du Bois emphasizes their desire for education and describes how the newly elected legislatures in the South where the Black population held a majority, such as in South Carolina, developed public schools and public education. Indeed, he asserts that the development of public education was the biggest contribution of Reconstruction-era governments. But for emancipated Black workers to achieve full political participation, formal freedom alone was not sufficient. Emancipated Black workers were still subject to the whims of the ruling white power bloc. Du Bois suggests that the freed people needed access to land so they could have their own economic base to stand on and would not have to depend on the goodwill of landowners, employers, or politicians. As he writes in *Black Reconstruction*, "The Negroes were willing to work and did work, but they wanted land to work, and they wanted to see and own the results of their toil. . . . Here was a chance to establish an agrarian democracy in the South: peasant holders of small properties, eager to work and raise crops, amenable to suggestion and general direction. All they needed was honesty in treatment, and education."[85]

The possibility of democracy in the United States depended on an agrarian reform that would give the formerly enslaved people "forty acres and a mule," as the phrase that would go on to become memorable put it. The economic empowerment of Black workers was necessary to both guarantee and solidify Black political power and to allow for a full democratization of American society.

Du Bois presents a theory of democracy that relies on the power of laborers, particularly Black laborers, to assert and protect their own interests. The economic empowerment of the Black laborers, however, depended on accessing political power. For Du Bois, this power could not be based on the union movement, as later social-democratic theories of democracy would argue, because most of the labor movement was racist.[86] Du Bois argues that a united bloc of Black and white laborers could have imposed a program of education and economic empowerment, but again, the working class was deeply and fundamentally divided along racial lines. The intersection of class and race in the lived experience of workers led to profound racial divisions in the labor movement.

A second source of power for the necessary structural transformation of society that would have empowered the Black worker could have been the forceful imposition of a program of reform by the federal government. Du Bois refers to this possibility as the dictatorship of labor: a temporary government based on the northern armies that would favor the economic and political development of Black and white labor and create the basis for substantive democracy to develop. Du Bois argues that this should have been the historical task of Reconstruction and that for a while the Freedmen's Bureau did try to fill this role. But the possibility of a full transformation of American democracy (in both the South and the North) rested on a fragile racial and class alliance. Confronted with resistance from the old planter class in the South at the end of the Civil War, the northern industrial bourgeoisie initially decided to rely on the voting power of the Black population to check the power of the southern elites and stop them from reasserting their power. As he adds, "It was because of this thought that Northern industry made its great alliance with abolition-democracy. The consummation of this alliance came slowly and reluctantly and after vain effort toward understanding with the South which was unsuccessful until 1876."[87]

But Du Bois asserts that this was a problematic strategy for the northern economic elites because it relied on the empowerment of Black labor. Eventually, the northern industrialists came to terms with the new southern elites and left to them the control of southern politics: "Meanwhile, the leaders of Northern capital and finance were still afraid of the return of southern political power after the lapse of the military dictatorship. . . . It was, therefore, necessary for Northern capital to make terms with the dominant south."[88] The consequence of this agreement between the white North and the white South was the abandonment of the recently emancipated Black laborers to the will of the rising white southern political power. Once this happened, it did not take long for the reconstituted southern white ruling bloc to move toward Black disenfranchisement. The result was the end of Reconstruction, the institutionalization of Jim Crow, and the failure to establish full democracy in the United States: "Thus, both the liberal and the conservative North found themselves willing to sacrifice the interests of labor in the South to the interest of capital."[89] The agreement between the northern and southern white elites took place at the expense of Black labor.[90] While the northern bourgeoisie and the southern planters sought to weaken labor in both the North and the South, the concrete form that strategy

took was the disempowerment and disenfranchisement of Black workers. As Du Bois wrote, "It did not go to the length of disfranchising the
whole laboring class, black and white, because it dared not do this, although this was its logical end. It did disfranchise black labor with the
aid of white Southern labor and with the silent acquiescence of white
Northern labor."[91]

The planters opposed the empowerment of Black labor because they
sought cheap labor and because they did not see Black people as equals.
Except for the radical abolitionists, the northern bourgeoisie also did
not fully believe in racial equality, and thus could easily accept southern
complaints about "black laziness" at work and corruption in politics. As
Du Bois put it,

> It happened that the accusation of incompetence impressed the North
> not simply because of the moral revolt there against graft and dishonesty
> but because the North had never been thoroughly converted to the idea
> of Negro equality. . . . Under such circumstances, it was much easier to
> believe the accusations of the South and to listen to the proof which biol-
> ogy and social science hastened to adduce of the inferiority of the Negro.
> The North seized upon the new Darwinism, the "Survival of the Fittest,"
> to prove that what they had attempted in the South was an impossibility;
> and they did this in the face of the facts which were before them, the ex-
> amples of Negro efficiency, of Negro brains, of phenomenal possibilities
> of advancement.[92]

Reading Du Bois's analysis of Reconstruction is like reading a history
of the present. Du Bois wrote about the Reconstruction period thinking
about the continuing civil rights struggle in his time, but his analysis of
the process of Reconstruction was prescient about the possibilities and
constraints of our "post–civil rights" period. The civil rights movement
abolished the political boundaries of the color line, but it only scraped
its economic boundaries. And much as in the Reconstruction period,
the white sectors that supported the civil rights movement abandoned
the movement when the struggle moved from the political arena to the
economic and social arenas. The result was partial political and economic inclusion coupled with the marginalization of large sectors of the
African American population.[93]

The failure to establish democracy in the United States did not only have local consequences. By 1935, when he published *Black Reconstruction*, it was clear to Du Bois that racial and colonial capitalism was global. The failure of Reconstruction made the United States a part of the rising forces that shaped the late-nineteenth-century world order. As he put it, "The United States was turned into a reactionary force. It became the cornerstone of that new imperialism which is subjecting the labor of yellow, brown and black peoples to the dictation of capitalism organized on a world basis; and it has not only brought nearer the revolution by which the power of capitalism is to be challenged, but also it is transforming the fight to the sinister aspect of a fight on racial lines embittered by awful memories."[94]

In *Color and Democracy*, published in 1945, Du Bois addresses the intersection of class and race in the construction of global colonial power. He contends that colonial policies were the result of the political control of the metropolitan and colonial states by economic elites, and asserts, "There can be no question that most modern countries are in the hands of those who control organized wealth, and that the just and wise distribution of income is hindered by this monopoly. This power is entrenched behind barriers of legal sanction, guarded by the best brains of the country trained as lawyers, appointed to the bench, and elected to the legislature. The retention of this power is influenced tremendously by the propaganda of newspapers and news-gathering agencies, by radio, and by social organization."[95] Du Bois links political power to class power that is organized and maintained through a state apparatus that includes the legal system and public opinion. But class power is limited domestically by the strength of labor. Full class and racial power could be exercised against colonial populations only with the support of the metropolitan white working class. As he explains,

> Within the imperial nations, the status of colonies has been determined largely by the attitude of the mass of the working people, whereas in Spain, where workers were disfranchised and had little power, colonial labor conditions prevailed even in the mother country. In the British Empire colonialism could be carried through only when it was applied to alien peoples and not to white people, especially those of English descent. The growing home vote vetoed this.

In the United States fear of European aggression was back of the Monroe Doctrine, but later the doctrine was continued as the white laborers tried to establish in the United States and under American control outside the United States, colonial labor conditions bordering on slavery. They were following unconsciously the later labor patterns adopted by the Union of South Africa.

Today the American Federation of Labor, with its exclusion of Negro members in many of the powerful unions, is still following that pattern, and this is the reason that the AFL will not make common cause with Russian labor. The CIO is trying to recognize depressed labor in the United States and in colonial areas dominated by the United States, as part of the national labor problem. The Labor party in England, while giving theoretical assent to this attitude, has never had courage to follow it up with action.[96]

For Du Bois, the alliance between the economic elites and the labor movement of the colonial powers allowed for the continuation of colonialism. The racial character of the European states perpetuated the system of global exploitation of colonial workers. And again, as in *Black Reconstruction*, Du Bois asserts the need for an economic anchor to achieve democracy. In *Black Reconstruction*, he suggests that access to land would have helped to establish democracy in the United States. In *Color and Democracy*, he emphasizes the need to end colonial rule and the importance of industrial democracy and planning to guarantee full democracy in both the colonial powers and the colonies. These are points that he also made in *Dusk of Dawn*, in which he advocates economic democracy and the need for community control of economic life for Black subsistence and to develop an economic platform for the struggle for racial equality in America.[97]

Du Bois explains the failure of democratization in the United States and globally by analyzing the racial and class character of politics and the state. Because he accounts for the racial bases of political alliances and the fractures that racial divisions cause among workers, Du Bois's analysis of the state is more sophisticated and accurate than Marx's. Du Bois's analysis is also ahead of liberal and social-democratic theorists who consistently ignore racial and colonial exclusions in their analysis of democracy. For Du Bois, there is no true democratization of political life without addressing the racial character of the state and the question of economic power and economic democracy.

A Contemporary Du Boisian Global Sociology

Du Bois's sociology emphasizes the colonial and racial character of capitalism. If for Marx the archetypical figure of historical capitalism is the wage worker in the factory, for Du Bois it is the enslaved and the colonial worker on the plantation and in the mines. A contemporary Du Boisian global sociology would expand the four areas we have discussed in this chapter.

First, it would examine historical and contemporary forms of racial and colonial dispossession and exploitation. Although colonial empires have to a large extent disappeared, neocolonialism and coloniality are central features of the contemporary world, making these important subjects of study for Du Boisian sociologists. Furthermore, a contemporary Du Boisian global sociology would have to go beyond Du Bois's own analysis and consider processes of dispossession and displacement of indigenous people and historical and contemporary forms of settler colonialism.

Second, a contemporary Du Boisian sociology would search for the links between global structures and the phenomenology of lived experience. Racial schemes and colonial categories continue to shape subjectivities and identities. A Du Boisian sociology would examine the subjectivity and agency of the subaltern groups of contemporary capitalism, exploring how they construct their world and struggle for dignity, and how the veil blinds dominant groups to the plight of racialized others—others such as racialized workers, migrants, prisoners, and marginalized people. A contemporary Du Boisian sociology would also examine and critique the construction of racial and colonial forms of knowledge in the sciences and the public sphere.

Additionally, a contemporary Du Boisian sociology would analyze the historical and contemporary forms of the intersection of race, class, and gender. It would go beyond Du Bois's own limitations and fully incorporate the analysis of intersectionalities, both in the formation of inequalities and in the interpersonal and experiential dimensions. Furthermore, it would explore also the construction of intersectional solidarities.

Finally, a contemporary Du Boisian sociology would study the historical and present forms of the racial state. It is the task of Du Boisian sociologists to investigate the configurations of racial and class political power that maintain racial inequality and coloniality in the United States and globally. A Du Boisian political sociology should examine the racial logics of state bureaucracies and institutions, to document how they reproduce and recreate racial inequalities. A contemporary Du Boisian sociology would also go beyond Du Bois's and develop an analysis of settler colonial states.

Methodologically, a contemporary Du Boisian global sociology should be guided by a theoretical understanding of racial and colonial capitalism, rooted in historical analysis. For Du Bois, the analysis of contemporary institutions and structures could be conducted only by understanding how history constructs the present. A contemporary Du Boisian sociology does not seek generalizable ahistorical concepts or mechanisms but rather understanding of the structures of exploitation and oppression, as well as analysis of forms of agency and subjectivity, in their historical context. This does not mean that concepts cannot be generalized, but rather that one needs to account for the historical contexts in which concepts are developed and applied.[98]

A Du Boisian global sociology is also relational. It looks at peoples and social and cultural formations in their local and global connections. A contemporary Du Boisian sociology is attuned to the presence of diverse local histories and relational configurations. But local histories cannot be analyzed in isolation. The global system of relations in which they are embedded is fundamental to their analysis. A Du Boisian global sociology seeks to explore the relations between the global characteristics of racial and colonial capitalism and its local concrete manifestations. Much as with the tension between chance and law in Du Bois's theory of agency, Du Boisian sociology accepts the fact that a tension exists between local processes and global pressures. The two are interconnected, although not in a deterministic way. The degree of influence of global structures and the space for local agency must be explored through empirical historical and relational research. Du Boisian sociology thrives in those tensions, tensions that other sociological approaches may try to resolve by taking a position—either for law or chance, for structure or agency, or for global determination or local contingencies.[99]

A Du Boisian global sociology would conduct its analysis from the standpoint of different peripheries and different racialized peoples. Sociological theories emerging from the core are limited because of the presence of the veil and by the inability of scholars to see their positionality. The goal of a Du Boisian analysis is to reconstruct sociological analysis from the perspective of the racialized and colonized subjects of historical capitalism. In this sense, a contemporary Du Boisian sociology is close to the postcolonial sociology proposed by Julian Go.[100] For Julian Go, the goal of postcolonial sociology is to expand the conceptual and epistemological boundaries of sociology by bringing forward perspectives ignored by metrocentric claims to universalism. Go advocates a perspectival realism that would bring multiple standpoints into sociological analysis. A contemporary Du Boisian sociology embraces Go's multiple-perspectives approach, but it purposefully takes the position of racialized people in contemporary capitalism. It does so because this standpoint helps Du Boisian sociologists better understand the structures of oppression and exclusion of racial and colonial capitalism and the subjectivities that emerge in different historical contexts.

A final issue we must address concerns a tension that surrounds Du Bois's work as a global theorist. We have emphasized that for Du Bois the color line was a global structure that transcended the experience of Black communities in the United States. Some scholars take an either/or position on these questions, understanding our focus on Du Bois's global analysis to mean that we are arguing that Du Bois was not concerned with the African American experience of Black communities in the United States. We believe that a "both/and" approach is needed here. Du Bois's analysis was most definitely rooted in the African American experience. That was his initial standpoint, and Black communities in the United States were always central to his scholarship and activism. But Du Bois's analysis of the condition of Blackness transcended the United States and encompassed the whole of the Africana diaspora. And his concern with the color line addressed the experiences of people of color in the entire world. His life was quintessentially American and at the same time global. Du Bois was an activist fighting for the rights of Black people in the United States and at the same time a Pan-Africanist, and an anticolonial theorist and organizer. His death in Ghana was not a random event but the culmination of a life of global anticolonial thought and praxis.

3

Du Bois's Urban and Community Research Program

His first job offer came via telegram on August 17, 1894, shortly after his return from his postgraduate studies in Berlin, from Samuel Thomas Mitchell, the president of Wilberforce University, a historically Black institution in Ohio. W. E. B. Du Bois, the newly minted Harvard PhD, was offered a faculty appointment to serve as the chair of the classics department, where his primary responsibilities would include teaching Latin and Greek, at a meager salary of eight hundred dollars a year.[1] Du Bois accepted immediately. In the coming weeks he would also receive offers from the Lincoln Institute in Missouri and from Tuskegee University by way of a personal invitation from his soon-to-be adversary, Booker T. Washington. However hastily he had made the decision, Du Bois chose to stick to his initial commitment to Wilberforce, and began teaching there in the autumn of 1894.

He arrived at Wilberforce with an impressive pedigree, having come straight from Friedrich Wilhelm University, one of the most prestigious academic institutions in Germany, by way of Fisk and Harvard. Not surprisingly, he arrived displaying an air of cockiness and disdain for his position as it was described.

A self-proclaimed social scientist, Du Bois was determined to follow his dream of implementing a sociological research program on the empirical study of the "Negro problem" in America. He erroneously thought that once he was in the door of an institution like Wilberforce, he would be able to convince the administration to expand his role to include building such a program, even if it were to be done on his own time and at his own expense. Wilberforce mirrored most American universities at the time in that it did not yet have a sociology department in which Du Bois could build such a research program, nor was the institution asking for one. Needless to say, Wilberforce at the time was not a good match for W. E. B. Du Bois. As he lamented nearly fifty years later, in his reflective essay "My Evolving Program for Negro Freedom,"

"Try as I might . . . the institution would have no sociology, even though I offered to teach it on my own time. I became uneasy about my life program. I was doing nothing directly in the social sciences and saw no immediate prospect. Then the door of opportunity opened: just a crack, to be sure, but a distinct opening. In the Fall of 1896, I went to the University of Pennsylvania as 'Assistant Instructor' in Sociology."[2]

Du Bois burst through that door of opportunity to officially begin his sociological career. It was in Philadelphia that Du Bois conducted his first empirical sociological study of a Black community. Before leaving Ohio, as he was about to embark on his journey to Philadelphia to take up his one-year appointment at Penn, Du Bois married a young woman three years his junior, Nina Gomer, who had been one of his undergraduate students at Wilberforce.

The "Assistant Instructor" post was not a faculty position, and Du Bois was not even offered so much as an office in the university's Sociology Department. However, he did get a small research fund and full license to carry out a study of the social and economic conditions of the growing Black population in Pennsylvania's largest city, then with a population of a bit more than one million people, out of which close to forty thousand were Black. Philadelphia then had the second largest urban Black population in the United States.[3] Three years later, in 1899, this study would be published under the title *The Philadelphia Negro*.

Many factors make this a remarkable feat. Du Boisian scholars often note the facts that Du Bois conducted a complete sample population study, that his research findings were both broad and deep, or that it was the very first empirical study of an urban community carried out in the history of American sociology. In this chapter we propose that it was from this early study that Du Bois developed a methodological approach for the empirical study of populations and communities.

* * *

In the previous chapters we examined aspects of Du Boisian sociology that are theoretically and methodologically central to his approach yet unrecognized by the discipline; here we shall consider the aspects of his work that sociologists acknowledge but often misrecognize: his empirical community and urban studies. These works are bookended by the beginning and end of his employment with two university departments intermittently from 1896 to 1944, and they provide in-depth, systematic, and historically rooted analyses of the state of Black America at the time of his work. From independent place-based studies of the socioeconomic conditions of African Americans in "Chocolate Cities"[4] such as Philadelphia and Farmville, Virginia, to large-scale collaborative studies of different aspects of Black life conducted through the Atlanta University Studies, this body of work is most credited for representing Du Bois's sociology.

The body of writings focused on Du Bois's empirical community and urban studies is by far the most substantial portion of the sociological literature on his work. Much is known about the profound contributions that these studies have made to the discipline—most notably those of *The Philadelphia Negro* and the Atlanta University Studies—but as the sociologist Alford Young points out, "Much more could go into defining precisely what constituted the Du Bois school of sociology."[5] In the following discussion, we seek to answer Young's challenge as it pertains to Du Bois's urban and community research program.

We propose to look at Du Bois's early urban and community studies in light of his later global sociology. Although his early research was often read this way by his white counterparts, Du Bois was not only doing Black sociology for Black people. Even in his early work, he was a theorist of racialized modernity—asserting that the color line structured the world in which he lived—and he argued that the systematic disfranchisement, exclusion, and oppression of a significant portion of its population kept his country from realizing its stated ideals of democracy, equality, and freedom. His understanding of racialized modernity changed over time, from his early critique of the racial order as impeding the incorporation of Black Americans into the nation's capitalist economy and the democratic political system to his later critique of racial and colonial capitalism. But a critique of racialized modernity was already present in his early urban and community studies.

Going forward, we shall articulate the pillars of Du Bois's analytical method, outline the core tenets of his urban and community studies research program, and clarify how that program—"the path not taken"—differs from the major "schools" of sociology that developed at the University of Chicago and Columbia University. Finally, we shall demonstrate how taken-for-granted origin stories about the founding of the discipline of sociology in the United States affect our thoughts and actions as sociologists in the twenty-first century; as these narratives solidify the legacies of accumulated affirmation and erasure that result from what we tell ourselves about who we are and from whence we came.

Du Bois's urban and community studies present us with a coherent research program that systematically studied the social and economic conditions of Black communities, Black institutions, the inner workings of the Black social world, and the social forces that shaped that world. His analytical approach was based on three elements, beginning with a strong focus on the forms and possibilities of agency of Black communities. Du Bois understood this agency as conditioned by the second element, the presence of the color line as a historical structure affecting the lives and opportunities of racialized people. This tension between the possibilities of community agency and the historically constructed structural limits is a hallmark of Du Bois's analytical approach. The third element was his multimethod strategy of data collection, which privileged historical analysis and contextualization of sociological research and findings. Du Bois's approach may help us rethink the kind of sociology we practice now.

Defining the Problem

Du Bois defined a social problem as "the failure of an organized social group to realize its group ideals, through the inability to adapt a certain desired line of action to given conditions of life."[6] Using the example of democracy, he wrote, "If, for instance, a government founded on universal manhood suffrage has a portion of its population so ignorant as to be unable to vote intelligently, such ignorance becomes a menacing social problem."[7] Yet, the "Negro problems" that were the concern of Du Bois's sociology were not some sort of social pathologies or moral ills inherent to Black people. As he saw it, the "Negro Problem" was instead the failure of American society to include Black people. The Black community's difficulty in realizing its group ideals was for Du Bois an indictment of American democracy. Why, in a country founded on ideals of equality, life, liberty, and the pursuit of happiness, was nearly 20 percent of its population systematically and legally treated unequally, made to live in mean and often punitive circumstances from cradle to grave, and denied the basic freedoms afforded to the rest of its citizenry?

In his analysis of the "Negro problems," Du Bois makes it clear that the issues that affected Black people were the result of racism and segregation rather than any inherent racial difference. He states,

> Let us inquire somewhat more carefully into the form under which the Negro problems present themselves today after 275 years of evolution. Their existence is plainly manifested by the fact that a definitely segregated mass of eight millions of Americans do not wholly share the national life of the people; are not an integral part of the social body. The points at which they fail to be incorporated into this group life constitute the particular Negro problems, which can be divided into two distinct but correlated parts, depending on two facts:
>
> First—Negroes do not share the full national life because as a mass they have not reached a sufficiently high grade of culture. Secondly— They do not share the full national life because there has always existed in America a conviction—varying in intensity, but always widespread— that people of Negro blood should not be admitted into the group life of the nation no matter what their condition might be.[8]

Du Bois argued strongly that Black people are both African and American, and have something to contribute to society as full political, economic, cultural, and social participants. This was his main argument with the views offered by Booker T. Washington, as Du Bois was vehemently against the strategy of entering the national body politic as an ontologically compromised subject.

For the early Du Bois, the Du Bois of *The Philadelphia Negro* and the Atlanta University Studies, a body of work spanning from 1898 to 1910, deviant behavior in the Black community, such as crime, poverty, and alcoholism, was the historical result of the uneven power dynamics created by the color line. He acknowledged that a disproportionate segment of the Black population was plagued by social ills such as crime, "sexual immorality," and the like. Yet he asserted that the "Negro Problem" was singularly due to the social fact of anti-Black racism, a foundational tenet of the American racial state. He demanded that the social force of racism be included in empirical studies of the condition of Black people in America. In doing so, W. E. B. Du Bois was the first sociologist to study racism and to name it for what it was:

> These problems of poverty, ignorance and social degradation differ from similar problems the world over in one important particular way, and that is the fact that they are complicated by a peculiar environment. This constitutes the second class of Negro problems, and they rest, as has been said, on the widespread conviction among Americans that no persons of Negro descent should become constituent members of the social body. This feeling gives rise to economic problems, to educational problems, and nice questions of social morality; it makes it more difficult for black men to earn a living or spend their earnings as they will; it gives them poorer school facilities and restricted contact with cultured classes; and it becomes, throughout the land, a cause and excuse for discontent, lawlessness, laziness and injustice.[9]

Du Bois identified the "peculiar environment" in which Black people in America lived as the underlying cause of social deviance. While he did not withhold his criticism of the social problems that negatively affected the lives of Black Americans, he always emphasized the pervasive effects of racism. To that end, W. E. B. Du Bois was doing with science what Martin Luther King Jr. would do, nearly half a century later, with oration and organizing—he was calling on the United States of America to, as King stated, "cash its promissory note"[10] and give its Black citizenry their due.

The Analytical Pillars of Du Bois's Urban and Community Studies

Du Bois's urban and community studies were guided by four assumptions: (1) communities and environments are dynamic, and therefore cannot be studied as monoliths in space and time; (2) sociology is a science; (3) because sociology is a science it should be driven by facts and truth, not by ideology and prejudice; and (4) Black people are human beings, Americans, and are and will remain an integral part of the nation. These ideas may seem like foregone conclusions to a contemporary audience. However, in 1894, at the time Du Bois started his career, they were considered radical, and unscientific. It is useful to examine each of these assumptions before moving on to his methodological approach.

History, Social Change, and Heterogeneity

Du Bois's urban and community studies account for history, change, and heterogeneity. Du Bois was adamant about locating people and places within their historical contexts, and therefore his empirical studies had to acknowledge the fact that people and places change and it cannot be assumed that they are all the same. In this way Du Bois's empirical community studies are steeped in pragmatist principles of creativity and human action. As he wrote in his 1898 speech and essay, "The Study of Negro Problems,"

> Thus a social problem is ever a relation between conditions and action, and as conditions and actions vary and change from group to group from time to time and from place to place, so social problems change, develop and grow. Consequently, though we ordinarily speak of the Negro problem as though it were one unchanged question, students must recognize the obvious facts that this problem, like others, has had a long historical development, has changed with the growth and evolution of the nation; moreover, that it is not one problem, but rather a plexus of social problems, some new, some old, some simple, some complex; and these problems have their one bond of unity in the act that they group themselves about those Africans whom two centuries of slave-trading brought into the land.[11]

Du Bois's sociology required as much attention to the history, change, and heterogeneity of Black people as it did to "Negro problems." His empirical community studies always consider subjective questions of being and becoming—analyzing who Black people are, where they are going, and from whence they came. He found fault in studies, typically conducted by white sociologists, that focused only on what Black people were doing—that is, from the perspective of their deviance from social norms—without also paying attention to how they came to be the way they were and what the nature of Black life entailed. To this approach he offered a strict criticism:

The widespread habit of studying the Negro from one point of view only, that of his influence on the white inhabitants, is also responsible for much uncritical work. The slaves are generally treated as one inert changeless mass, and most studies of slavery apparently have no conception of a social evolution and development among them.

The slave code of a state is given, the progress of general influence of man on master are studied, but of the slave himself, of his group life and social institutions, of remaining traces of his African tribal life, of his amusements, his conversion to Christianity, his acquiring of the English tongue—in fine, of his whole reaction against his environment, of all this we hear little or nothing, and would apparently be expected to believe that the Negro arose from the dead in 1863. Yet all the testimony of law and custom, of tradition and present social condition, shows us that the Negro at the time of emancipation had passed through a social evolution which far separated him from his savage ancestors.[12]

Du Bois's sociology does not treat Blackness as a monolithic social category. He found this type of study to be dehumanizing and logically flawed, and for that reason he expressed moral, ethical, and scientific concerns about such an approach. He bemoaned the fact that "the work done has been lamentably unsystematic and fragmentary," asserting that "scientific work must be subdivided, but conclusions which affect the whole subject must be based on a study of the whole. One cannot study the Negro in freedom and come to general conclusions about his destiny without knowing his history in slavery."[13] Black people, like all social groups, vary and change across time and place, and Du Bois's community studies were attuned to the specificities of different populations and communities and to their sociohistorical contexts.

Sociology Is a Science

Du Bois saw sociology as the attempt "to make a science of human action."[14] This belief informs all of his work in the discipline, and stands at the center of his urban and community studies. Drawing upon the arguments laid out in "Sociology Hesitant," written circa 1905, Du Bois asserts that "sociology is the science that seeks to measure the limits of chance in human action, or if you will excuse the paradox, it is the science of free will."[15] He saw in sociology the potential to analyze, with exacting scientific measurement, the scope of people's ability to shape their lives—which he called Chance—within all of the various historical constraints—which he called Law.[16]

Du Bois believed that the study of Black people was central to developing social scientific inquiry writ large. To this effect he argues,

> The action and reaction of social forces are seen and can be measured with more than usual ease. What is human progress and how is it emphasized? How do nations rise and fall? What is the meaning and value of certain human action? Is there rhythm and law in the mass of the deeds of men—and if so how can it best be measured and stated—all such questions can be studied and answered in the case of the American Negro, if he shall be studied closely enough in a way to enlighten science and inspire philanthropy.[17]

For the early Du Bois, a systematic and exhaustive study of Black people was the key to building sociology as a scientific discipline and to convincing white elites to enact social reform and undo the color line. He saw the "Negro Problem" as one with which enlightened elites should be deeply concerned because the systematic exclusion and oppression of people of color kept the mass of Black people in poverty and deprived the country of the insights of educated Black people who could make important contributions to the general progress of the nation.

At the time of these writings, at the turn of the twentieth century, 90 percent of African Americans still lived in the South under Jim Crow. Du Bois believed that nothing good could come from segregation in terms of perfecting the nation, and he believed that science offered the first building block towards comprehensive social reform and progress. The early Du Bois was convinced that if the public and the scientific community could see the truth and the facts about racism and its detrimental effects on the nation, surely they would come together in the interests of society and humankind to ameliorate this problem. In a hopeful statement, he writes, "It would seem to be the clear duty of the American people, in the interests of scientific knowledge and social reform, to begin a broad and systematic study of the history and condition of the American Negroes. The scope and method of this study, however, needs to be generally agreed upon beforehand in its main outlines, not to hinder the freedom of individual students, but to systematize and unify effort so as to cover the wide field of investigation."[18]

Du Bois agreed with scholars who were his contemporaries, such as his mentor Gustav von Schmoller and his acquaintance Max Weber, who argued that sociological inquiry had to be objective to be scientific. For Du Bois, sociological inquiry need only seek the truth, and its findings need only to be supported by rigorous empirical observations and facts—even if those findings dismayed the researcher. His thinking departed from that of his peers, however, on the question of the social and moral aims of social science research: What is to be done with the findings of sociological scientific inquiry? The aim of Du Bois's sociology was always to undo the color line and advance the causes of the oppressed. The thinking of his peers, however, still plagues the discipline, in that many sociologists are comfortable studying structural inequalities yet uncomfortable with scholar activism. In their view, in-activism is the ultimate badge of scientific honor.

Willful Ignorance and Prejudice Hindering Research

In Du Bois's view, the great American project of democracy hinged on erasing the barriers to equality posed by the color line. Prejudice and willful ignorance stood in the way of any meaningful progress: "No subject is so intricate and dangerous, as not to be infinitely more approachable in the clear light of knowledge than in the fog of prejudice and bitter feeling, and . . . the first business of any nation distracted by a great social problem is thoroughly to study and understand this problem."[19] However, in the early decades of the twentieth century, sociologists were mired in prejudiced thinking about race, as were most of their compatriots, and they allowed these biases to determine their findings before the facts were revealed. This meant that Black people were studied as an assumed problem. Inherent inferiority, rather than socioeconomic conditions, historical formations, or their own agency and activity, was the object of analysis. Of this he writes,

> The scope of any social study is first of all limited by the general attitude of the public opinion toward truth and truth-seeking. If in regard to any

social problem there is for any reason a persistent refusal on the part of the people to allow the truth to be known then manifestly that problem cannot be studied. Undoubtedly much of the unsatisfactory work already done with regard to the Negro is due to this cause; the intense feeling that preceded and followed the war made a calm balanced research next to impossible.[20]

The early Du Bois believed that the longitudinal, systematic study of "Negro problems" would change public opinion about racial inferiority and lead to social reform, namely, the true and earnest incorporation of Black people into American society. Although he never gave up his belief in science, as he aimed to restart his community studies during his second term as a professor at Atlanta University from 1934 to 1944, he came to realize that the white public's commitment to white supremacy superseded its desire for scientific truth and true democracy.

Black People Are Human Beings, American Citizens, and Part of Society

The last set of tenets that prefigured Du Bois's empirical community studies were that Black people are human beings, American citizens, and full members of American society. Du Bois came to the discipline in a time when biological racism and eugenicist thinking dominated the spheres of science, law, and public opinion. The notion of inherent racial inferiority, or white supremacy, had multiple impacts on Black lives—and still does. People from the bottom rungs of the socioeconomic strata to the upper echelons of academia and industry held these views, which in turn shaped the policies, studies, and social environments they created.

Furthermore, from the time of the nation's independence until well into the early decades of the twentieth century, there was a widely held view among whites that Blacks, once freed, would either repatriate to Africa, the Caribbean, or some other place outside the United States, or simply die off. This belief was espoused by statesmen such as Thomas Jefferson and James Monroe, as well as industry barons, judges, and even abolitionists. Du Bois opposed this view, and stated his opinion in this regard early and often: "We have assumed that the Negro is a constituent member of the great human family, that he is capable of advancement and development, that mulattoes are not necessarily degenerates and that it is perfectly possible for the Negro people to become a great and civilized group. In making these assumptions we have kept before us the facts that every student knows, namely: That there is no adequate historical warrant for pronouncing the Negro race inferior to the other races of the world in a sense of unalterable destiny."[21]

The idea that freed Blacks would simply "go back to Africa" or perish as a people was fueled by the widely held public opinion that Black people had no claim to the United States, and thus had none of the duties or rights of an American citizen. Du Bois addressed this denial of citizenship claims with a sobering reminder to his audience:

> It must be remembered that these persons are Americans by birth and descent. They represent, for the most part, four or five American born generations, being in that respect one of the most American groups in the land. Moreover, the Negroes are not barbarians. They are, as a mass, poor and ignorant; but they are growing rapidly in both wealth and intelligence, and larger and larger numbers of them demand the rights and privileges of American citizens as a matter of undoubted desert.[22]

Du Bois was clear and unwavering in his position. He understood, however, that what he deemed a foregone conclusion was still up for debate among the vast majority of white Americans. He articulated this point in powerful words: "Whether at last the Negro will gain full recognition as a man, or be utterly crushed by prejudice and superior numbers, is the present Negro problem of America."[23]

The Social Study

"The social study" served as the primary analytical tool Du Bois used for his community and urban studies. With each study, he aimed to empirically trace the socioeconomic conditions of Black people in America over space and time as well as the inner workings of their social worlds, including their characteristics, group organization, customs, and behavior. Beyond merely using statistics to determine how a population was behaving (for example, determining rates of migration, employment, crime, and fertility), Du Bois saw the social study as a robust analytical tool with which to study social problems, the conditions under which they emerge, and the way they are subsequently reproduced. Advocating for the use of the social study as an analytical tool, he writes,

> The rather indefinite term "Social Study" has come to be applied to such investigations that seek to go further and deeper than a national census and study definitely and, within limits, exhaustively, the conditions of life and action in certain localities. Such difficult undertakings have very obvious limitations: they must necessarily be confined to small geographical areas; they can after all measure only the more powerful economic and social forces and must largely omit the deeper spiritual and moral impulses; and above all they require for their successful pursuit a high order of ability, insight, and tact. They are also very costly when the paucity of definite or immediately usable results is considered. Nevertheless the Social Study manifestly approaches as nearly as anything the ideal of measuring and classifying human activity.[24]

So sure was Du Bois of the analytical power of the social study that he proposed lending his research design to the United States Census Bureau as early as the twelfth census of 1900. While he saw great value in the US Census, conducted every ten years on the nation's population from 1790 to the present, he recognized also its limitations, thus arguing for the use of the "social study":

> As an instrument for social investigation there are certain obvious limitations to the national census. It can successfully measure only the broader and simpler aspects of human society—the number, distribution, age, sex, conjugal condition, and occupations of men. Such matters are easily counted, there is, comparatively speaking, small room for error, and no other agency but the government could command the requisite funds and authority for covering so vast a field. Other data such as those relating to literacy, deaths, industries, etc. are less obviously suited to the census methods and yet we have just now no better agency. When, however, it comes to matters of land and property, education, crime, and the more delicate and intricate questions of social life, the ordinary machinery of the census is obviously unsuited to the work.[25]

The analytical power that census data offered in breadth, the social study offered in depth. Du Bois thought that by combining census data with the social study, social scientists could tackle the problem of the color line in a matter of decades. He believed that through these studies, sociologists could provide exacting scientific evidence that would inspire reformers to enact social change.

Just shy of forty years since Emancipation, at the dawn of the twentieth century, government, industry, and the general public had only a shallow grasp of the condition of the descendants of the enslaved, a group that represented nearly one fifth of the nation's population. Remarking on the cacophony of contradictory yet authoritative statements made about the life of the newly freed Black population and the conditions under which they lived, Du Bois writes,

> Just the other day two speakers in the University Extension Series of Philadelphia made substantially the following statements:

> The freedman bought land in Georgia, but his sons have not, and are even losing what he had owned. The later generation make such poor workmen that corporations often offer higher wages for convict than for free labor.

> The ownership of land by Georgia Negroes has increased by leaps and bounds, save at a few temporary periods of financial depression or political unrest, and the material advance of the great mass of the black people of that state cannot be denied.

> This is but a single instance of the almost daily contradiction as to the elementary facts which greet the layman who seeks lights on the present condition of the Negro. . . . Is the Negro buying land or is he not? Is he losing or gaining in the skilled trades? How does his physical health compare with that of the past? Does he receive living wages? Can he vote? What does the graduate of the schools find to do?—all these are specimens of the important questions which to-day can be given no comprehensive or authoritative answer covering large and typical areas. And yet most of them are vitally necessary to a preliminary understanding of the Negro problems, not to say to intelligent plans for reform.[26]

In his early career, from 1894 to 1910, Du Bois tried to redress what he identified as the problem of "car window sociology," by which he meant harmful studies whose findings were based on opinion, prejudice, and first-glance assumptions about entire populations of people. Du Bois understood that such studies made the goal of achieving freedom and equality for Black people nearly impossible, as they legitimated and perpetuated racial myths that justified his people's oppression. Du Bois challenged white social scientists to approach the study of Black communities and their lives objectively and using the most advanced scientific tools, convinced that if they did so they would realize the destructiveness of racism and lift the barriers to fully incorporate Blacks in public life.

Du Bois's dream was to build the discipline of sociology through the study of Black communities in America. Financial constraints, race prejudice, and general apathy turned his dream into one that would be forever deferred. However, he was able to implement some of his ideas through the Atlanta University Studies, and he hoped that they would eventually evolve into a hundred-year longitudinal study of the socioeconomic conditions, practices, and progress of America's Black population.

> The object of the Atlanta Conference is to study the American Negro. The method employed is to divide the various aspects of his social condition into ten great subjects. To treat one of these subjects each year as carefully and exhaustively as means will allow until the cycle is completed. To begin then again on the same cycle for a second ten years. So that in the course of a century, if the work is well done we shall have a continuous record on the condition and development of a group of 10 to 20 millions of men—a body of sociological material unsurpassed in human annals.
>
> Such an ambitious program is of course difficult to realize. We have, however, reached already the eighth year of the first cycle and have published seven reports and have the eighth in preparation; the sequence of subjects studied has not been altogether logical but will in the end be exhaustive.[27]

For the Atlanta University Studies, Du Bois proposed that the following ten topics be studied: population distribution and growth, the health and physique of Blacks, socialization, cultural patterns of morals and manners, education, religion, crime, law and government, literature and art, and a bibliography and summary.[28]

What the early Du Bois proposed was to produce fact-based longitudinal social studies of the African American population that would eventually lead to social reform. At this point in his life, however, Du Bois was adamant in his belief that social science and activism were two separate enterprises. Du Bois believed that to make an airtight argument for change, sociologists needed reliable, systematically collected data. Activists and reformers, he believed, could not take up the task of eradicating the problem without first defining and studying it scientifically. And he further believed that the findings from his studies would lift the veil from people's eyes, leading American citizens, both Black and white, to work together towards the shared goal of dismantling the color line. He saw the social study as a powerful tool for analysis, and by extension, a vehicle that would inspire social reform and free America from the ills of race prejudice.

But, as he articulates in his 1944 essay "My Evolving Program of Negro Freedom," and in his 1940 book *Dusk of Dawn*, the practice of social science in Philadelphia and Atlanta at the turn of the twentieth century made him realize that he could not convince the white elites to eliminate the barriers to Black progress simply through the presentation of scientific knowledge. He became convinced that racism was deeply rooted in habits, interests, and what he would term in *Dusk of Dawn* the irrationalities that sustain white subjectivity.

Du Bois's Methodological Approach to Urban and Community Studies

Du Bois articulates his empirical research program in his 1898 speech and essay, "The Study of Negro Problems,"[29] written at the end of his research for *The Philadelphia Negro*. This is by far his clearest and most detailed articulation of his methodology for urban and community studies. In this essay Du Bois argues that the study of Black communities should account for the historical and social conditions that define their environment, the intangible social forces of racism and prejudice, and the inner workings of the Black social world.

Furthermore, in this essay Du Bois advocates for a mixed-methods approach, one that includes (1) the history of communities, (2) statistical investigation, (3) anthropological measurement, and (4) sociological interpretation.[30] As we have seen, for Du Bois the historical construction of social situations was central to understanding the conditions under which Black lives developed. Such a conclusion may seem obvious, but an indifference to history continues to plague contemporary sociological analyses. Du Bois argued that there was no excuse for bypassing this crucial component:

> The material at hand for historical research is rich and abundant; there are the colonial statutes and records, the partially accessible archives of Great Britain, France and Spain, the collections of historical societies, the vast number of executive and congressional reports and documents, the state statutes, reports and publications, the reports of institutions and societies, the personal narratives and opinions of various observers and the periodical press covering nearly three centuries.
>
> From these sources can be gathered much new information upon the economic and social development of the Negro, upon the rise and decline of the slave-trade, the character, distribution and state of culture of the Africans, the evolution of the slave codes as expressing the life of the South, the rise of such peculiar expressions of Negro social history, as the Negro church, the economics of plantation life, the possession of private property by slaves, and the history of the oft-forgotten class of free Negroes.
>
> Such historical research must be subdivided in space and limited in time by the nature of the subject, the history of the different colonies and groups being followed and compared, the different periods of development receiving special study, and the whole subject being renewed from different aspects.[31]

Du Bois's methodology also includes statistical analysis as a key element, and focuses on measuring "the size and condition of families, the occupations and wages, the illiteracy of adults and education of children, the standard of living, the character of the dwellings, the property owned and rents paid, and the character of the organized life"[32]—in other words, examining the issue by starting with data gleaned at the local community level rather than national aggregated numbers. Du Bois advocated for community-level studies conducted in multiple locations to capture the diversity and heterogeneity of living conditions of Black Americans: "Such investigations should be extended until they cover the typical group life of Negroes in all sections of the land and should be so repeated from time to time in the same localities and with the same methods, as to be a measure of social development."[33]

He believed that "general averages in so complicated a subject are apt to be dangerously misleading,"[34] and that to make broad generalizations about groups of people based on singular observations of a few who were members of this group was irresponsible. Influenced by Gustav von Schmoller, his mentor during his studies in Germany, Du Bois believed that sociological studies should be empirically based, systematically conducted, and inductive in their reasoning.

The third methodological component proposed by Du Bois was anthropological measurement, or the "scientific study of the Negro body." Much like his contemporary Franz Boaz, the Columbia University anthropologist who was in large part responsible for steering his discipline away from biological understandings of race, Du Bois aimed to fight scientific racism by showing that there are no measurable physical differences between Blacks and whites. He dedicates the 1906 Atlanta study to this issue, aiming to use physical measurements to debunk "scientific" claims about biological racial differences. This methodological approach seems to have been a product of Du Bois's faith in science at the time, but he soon abandoned this strategy of fighting "scientific" racism, and focused on the analysis of the social and historical construction of race.

The fourth methodological element of Du Bois's urban and community studies is sociological interpretation. For Du Bois, this amounts to the study of the lived experience and social organization of Black communities, and he contended that such study should be based in the investigation of "their hundred newspapers, their considerable literature, their music and folklore and their germ of esthetic life."[35] This component is strongly present in *The Philadelphia Negro* and the Atlanta Studies, in which Du Bois used interviews and secondary materials to give a sense of the texture of community life. This element became increasingly important to his sociology as witnessed by his use of auto-ethnography, a form of ethnographic analysis generated by the observer's own experience, in *Dusk of Dawn*, and the emphasis on writing the history of Reconstruction from the standpoint of the enslaved, in *Black Reconstruction*.

Du Bois asserted that community studies should consist of two related but different components: "The study of the Negro falls naturally into two categories, which though difficult to separate in practice, must for the sake of logical clearness, be kept distinct. They are (a) the study of the Negro as a social group, (b) the study of his peculiar social environment."[36] Du Bois admitted that it was difficult to separate the study of a group from the study of the context in which a group lives, but he emphasized that it was important to study these two aspects of social life separately. He believed that it would be impossible to understand the lives and lived experiences of Black people in America without studying the context in which their communities developed. He reminds us that "we must realize definitely that not only is he affected by all the varying social forces that act on any nation at his stage of advancement, but that in addition there is reacting upon him the mighty power of a peculiar and unusual social environment which affects to some extent every other social force."[37] Du Bois's approach to urban and community studies was historical and relational. The study of Black communities needed to be rooted in their history, based in the understanding of the broader historical times (racialized modernity), and embedded in the network of relations that constructed the place and at the same time limited the opportunities and constrained the lives of people. Still, in line with his goal of making sociology the science of human action, Du Bois's urban and community sociology always emphasized the importance of community organization in improving the lives of Black people.

Du Bois's Urban and Community Studies Program in Action

We can best illustrate the implementation of Du Bois's use of the social study and his methodological approach by examining his 1899 book, *The Philadelphia Negro*, and one of the Atlanta Studies, the 1904 study titled "Some Notes on Negro Crime. Particularly in Georgia."[38] We chose the latter because the question of crime remains central to contemporary community studies and therefore it is very interesting to observe how Du Bois approached this issue. *The Philadelphia Negro* is the most widely read of Du Bois's works in sociology, and there is a growing body of literature on the book.[39] Our contribution to this literature is to show how the book's analytical structure corresponds to the arguments Du Bois delineates in "The Study of Negro Problems." If the program that Du Bois articulates in "The Study of Negro Problems" feels familiar to the reader of *The Philadelphia Negro*, that is the case because in that essay Du Bois articulates the analytical and methodological basis for the research project that he had just concluded in Philadelphia.

The Philadelphia Negro begins with the history of Black people in Philadelphia since the beginning of slavery in Pennsylvania in the seventeenth century. The book describes the historically different forms of organization of the Black population, and examines how the Black community runs into structural constraints such as labor competition with immigrants and the system of white power. This historical context makes it clear that the imposed structural barriers to the progress of the Black community are manifestations of white supremacy and political power.

In his analysis of the historical construction of the Black community in Philadelphia, Du Bois emphasizes four broad processes: "1. The growth of Philadelphia; 2. The increase in the foreign population in the city; 3. the development of the large industry and increase of wealth; and 4. The coming in of the Southern freedmen's sons and daughters."[40] Du Bois argues that the predicament of Black Philadelphians can only be understood in the context of these larger trends. For Du Bois, sociological analysis was rooted in concrete historical processes.

The Atlanta study on Black crime begins with a historical analysis of the system of convict leasing as it developed after the end of Reconstruction. Du Bois states,

> *The courts* sought to do by judicial decisions what the legislatures had formerly sought to do by specific law—namely, reduce the freedman to serfdom. As a result, the small peccadilloes of a careless, untrained class were made the excuse for severe sentences. The courts and jails became filled with the careless and ignorant, with those who sought to emphasize their new found freedom, and too often, with innocent victims of oppression. . . . Throughout the South laws were immediately passed authorizing public officials to lease the labor of convicts to the highest bidder. . . . Thus a new slavery and slave-trade was established.[41]

Du Bois makes clear that the increase in Black crime in Georgia could only be understood as the product of the political defeat of Reconstruction, the aims of which were to rebuild the South after the Civil War while protecting the rights of the emancipated Black population. The end of Reconstruction in 1877 meant the official restoration of white power in the South. Again, we note that this analysis is rooted in specific historical developments.

After the historical sections, the two works go on to describe and analyze their subjects through a combination of detailed statistical descriptions, the use of secondary sources, and interviews. *The Philadelphia Negro* includes chapters on the demographic structure of the Black population, its education and health, the Black family, crime and poverty, and the organization and politics of Black Philadelphians. In these chapters, Du Bois follows his analytical approach of emphasizing agency and structural limits, or finding the boundaries of Law and Chance, as he writes in "Sociology Hesitant."

Describing the multiple occupations of Black Philadelphians in the seventh ward, an area that at the time was the heart of Philadelphia's growing Black and immigrant population, and in the city as a whole, Du Bois cites Black advances in many different occupations and businesses, as well as limits to Black progress. He attributes the limits principally to discrimination, although also in part to lack of skills. In addition, he describes how massive European migration displaced Black workers from several occupations and articulates a version of what came to be known later as split labor market theory.[42] As Du Bois writes,

> The real motives back of this exclusion are plain; a large part is simple race prejudice, always strong in working classes and intensified by the peculiar history of the Negro in this country. Another part, however, and possibly a more potent part, is the natural spirit of monopoly and the desire to keep up wages. So long as a cry against "Irish" or "foreigners" was able to marshal race prejudice in the service of those who desired to keep those people out of some employments, that cry was sedulously used. So today the workmen plainly see that a large amount of competition can be shut off by taking advantage of public opinion and drawing the color line.[43]

Exclusion from the labor market is thus the result of pervasive racism, wielded to protect certain types of job for white labor. This analysis of the labor market in *The Philadelphia Negro* already prefigures the analysis of the intersection of race and class that Du Bois would develop three decades later in *Black Reconstruction.*

Du Bois's discussion of Black organizations in *The Philadelphia Negro* strongly emphasizes their potential for agency.[44] Du Bois focuses on the history of the Black church in Philadelphia and its role in building community, presenting statistics on membership, the economic worth of different churches, and how congregations use their money. He writes, "All movements for social betterment are apt to centre in the churches. Beneficial societies in endless number are formed here; secret societies keep in touch; cooperative and building associations have lately sprung up; the minister often acts as an employment agent; considerable charitable and relief work is done."[45] Du Bois also describes the histories and actions of other types of organization, such as mutual aid associations, cooperatives, unions, and secret societies. He sees limits to Black organizational life, arguing that the Black community is less well organized than the white community in Philadelphia, and that the organizations of the Black community may be weaker or experience more problems than their white counterparts. Nonetheless, he is adamant that "the largest hope for the ultimate rise of the Negro lies in this mastery of the art of social organized life."[46]

In *The Philadelphia Negro*, Du Bois defines crime as a rebellion of individuals against their environment and attributes this rebellion to the fact that it is difficult for migrants to adapt to urban life. The book presents detailed statistical tables on types of crime and arrests, graphs presenting trends in different types of crimes, and newspapers' descriptions of crime "to give a more vivid idea than the abstract statistics give."[47]

In Du Bois's analysis, the number of crimes committed by Blacks was disproportionate to their percentage of the population, and he notes that crimes are committed by a specific group of people, mostly young men. But he also cautions that the overrepresentation of Blacks in crime statistics may not represent faithfully the real situation of crime in the city. Du Bois poses the possibility that racial and class power may be distorting the portrait of crime in the city. "In convictions by human courts," he asserts, "the rich always are favored somewhat at the expense of the poor, the upper classes at the expense of the unfortunate classes, and whites at the expense of the Negroes."[48] In other words, Du Bois suggests that crime statistics may be reflecting who is convicted rather than who commits crimes. As we have seen, the 1904 Atlanta study on crime began with an analysis of the convict-lease system, a system that Du Bois referred to as the spawn of slavery, as a historical practice that emerged in the process of reasserting white power in the American South. In addition, the study emphasized the fact that southern states profited from the imprisonment of Black people.

The 1904 study also analyzed census data on incarceration, but Du Bois and his collaborators were highly critical of and doubtful about the accuracy of census data given the ad hoc and often inaccurate work of census enumerators at the turn of the twentieth century, especially when it came to the classification of racial and ethnic minorities. Instead they chose to rely on local and court reports on incarceration and focus the study on the state of Georgia. The study also included a survey of young people (schoolchildren in Atlanta public schools and students throughout Georgia) on their opinions on the causes of crime, the police, and the courts.

The study presents some tentative conclusions regarding the causes for crime in the Black community. Du Bois attributes different responsibilities to Blacks and whites. The "faults" that he attributes to Blacks concern attitudes, including "lack of proper self-respect; low or extravagant ideals" or "lack of thrift and prevalence of the gambling spirit."[49] As always, however, Du Bois asserts that these attitudes have historical roots in slavery and the failures of the larger society.

The causes of crime attributed to whites involve the reconstruction of white power and include "the taking of all rights of political self-defense from the Negro either by direct law, or custom, or by the 'white primary' system" and "the punishment of crime as a means of public and private revenue rather than as a means of preventing the making of criminals."[50] In this study we can observe Du Bois's analytical and methodological approach: studying communities in depth, analyzing their structural context, and seeing that context as historically constructed through the action of a racialized society and the racial state.

While at this point Du Bois's politics focused on uplifting the Black community and incorporating that community into the economic order of American society, he realizes that this incorporation cannot occur without a change in the white-supremacist social order. The conclusions of the Ninth Atlanta Conference Study offer some hope for progress but also allude to clear and present dangers. As the study states, "In Georgia the tendencies are overwhelmingly in the right direction; crime is decreasing, property and education increasing. The danger lies in the environing white population with their tendency toward the unfair treatment of blacks."[51] The racial state and racial inequality are at the center of Du Bois's analysis of crime.

In its conclusion, *The Philadelphia Negro* poses the question, "What is the Negro problem?"[52] Du Bois's answer is that the problems of the Black community are, on the one hand, the traditional problems of human societies—"the old world questions of ignorance, poverty, crime, and the dislike of the stranger"[53]—and adds that these questions must be addressed together, given their interconnection and their complexities. But he asserts that ultimately the problems of the Black community come down to "that question of questions: after all who are Men?"[54] That is, at the root of the so-called Negro Problem is the question of equality among humans. Addressing this question means addressing the fundamental source of exclusion—the color line.

Du Bois puts forth a list of duties that Blacks and whites must assume to achieve equality. Following his politics of racial uplift at the time, this list emphasized bringing Black communities and individuals to work effectively on the terms of US society. Du Bois argues that it is "the duty of the Negro to raise himself by every effort to the standards of modern civilization and not to lower those standards in any degree."[55] Du Bois emphasized that achieving this goal required economic cooperation designed to create employment and business opportunities. In line with his belief that the Talented Tenth would lead the way in this and other endeavors, he also emphasized the duty of Black elites toward the masses. He asserts that the elites "should not forget that the spirit of the twentieth century is to be the turning of the high toward the lowly, the bending of Humanity to all that is human; the recognition that in the slums of modern society lie the answers to most of our puzzling problems of organization and life, and that only as we solve those problems is our culture assured and our progress certain."[56] But eliminating barriers to Black employment opportunities, he contended, was the task of whites.

As he wrote, "There is no doubt that in Philadelphia the centre and kernel of the Negro problem so far as the white people are concerned is the narrow opportunities afforded Negroes for earning a decent living."[57] Exclusion from opportunities was the root cause of the social problems of Black communities, which, as we have seen, was the result of white political power and a social order defined by race.[58]

The Sociology Chicago Made

Du Bois was the first sociologist to develop a scientific school of empirical sociology in the United States. Yet, his sociology was, as the sociologist Aldon Morris stated, a "path not taken."[59] In the story of origin that American sociologists tell, sociology became a professionalized discipline in Chicago in the late 1910s and the 1920s. And it is indeed true that the discipline, as it is practiced today, was to a large extent shaped by scholars associated with the University of Chicago, namely, Robert Park, Ernest Burgess, W. I. Thomas, and their students. It was at that university that some key practices that continue to structure the discipline even today were formed.

Robert Park was the main scholar among those that created the Chicago School, and he was definitely aware of Du Bois and his sociological work.[60] Park was Booker T. Washington's ghost writer and publicist for seven years, from 1905 to 1912. In his personal notes he compared Washington and Du Bois in the following terms: "These two men have divided the white and dark world between them. Du Bois has defined the relationship as one of radical and irreconcilable opposition. Washington is cooperative despite divergences and differences, not, however, minimizing the conflict of interest where it exists."[61] Winifred Raushenbush's biography of Park leaves no doubt that as someone who was very close to Booker T. Washington and held an assimilationist/accommodationist view of race and racial inequalities, Park was familiar with Du Bois and predisposed against his understanding of race and his political positions. So it is not surprising that in shaping the discipline of sociology at the University of Chicago, Park ignored Du Bois's work and insights. Yet, the result of Park's omission of Du Bois's work is a much impoverished discipline, as Park's sociology lacked the methodological complexity and theoretical sophistication of Du Bois's approach.

A main difference between Du Bois's sociology and that of the Chicago School was their relationship to history.[62] Whereas Du Bois's sociology was rooted in a thorough analysis of historical processes and historically constructed social contexts, Chicago's approach was to search for patterns and regularities that characterize social life regardless of its specific historical context. As Park asserted, "The sociologist is interested in the particular experience only so far as it enables him to say something about human nature in general, irrespective of any particular time and place."[63] To be sure, Park did not ignore history. His writings contain multiple historical references, and he focused on specific locations; for example, he analyzed race relations as they played out in different places.[64] Similarly, Chicago ethnographies make multiple references to processes of historical change. But those historical references are presented as teleological processes of transformation between stages of social evolution or as processes of social change understood as natural histories. For Park, societies changed and grew on predicable pathways that could be explained, much like the natural sciences, in ecological terms.

Rather than seeing modernity as a historically contingent social formation structured by the color line and racial colonial capitalism, as Du Bois did, Park saw the history of human societies as a natural process of change between two ideal types: culture (close-knit societies held together by a moral order) and civilization (territorial societies integrated by markets). Park understood this evolution as taking place through processes of competition, accommodation, and assimilation that he and Burgess described in their seminal *Introduction to Sociology* textbook.[65] As Park asserted, "What we call civilization is a territorial affair. It comes about by trade and commerce. . . . Civilization is built up by the absorption of foreign ethnic groups, by undermining them, and by secularizing their cult and sacred order."[66] Park analyzed specific cases of race relations as instances of the general process he postulated. The natural process of the development of civilization, he believed, would lead to the assimilation of ethnic groups. He was aware, however, that racial differences in the United States did not follow that path, and suggested the possibility of an alternative path, one that led to a binational society divided by vertical rather than horizontal lines of division. But he did not account for the power relations that made the American racial system not only separate but also highly unequal and unjust.

For Park, the city was the quintessential territory in which civilization developed and where the key social problems of American industrializing society played out. Park and Burgess sent their students to observe and record the social changes and interactions that were taking place in Chicago. In his introduction to the 1923 text *The Hobo*, the first of the Chicago ethnographic studies, Park argues that the old and familiar problems of crime, vice, and poverty take new forms in modern cities and that his new series of studies will investigate the various aspects of city life and its problems.[67] But again, he saw those processes as instances of a general natural process of change in the city: "There are forces at work within the limits of the urban community—within the limits of any natural area of human habitation, in fact—which tend to bring about an orderly and typical grouping of its populations and institutions."[68]

Ernest Burgess proposed to look at the process of city growth as analogous to biological metabolism. This process was characterized by a constant and recurrent sequence of disorganization and organization, an unstable equilibrium that sorts people across the city space into different groups. He describes modern cities as typically organized in four concentric areas—the main business district, a transition area of business and light manufacturing, a residential area for working people, and an upper-middle-class residential area. He asserted that the expansion of the city was characterized by "the tendency of each inner zone to extend its area by the invasion of the next outer zone. This aspect of expansion may be called succession, a process which has been studied in detail in plant ecology."[69] Burgess saw the process of urban change as equivalent to a process of change in a natural ecological system. This is a fundamentally ahistorical sociology, a sociology that looks for generalizable ideal types and regards change as a natural process.

Andrew Abbot presents a different interpretation of the Chicago School. In his view, "Chicago felt that no social fact makes any sense abstracted from its context in social (and often geographic) space and social time."[70] Abbot emphasizes that in addition to natural histories, Chicago scholars also focused their analysis on careers and interactional fields, concepts that allowed for much more contextuality and analysis of localized and temporal processes that make it impossible to separate social facts from their places and times.

Despite Abbot's interpretation, the fact is that Park and his students chose to fold the social tensions that they were indeed observing into natural history patterns. As historian Dorothy Ross observed in her 1991 book, *The Origins of American Social Science*, for Park, "Individual subjectivity and social attitudes were specified as the significant area of sociology only to be declared in the end to mirror and largely depend upon the competitive ecological process. . . . Park was prevented by his own positivism from adequately defending or enlarging the role of interpretative and historical method in Sociology."[71]

The teleological ideal-typical model of historical change proposed by Park is also seen in the monographs produced by his students that made the school famous during its rise to dominance through the 1920s and 1930s. For example, Harvey Zorbaugh's *Gold Coast and the Slum* includes sharp observations and descriptions of the many areas that comprised the North End of Chicago in the 1920s.[72] The North End was then a very diverse urban area, home to different ethnic groups and social classes. Zorbaugh, who was an acute observer and a gifted writer, documented the richness and diversity in the area's social life. Yet, at the same time, he tried to contain all the dynamism and tensions that he observed within the analytical "natural history" model of his mentors. The history of different areas of the city is presented as the unfolding of a teleological process of growth rather than a process of political construction of exclusion and access. The richness of the empirical analysis is subsumed under the straitjacket of the ecological model. Zorbaugh admitted that each city had its own peculiarities, the result of the combination of their topography, their type of industry, and their systems of transportation. Nonetheless, he asserted that "segregated areas of a given type, wherever they may be located in a given city with respect to other such areas, invariably fall, in every city, within one of these larger and well-defined zones."[73] The "natural history" understanding of social processes is also seen in Louis Wirth's *Ghetto*. A subsection in the book's introduction bears the precise title "The Natural History of the Ghetto." In this section, Wirth argues that the richness and detail of the ghetto's life—its poetry, fiction, and philosophy, its biographies and lives—should not be analyzed simply like the particular history of the Jewish ghetto (or any Jewish ghetto in particular) but as a type of cultural community. Wirth clearly adopts the Chicago ideal-typical approach to community studies, stating, "The study of the ghetto, viewed from such an angle, is likely to throw light on a number of related phenomena, such as the origin of segregated areas and the development of cultural communities in general; for, while the ghetto is, strictly speaking, a Jewish institution, there are forms of ghettos that concern not merely Jews. There are Little Sicilies, Little Polands, Chinatowns, and Black belts in our large cities, and there are segregated areas, such as vice areas, that bear a close resemblance to the Jewish ghetto."[74]

Park and his fellow Chicago scholars instituted a disciplinary approach based on the search for abstract patterns and ahistorical generalizations, an approach that ignored processes of interaction and conflict between situated actors. If it can be said that American empirical sociology started at Chicago, that is the case because, although Du Bois conducted his work first, the sociology that we practice today derives much more from Chicago than from Atlanta. While Park and the Chicago monographs are little read today, their influence is keenly recognized in many of the discipline's contemporary practices. Park and the Chicago School focused on social problems such as crime, marginality, social disintegration, assimilation, and urban succession that are still major subjects of study in the discipline. And a reader of the Chicago monographs will find that the concepts and methods that Park and his students used to write about those topics are not very different from those that contemporary sociologists use.[75]

Moreover, we see the lasting power of the Chicago approach in the discipline's mainstream search for ahistorical patterns and regularities, in the lack of theorization and analysis of racialized modernity and different historical forms of exclusions, in the lack of serious engagement with agency, and in the delegitimating of the subaltern standpoint in scholarship. Du Bois, on the other hand, proposed historically and contextually situated studies, conducted within the broad theoretical frame of racialized modernity. His analysis of Philadelphia's Black community is not rooted in a natural history of race relations or city change, but on the struggles of the Black community to make a place for itself in the city and the actions of the white population to maintain the color line and protect it from challenges.

Yet, for all its problems, Abbott is right that the Chicago School was more conscious of the importance of historical context and processes than much of contemporary sociology has been, even if it subsumed them as natural processes and set patterns of change. As Abbott points out, much of the current reasoning in contemporary sociology derives from the so-called variable revolution that was the result of the influence of Paul Lazarsfeld at Columbia.[76]

Variable-oriented sociology focuses on the effect of supposedly independent social forces, codified as measurable variables, that shape the behavior or opinions of actors who are analyzed detached from their social and historical contexts. These types of variable-oriented studies have come to dominate research on important contemporary issues such as migration, neighborhood change, and social inequalities. Historical and social contexts are codified as control variables. As Abbott, and C. Wright Mills before him, point out, the importance, richness, and specificity of context and history are lost in this type of research. As a result of this approach, much of American sociology has become a "one case study" research enterprise that ignores the specific historical and contextual characteristics of its case.

Du Bois's sociology has little in common with the variable-oriented research model and decontextualized analysis that emerged from Columbia. And although it was closer to the Chicago approach, it differed from it in three very important ways: first, it was rooted in historical and contextual analysis that highlighted both agency and power differences; second, it took the color line and racialized modernity as its theoretical framework; and third, it developed a specific mixed-methods methodology. Du Bois's research methodology was based on thorough and detailed descriptions and interpretations of communities, their social and historical contexts, and the actions of the people who lived within them.

Like Abbott's description of Chicago sociology, Du Bois's sociology was not based on an understanding of causality as the effect of a set of independent variables on a dependent variable, nor did he set out to test low- or middle-range theories in this way.[77] Rather, he saw science as the detailed examination of the predicament and lived experience of people, as the search for the realm of chance in a world of law, and he conducted this search within the theoretical frame of racialized modernity. This is not to say that he rejected statistics—statistical description of local contexts was part of his research program—but he warned that the broad use of data unmoored from the context in which it was collected did not produce accurate descriptions of social situations.

A Contemporary Du Boisian Urban and Community Sociology

The limits and deficiencies of the Chicago-inspired urban and community sociology have important consequences: This approach pushes work that centers on the analysis of racism and coloniality to the margins of the discipline, and fails to address how history shapes the contemporary moment. At least in theory, mainstream sociology takes a liberal reformist stand—books and articles conclude with policy recommendations aimed to address various social problems—but it does not address the power structures that create those social problems or the politics necessary to put those policies in action. As a result, this seemingly reformist stance simply fails to provide any answers as to how to change the status quo.[78]

These limitations also take a toll on graduate students and young faculty of color, who find their experiences marginalized, discredited, or even negated. If they want to address their own experiences of inequality, if they want to work on the construction of subaltern subjectivities or memories of oppression, or if they want to question methods to include subaltern experiences or to expand the archives that sociologists use, they are often told that their work is not sociological. They are forced into a pattern of disciplinary work that denies their experience or standpoint as a source of knowledge. Or they are told that their work belongs in the humanities or in ethnic studies, not in sociology. As a result, many promising students or young sociologists are pushed away from the discipline.

We assert that an engagement with Du Bois's sociology is necessary to expand the boundaries of what is possible and legitimate in the discipline. A contemporary Du Boisian urban and community sociology would build on both Du Bois's early analytical and methodological approaches to community studies and his late theoretical analysis of racial and colonial capitalism and the racial state. It would address the issue of agency with utmost seriousness, and would identify different forms of agency, organization, and community self-making within subaltern groups. In focusing on the forms of agency of the subaltern, it would not lionize or romanticize "resistance," but carefully observe how these communities aim to shape their own lives, with their achievements, their limitations, and their defeats.

A contemporary Du Boisian sociology would also examine historically constituted social relations of inequality and exclusion, rather than seeking ahistorical patterns and regularities. It would take structure and power seriously, remembering that structures are relational and historical constructions, not natural processes. A contemporary Du Boisian urban and community sociology would take the historical constitution of these power structures as one of its key objects of study and demand that we critically examine racial and colonial capitalism, and the intersections of class, race, and gender. The analysis of "social problems" would expand from looking only at the poor to looking also at the powerful, including their ideologies and practices of exclusion.

A contemporary Du Boisian urban and community sociology should also follow a multimethod strategy. First, it would root its analysis in the historical context. At the same time, it would be eclectic concerning the forms of data collection. It should embrace sophisticated quantitative methods. We believe that Du Boisian sociologists should learn and be proficient in advanced quantitative techniques of analysis, but not employ quantitative methods for method's sake.[79] Furthermore, quantitative analysis should be conducted applying a Du Boisian methodology, that is, quantitative analyses of communities or social inequalities should be rooted in their social and historical contexts. Race and gender (or any other social category of difference and inequality) are not just variables that affect outcomes regardless of context and power relations. They are forms of social relations rooted in place and time, mechanisms of exclusionary power, and bases for social action, and those need to be explicitly addressed in any quantitative or qualitative urban or community study.

The Du Boisian sociology we propose would emphasize description and the link between local experiences and the sociohistorical context. Furthermore, comparisons and generalizations would be inductive, based on a thorough search for commonalities and differences through a strategy of contrasts. This approach would be guided by the overall theoretical framework of racialized modernity. Similarly, a contemporary Du Boisian urban and community sociology would embrace a critical ethnography that accounts for the historical context that produced the case that is being researched. Rather than trying to explain how "the other half" lives, this ethnography would aim to explain how people are pushed to live under certain conditions and how people respond to those conditions. A contemporary Du Boisian sociology would also welcome other methods, such as auto-ethnography, and would question the archive upon which we build our knowledge.

Finally, a contemporary Du Boisian community sociology would also be a public sociology. It would be concerned with the fundamental questions of change and equality—that is, "Who is a human?" and "What is a just society?" Contemporary Du Boisian sociologists would work with communities that struggle for justice, equality, and emancipation. And they would fight passionately and strenuously to help them achieve those goals.

4

Public Sociology and Du Bois's Evolving Program
for Freedom

In the summer of July 1894, at age twenty-six, W. E. B. Du Bois traveled home from his two years at Friedrich Wilhelm University in Berlin, Germany, where he had been furthering his postgraduate coursework en route to his PhD. He returned home by boat, in the ship's steerage deck, along with the other impoverished passengers, the rats, and the cargo. But the accommodations did not bother him because he truly believed that he was returning home on a mission.

Reflecting on that young version of himself, Du Bois recalled in his 1944 essay, "My Evolving Program for Negro Freedom," "I returned ready and eager to begin a life-work, leading to the emancipation of the American Negro. History and the other social sciences were to be my weapons, to be sharpened and applied by research and writing. Where and how, was the question in 1894."[1]

It did not take long for Du Bois to find his way. By the turn of the twentieth century, and in six short years, Du Bois had achieved a growing reputation as a sociologist, despite the caste system based on race that was designed to relegate him and his research to the margins of his budding discipline. Within that short period of time, between 1894 and 1900, Du Bois had earned his PhD in history from Harvard, the first Black person to be awarded a doctorate at that institution, and he had published both his dissertation, titled *The Suppression of the African Slave Trade to America*, and a second major study, *The Philadelphia Negro*.[2] He had also earned a faculty position at Atlanta University, a Black college founded in 1865 by the American Missionary Association and the Freedman's Bureau in the aftermath of the Civil War, where he was appointed to teach social science and direct the Atlanta University Studies.

Even in those early years it was clear to Du Bois that although chattel slavery in America had been abolished some three decades earlier, his people were still not yet free. A strict and often punitive system of Jim Crow discrimination and racial violence prevailed throughout the South, and conditions for Black people in the North, where de facto segregation relegated them to poor neighborhoods, inadequate schools, and the lowest of jobs, were not much better. But like most young people, Du Bois was hopeful and full of earnest conviction. Armed with his mighty "weapons," as he described them—history and the social sciences—he believed that he could lead Black folks in America to freedom.

How did he seek to achieve this? As we shall see, Du Bois embarked upon a long and peripatetic journey in search of freedom, liberty, peace, and humanity for the darker races of the world who lived, as he described their situation, behind the veil of the color line. This journey can be understood by braiding together two separate yet inextricable aspects of his work: his evolving philosophy of freedom and his public commitment. To truly understand Du Bois's lifetime achievements and public works, we believe that it is critical to understand the link between Du Bois's public sociology and his evolving program for freedom.

As for the latter, Du Bois wrote early and often about his shifting program and the world-historical events that prompted those shifts. The former dimension, his public sociology, is by far the most contested aspect of Du Bois's career in this field. Public sociology is often greeted with skepticism from the mainstream members of the discipline. Institutionally, it is often rendered illegible or is often discounted among academics, making it difficult for work in this area to help a sociologist reach critical professional milestones, such as tenure and promotion. Yet, public sociology is rooted in the origins of the discipline, and for that reason, it is one of many tools available to its practitioners. Du Bois's works in this area were underpinned by theory. As we will show, every one of his public endeavors was informed by a deep reservoir of his philosophy about freedom, which he developed, cultivated, pruned, and replanted over his long life.

Up to this point, we have tried to distill and systematize Du Bois's sociological program under broad topics, specifically his phenomenology, his formulation of theories about racial and colonial capitalism, and his approach to urban and community studies. Previous chapters have been organized thematically to help us explore the ideas, concepts, and theoretical frameworks that make a Du Boisian sociology unique. In this chapter, however, instead of discussing the themes that Du Bois's public sociology encompasses, we trace the development of those themes chronologically, following the arc of his evolving thought. We describe these Du Boisian "eras" of thought by drawing from his biographical works in which he self-narrates his own intellectual genealogy, specifically his essay "My Evolving Program for Negro Freedom" and three of his autobiographies, *Dusk of Dawn: An Essay towards an Autobiography of Race Concept*, *In Battle for Peace: The Story of My 83rd Birthday*, and *The Autobiography of W. E. B. Du Bois*. Du Bois wrote several autobiographical reflections over the course of his lifetime. The fact that there are so many such works suggests that he wanted those who followed him to explore how world events, his life experiences, and his philosophies intersected to inform his actions.

It is important to point out that in exploring these issues, we are not writing Du Bois's biography. Others have done so before, notably David Levering Lewis in his two-time Pulitzer Prize–winning works, *W. E. B. Du Bois: Biography of a Race, 1868–1919* and *W. E. B. Du Bois: The Fight for Equality and the American Century, 1919–1963*. Rather, we seek to describe some of the critical events and actions in Du Bois's life that demonstrate and elucidate how he addressed in his life the question of the relationship among being a scholar, being an activist and organizer, and being a person who thought about freedom for people who were shackled by racism and oppressed by colonialism. We want to show how these different threads came together in Du Bois's life through the examination of selected moments in his life. And to explore these issues, it is important to situate Du Bois within the historical context within which his sociology and intellectual commitments emerged.

The Intellectual and American Sociology

Du Bois began practicing sociology even before it was considered an academic discipline. Harvard, his alma mater, did not have a department dedicated to the discipline. Among sociology's founders, this route to being a practitioner of the discipline is not unique. The social psychologist and sociological theorist George Herbert Mead studied psychology and philosophy at Harvard and later at the University of Leipzig, but never finished his dissertation or earned a doctorate degree. Robert Ezra Park also earned his PhD in philosophy, and like Du Bois, studied under William James at Harvard. Across the Atlantic, Karl Marx and Emile Durkheim earned PhDs in philosophy, and Max Weber earned his in history and law. These pedigrees illuminate the fact that, like his fellow founding sociologists, Du Bois was not a product of the discipline but rather one of its architects.

These early practitioners came to the field of sociology largely from other disciplines, namely, philosophy, history, and psychology, and shaped what would become the field of sociology as it is known today. Each scholar came with his own vision for what sociology could be, and all of them had specific interests that influenced their priorities and their approaches. Park, along with his colleagues at the Chicago School, shaped urban ethnography and promoted imposing ecological frameworks onto the study of social relations. Mead's emphasis on the mind, the social self, and consciousness would eventually lead to a line of sociological inquiry that came to be known as symbolic interactionism, an approach that also came from Chicago. And thanks to his seminal writings, Marx is claimed by almost every discipline in the human sciences as a founding father, even though he never even taught at a university.

Today the discipline of sociology is in fact a conglomerate of subfields, with some that speak to one another and others that do not. As a result, the leading contemporary sociologists are increasingly specialists. In contrast, Du Bois and his contemporaries founded a discipline under a different "landscape of meaning"[3] in that the human sciences and their disciplines evolved in the late nineteenth and early twentieth centuries at the same time that that generation of scholars came to them.[4]

Each of these early scholars came to the field with a particular perspective. Du Bois was first and foremost a scholar of racialized modernity, and his concerns lay with the global color line and the racial and colonial capitalist system that conditioned and sustained it. Because he wanted to undo these structures, his was always an emancipatory sociology. While Du Bois's work was read within the academy, by no means did he limit his audience to the ivory tower. He understood that if his mission was to lead his fellow racialized and colonized peoples to freedom, he had to awaken public opinion, Black and white. To this end, a Du Boisian sociology is necessarily dependent on public engagement.

Era I: Science, Truth, and the Negro Problem (1900–1910)

The Exhibit of American Negroes

In April of 1900, Du Bois found himself repeating the journey across the Atlantic that he had taken just six years earlier, again traveling by ship, again in steerage, and again on a mission to "free" the American Negro.[5] However, this time he was journeying not to the United States but back to Europe. At the invitation of Thomas Junius Calloway, a Washington lawyer, Du Bois had joined a team of Black intellectuals, including Calloway and the assistant librarian of Congress, Daniel Murray, to curate a display titled "The Exhibit of American Negroes" for the 1900 World's Fair in Paris.[6]

This World's Fair was a monumental international event, drawing an estimated fifty million visitors from around the world to admire the accomplishments of humankind as the world stood on the brink of the twentieth century. Calloway, who was Du Bois's friend and former Fisk classmate, understood the significance of this event, and thus urged members of the African American intelligentsia to insist that an exhibition dedicated to the accomplishments of Black Americans be installed on behalf of the United States government. With the personal support and advocacy of Booker T. Washington, who held the role of power broker between the white elite and Black worlds, Congress committed fifteen thousand dollars to fund the project and named Calloway as special agent to the United States for the exhibit.

Receiving the money just two months before the opening, Calloway, Murray, and Du Bois scrambled to produce what proved to be a brilliant exhibit. As a librarian, Murray contributed an extensive bibliography of literary and scientific publications by African Americans and sent a sample of two hundred books to put on display. Du Bois assembled 363 photographs into two series, entitled "Types of American Negros, Georgia U.S.A." and "Negro Life in Georgia U.S.A.," and produced sixty colorful handmade data visualizations depicting charts and graphs related to the Black American population.[7]

Unlike nearly all such exhibitions, Du Bois's display included no descriptions of the photographic and other images. The graphs on display described the demographic and economic characteristics of African Americans in Georgia, and showed the drastic population increases within this group. To give his audience a sense of the historical and political context of these images, he also displayed a three-volume compilation of Georgia's Black Codes, spanning the period from the colonial era to his present day. However, he let the photographs speak for themselves.

This was Du Bois's first documented work of what we would now call public sociology. In an article about the event, published in the *American Monthly Review of Reviews*, Du Bois stated, "In the right-hand corner . . . as one enters, is an exhibit which, more than most others in the building is sociological in the larger sense of the term—that is, is an attempt to give, in as systematic and compact a form as possible, the history and present condition of a large group of human beings."[8]

Depicted in these images were Black folks in all their heterogeneity—representing various characteristics, such as class standings, and occupations. The people depicted in these photographs did not conform to the derogatory stereotypes that were often evoked in popular representations of Black people, for example, the barbaric mongrel, the minstrel, the coon, or the mammy, all of which were overrepresented in media in America and around the world at that time. Instead, the images that Du Bois presented were of everyday Black people, many of whom were middle class and who had their photographs taken by the local photographer in Atlanta, family photographs having by this point become popular among the middle class.[9] Through this exhibition, Du Bois reiterated his simple yet powerful argument on a world stage: African Americans were human beings just like everyone else. For this display, Calloway, Murray, and Du Bois won the gold medal in their category.

In her 2004 book, *Photography on the Color Line: W. E. B. Du Bois, Race, and Visual Culture*, Shawn Michelle Smith, a professor of visual and critical studies, argues that "the 363 photographs Du Bois procured for the American Negro Exhibit collectively function as a counter archive that challenges a long legacy of racist taxonomy, intervening in turn-of-the century 'race science' by offering competing visual evidence."[10] Without comment, Du Bois simply placed the photographs, the volumes of oppressive Black Codes, and the data before the viewers to interpret. Through the exhibition in Paris, Smith argues, "Against [the] vision of scientifically legitimized white supremacism, Du Bois wields his own science in the Georgia Negro studies. He de-naturalizes the color line, wrenching it from biology and biological explanations, to relocate it back in the terrain of social history, economics, and global politics."[11] In so doing, he translated his sociology so as to make it accessible to an international lay public. Through the Paris exhibition Du Bois was seeking to assert the humanity and complexity of Black life within, and the oppressive structures of, the color line.

"The Exhibit of the American Negroes" at the World's Fair was not the only business matter Du Bois attended to during his voyage to Europe in 1900. In the middle of the fair, in late July, he took a side trip to London, where he attended the first Pan-African Conference. The conference, primarily organized by Sylvester Williams, a London attorney, was convened to discuss the common issues facing people of African descent, whether they lived on the continent or abroad, and whether in circumstances of slavery or in circumstances of colonialism. In the years leading up to the gathering, Williams had curried much favor among the Black elite of Europe, the West Indies, and the United States.

Du Bois served as chairman of the Committee on Address, a role in which he was charged with writing the official statement that emerged from the discussions at the conference. This statement, titled "To the Nations of the World," was read to the group at the last session of the conference, and a copy was subsequently sent to the queen of England.[12]

This statement represents the first time Du Bois formulated his claim that "the problem of the twentieth century is the problem of the color line."[13] However, despite the general enthusiasm for the mission and aims of the conference, not much came of the first meeting, and the organization fizzled out soon after. However, the Pan-African Conference planted a seed in Du Bois. It was here that he discovered his penchant for organizing, and here that he embraced the concept of Pan-Africanism. For him, this concept was not merely a theoretical formulation of identity throughout the Black diaspora. It also represented a worldview that would orient his thoughts and actions forever after. However, as we shall see, it would be nearly twenty years later, in 1918, before Du Bois revived the idea by founding the Pan-African Congress.

The Moon, the Horizon, and the Niagara Movement

In 1905 Du Bois expanded his sociological repertoire even further. That was the year when he founded his first periodical, the Moon, and in which he organized the inaugural meeting of the Niagara Movement, a US-focused civil rights organization. While Du Bois had participated in the organizing circuit in the past by speaking in 1897 at the American Negro Academy and in 1900 at the Pan-African Conference, the Niagara Movement was the first organized movement that Du Bois founded and led. Du Bois firmly believed that Black people needed to lift themselves up and produce solutions to their predicament within their community. In this way, Du Bois was becoming focused on the idea of influencing the way his people were educated; therefore he became increasingly focused on controlling the means of knowledge production for and about Black people.

Du Bois firmly believed that for his research and ideas to have a real impact on the betterment of Black people, he had to reach and engage a broad public. The main vehicle he used to reach this vast and heterogeneous audience was periodicals, founding three of them between 1901 and 1933.[14] Most notable was the *Crisis*, the official monthly magazine of the NAACP. He served as its editor-in-chief between 1910 and 1934, nearly a quarter of a century. However his career as an editor actually began in 1905 with the founding of the *Moon Illustrated Weekly*.

The *Moon* had its headquarters in Nashville, Tennessee, and had a small circulation of about five hundred regional subscribers. At the time he founded this publication, Du Bois was already well known in Black intellectual circles, having published two books, *The Philadelphia Negro* and *The Souls of Black Folk*, and was serving as a faculty member at Atlanta University and principal investigator of the Atlanta University Studies. Du Bois associated with two former students and the three bought a press in Memphis to get the magazine off the ground. To finance a magazine that focused on issues relevant to Black people in America, Du Bois tried to tap into the network of white philanthropists. His proposal for the journal to potential donors, written in 1904, stated his goals eloquently: "The present is a very central time for the American Negro and for the darker races in general. It is not simply a question of individual ability but of group cooperation and to initiate forward movements in culture and reform, and to repel unjust attack. To stimulate this cooperation wide self-knowledge within the race of its own need and accomplishments is demanded; and certain ideals, racial

and cultural, must be brought home to the rank and file. A proper journal would be the first step toward these ends."[15]

The idea was ultimately regarded as too radical, both because of its
stated aims and because Du Bois made it clear that he intended to have
full editorial control of the publication. The white northern financiers
whom Du Bois asked for financial help all declined. Still, with the support of some advertisers, Du Bois and his associates started publishing
the *Moon* in December 1905, but the magazine lasted just slightly over a
year and dissolved in early 1907, as the small group of subscribers could
not sustain the cost of operating the journal.

The dissolution of the *Moon* did not, however, deter Du Bois. In 1907,
the same year that the *Moon* died, he partnered with two of his fellow
Niagara Movement[16] founders, F. H. M. Murray and L. M. Hershaw,
to found a Black periodical: the *Horizon: A Journal of the Color Line.*
Du Bois, Murray, and Hershaw put up their own money to launch the
magazine and shared editorial responsibilities. Three columns were regular features: The Out-Look, the In-Look, and the Over-Look.[17] Each
column addressed Black issues from the perspective of outside, within,
and beyond the veil. The three editorial perspectives reflected the African American experience of "twoness," the unreconciled position of
simultaneously being both American and Black, presented in both *Souls*
and *Dusk of Dawn.* The Out-Look spoke from the former perspective,
while the In-Look spoke from the latter, from within the veil. The column Du Bois wrote, the Over-Look, offered a worldview that envisioned
life beyond the color line, what Du Bois described as second sight, that
is, the ability to see past the veil.

Like the *Moon,* the *Horizon* was considered too radical for the white
liberal elite. In addition, many issues of the publication openly criticized
Booker T. Washington and his Tuskegee Machine, which at this point
was involved in nearly every facet of Black political and economic life.
The editorial leadership of the *Horizon* held the position that Washington's compromising stance on race relations was detrimental to the social, economic, and political advancement of the Black race. And they
were not shy about saying so in the published periodical. Murray and
Hershaw bore the brunt of the backlash that greeted the views expressed
in the journal, as both were among the few Black civil servants hold-
ing high-level positions in the federal government during the Theodore

Roosevelt administration.[18] Washington responded to the negative press about his politics by sending his assistant to the White House to demand that Murray and Hershaw be demoted on the grounds that civil servants should not express political concerns. And both men's careers suffered irreparable damage during this period as a result of their brazen editorials. Despite all this, the *Horizon* sustained itself for three years, largely at the personal expense of its three founders, and eventually morphed into Du Bois's most far-reaching Black periodical, the *Crisis*.

Although the *Moon* was short-lived and only reached a modest audience, the periodical's biography reveals Du Bois's long-lasting engagement with the public. His struggles with funding and controlling his own publication outlets lay bare another veil that Du Bois would encounter and speak openly about for years to come—the silent power and pervasive influence of the powerful philanthropic organizations of the North. By the end of the decade, Du Bois found himself less and less convinced that his "weapons of history and social science" alone were mighty enough to slay his arch enemy, the color line. This doubt started creeping into Du Bois's thinking as early as 1899, just two years into his post at Atlanta University, spurred by a specific incident.

Sam Hose, a Black man accused of murdering his white employer, had been lynched and burned to death that year in a public spectacle in rural Georgia. Upon learning about the alleged murder, Du Bois wrote an article about the incident to submit to the local newspaper, the *Atlanta Journal Constitution*. However, as he was walking over to the newspaper's office, Du Bois learned from a colleague that Hose had already been lynched, and that his dismembered knuckles were on display on the counter at the local grocery store as a trophy. As he realized instantly, there are some things one cannot un-see.

In that moment, the first whisper of doubt visited Du Bois. In *Dusk* he recollected that "one could not be a calm, cool, and detached scientist while Negroes were lynched, murdered and starved."[19] The persistence of racial oppression and violence in the South caused Du Bois to question what fruits his reliance on science and truth were bearing in terms of liberating Black people from their harrowing condition. Of all atrocities, it was the everydayness of lynching that made Du Bois retool his program: "It reached a climax in 1892, when 235 persons were publicly murdered, and in the sixteen years of my teaching nearly two thousand persons were publicly killed by mobs, and not a single one of the murderers punished."[20]

The 1906 Atlanta race riots marked a major turning point in terms of how Du Bois viewed the import of his sociological approach thus far. For two gruesome days, from September 22 to September 24, white mobs invaded the Black enclaves of the city of Atlanta and slaughtered their residents. The white perpetrators used the tried-and-true scapegoat idea of the alleged rape of white women to justify the wholesale killings of their Black neighbors. Whites lynched Black people, leaving their bodies hanging on trees and lampposts. For two long days Blacks were shot and stabbed, gang raped, and left for dead.

The body count for this all-too-common type of turn-of-the-twentieth-century massacre is still unverified to this day. The *New York Times* reported that at least twenty-five Blacks and two whites were murdered during the riot;[21] other accounts estimate that as many as one hundred Black people died. Du Bois, his wife, Nina, and the couple's six-year-old daughter, Yolanda, bore witness to this horrific event. So shaken was the Du Bois family that Nina and Yolanda left Atlanta and returned to Du Bois's hometown of Great Barrington, Massachusetts. In his stupor, Du Bois sought comfort in the one tool he knew he controlled completely—his writing. He wrote what would become one of his best-known poems to express his shock and rage. These stanzas of "The Litany of Atlanta" reveal a great deal about Du Bois's state of mind:

> Bewildered we are, and passion-tost, mad with the madness of a mobbed and mocked and murdered people; straining at the armposts of Thy Throne, we raise our shackled hands and charge Thee, God, by the bones of our stolen fathers, by the tears of our dead mothers, by the very blood of Thy crucified Christ: *What meaneth this?* Tell us the Plan; give us the Sign!
> *Keep not thou silence, O God!*
>
> Sit no longer blind, Lord God, deaf to our prayer and dumb to our dumb suffering. Surely Thou too art not white, O Lord, a pale, bloodless, heartless thing?
> *Ah! Christ of all the Pities!*

Forgive the thought! Forgive these wild, blasphemous words. Thou art still the God of our black fathers, and in Thy soul's soul sit some soft dark-enings of the evening, some shadowings of the velvet night.

Du Bois by no means gave up his research. On the contrary. During this first era of Du Bois's program for freedom, between 1900 and 1910, he would publish two additional books, the iconic *Souls of Black Folk* in 1903 and *John Brown* in 1909, as well as several articles in academic journals and essays in such esteemed publications as the *Atlantic* and the *Outlook*. However, Du Bois became jaded with the idea of science for science's sake and concluded that he could do more to help Black people achieve freedom from outside of the academy. Reflecting on that transitional moment he wrote,

It was of course crazy for me to dream that America, in the dawn of the Twentieth Century, with Colonial Imperialism, based on the suppression of colored folk, at its zenith, would encourage, much less adequately fi-nance, such a program at a Negro college under Negro scholars. My faith in its success was based on the firm belief that race prejudice was based on widespread ignorance. My long-term remedy was Truth: carefully gathered scientific proof that neither color nor race determined the limits of a man's capacity or desert. I was not at the time sufficiently Freudian to understand how little human action is based on reason; nor did I know Karl Marx well enough to appreciate the economic foundations of human history.[22]

In 1910 Du Bois resigned from Atlanta University and went to work as the editor of the *Crisis*, the journal of the NAACP.[23] This moment in Du Bois's career is significant because of his decision to leave the acad-emy, but even more so because it marked the first major watershed in his thinking when it came to his program for Negro freedom.

As he wrote, "On the other hand, gradually and with increasing clar-ity, my whole attitude toward the social sciences began to change: in the study of human beings and their actions, there could be no such rift between theory and practice, between pure and applied science; as was possible in the study of sticks and stones. The 'studies' which I had been conducting at Atlanta I saw as fatally handicapped."[24]

Era II: Pragmatism, Propaganda, and Pan-Africanism (1910–1928)

Du Bois left Atlanta University in part because he no longer believed that his purist approach to sociology would achieve freedom for Black people, as he originally thought it would. Data, facts, and analyses might have articulated the problem, but they did not move the hearts and minds of the white public. He arrived in New York City to assume his new position as director of publications and research for the NAACP with the same commitment to racial uplift; this time, however, he would implement a program that fused facts, theory, and action in real time.

He arrived at this post in the midst of a wave of citywide race riots, much like the one he had experienced first-hand in Atlanta. Such riots were sweeping the country. Lynching, murder, disenfranchisement, and abject poverty due to exploitative labor structures were just a few of the indignities that Black Americans were experiencing in systematic fashion throughout the country. Not surprisingly, Du Bois approached his new assignment with urgency. As he described his emotions at the time, "I faced situations that called—shrieked—for action, even before any detailed, scientific study could possibly be prepared. It was as though, as a bridge-builder, I was compelled to throw a bridge across a stream without waiting for the careful mathematical testing of materials."[25]

The strictures of the academy made it impossible for Du Bois to respond to these devastating situations in time to have any real effect. Furthermore, the audience for his initial program was primarily intended to be white liberals, with the belief that racism was merely a problem of ignorance. By 1910, when he left Atlanta University, Du Bois had abandoned that thinking. Although he still believed in building coalitions across racial and ethnic lines, he felt a moral and political obligation to struggle in and with his community. As he summed up his feeling, "I saw before me a problem that could not and would not await the last word of science, but demanded immediate action to prevent social death."[26] As we will see, this sense of sheer urgency would only be exacerbated by the coming of the First World War. If the universal laws of science were no longer sufficient for Du Bois, what approach to the acquisition of knowledge did he now embrace? At first he returned home to pragmatism. As he wrote in "My Evolving Program for Negro Freedom,"

Then, too, for what Law was I searching? In accord with what unchangeable scientific law of action was the world of interracial discord about me working? I fell back upon my Royce and James and deserted Schmoller and Weber. I saw the action of physical law in the actions of men; but I saw more than that: I saw rhythms and tendencies; coincidences and probabilities; and I saw that, which for want of any other word, I must in accord with the strict tenets of Science, call Chance. I went forward to build a sociology, which I conceived of as the attempt to measure the element of Chance in human conduct. This was the Jamesian pragmatism, applied not simply to ethics, but to all human action, beyond what seemed to me, increasingly, the distinct limits of physical law.[27]

His approach was no longer just about testing and proving but about acting and implementing. This represented a major shift in his thinking in that up to this time, Du Bois had been opposed to research that had an explicit reformist agenda. Although he had believed that the outcome of research would be reform, he had also believed that reform would be the result of the elite enlightenment produced by science.

With this new shift in Du Bois's program, he now believed not only that his research aim should be to produce social change but that it must. For this new Du Bois, it was not enough to view his research findings as one element to be integrated into some sort of social justice assembly line. At this point, whatever boundaries had existed between his research, his organizing, and his activism had completely dissolved. These were all key ingredients in a program designed to liberate his people.

A second major influence on Du Bois's new approach was the vibrant resurgence of Black intellectual and artistic production then concentrating in New York City. Du Bois moved to New York just as the extraordinary cultural movement known as the Harlem Renaissance was emerging, finding himself in the mecca of the Black intelligentsia of the moment. He was both shaped by and shaping the various ideologies that gripped and transformed Black thought from the turn of the twentieth century through the Great Depression. Especially influential at this moment was what was known as the New Negro ideology. The New Negro Movement was a fin de siècle and early-twentieth-century social movement promulgated by Black artists and intellectuals that promoted self-determined representations of Blackness to counter racist and dehumanized representations of Black people. In their 2007 anthology, professors of English and African American studies Henry Louis Gates Jr. and Gene Andrew Jarrett assert that "the New Negro was a major discursive cornerstone of racial representation in the late nineteenth and early twentieth centuries."[28] New Negro philosopher Alain Locke articulated the issue with the representation of the Negro figure in his 1925 essay, "The New Negro." There he wrote,

> For generations in the mind of America, the Negro has been more of a formula than a human being—a something to be argued about, condemned or defended, to be "kept down," or "in his place," or "helped up," to be worried with or worried over, harassed or patronized, a social bogey or a social burden. The thinking Negro even has been induced to share this same general attitude, to focus his attention on controversial issues, to see himself in the distorted perspective of a social problem. His shadow, so to speak, has been more real to him than his personality.[29]

The issue of representation was central to New Negro ideology, as its mission was to represent the "Negro figure" as a human being—one possessing dignity, self-respect, culture, capability, and rights and thus worthy of mutual recognition in the eyes of the "other." This formulation was the opposite of the post-Reconstruction representation of the "old" Negro as shiftless, abject, and childlike. Members of the movement promoted these representations mainly through the proliferation of uniquely Black literature, art, history, and music. Du Bois called such material propaganda. In his eyes, this did not imply making things up. Quite the contrary. He still believed in facts, truth, and the power of the social sciences. However, unlike previously, he also believed in propagating ideas and sending messages to the general public through his work.

The Economy of Knowledge Production and Its Problems

Du Bois's decision to shift his approach was not only a response to events and the changing environment. It was also due to his late realization of the elusive power structures that exerted undue influence on common knowledge. Through his debilitating encounters with Booker T. Washington and the "Tuskegee Machine," wavering northern philanthropists, and publishing-industry gatekeepers, Du Bois gained an understanding of the power of representation, aesthetics, and the means of knowledge production. In a way, his so-called second sight was awakened anew, and he was determined to speak truth to power.

Du Bois articulates this philosophy most clearly in "The Criteria of Negro Art," a speech he delivered in 1926 as the keynote address at the NAACP's Annual Spingarn Medal ceremony and later published in the *Crisis*.[30] The Black literati of the day—artists, poets, writers, scholars, and educators—constituted a large part of the original audience. In this piece, Du Bois encouraged the members of his audience to consider their works both within and outside of the economy of cultural production. The publishing industry was steeped in racial bias, and the bar for Black artists and writers to get their work out into the public was high, as they were encouraged to make their works conform to the distorted, degraded images used to reinforce negative stereotypes of Black people. This was the dilemma the Black artists faced.

Du Bois urged his fellow Black literati, whether they were artists, performers, or writers, to consider the stakes involved in dealing with this dilemma not only as a current social problem but as one that would extend into posterity:

> We can go on the stage; we can be just as funny as white Americans wish us to be; we can play all the sordid parts that America likes to assign to Negroes; but for anything else there is still small place for us. And so I might go on. But let me sum up with this: Suppose the only Negro who survived some centuries hence was the Negro painted by white Americans in the novels and essays they have written. What would people in a hundred years say of black Americans?
>
> Now turn it around. Suppose you were to write a story and put in it the kind of people you know and like and imagine. You might get it published and you might not. And the "might not" is still far bigger than the "might." The white publishers catering to white folk would say, "It is not interesting" to white folk, naturally not. They want Uncle Tom, Topsies, good "darkies," and clowns.[31]

The dilemma that Du Bois describes still plagues the media industry today,[32] and stood at the crux of Du Bois's 1926 message: He faced both a racist publishing industry and huge barriers created by various gatekeepers such as "the Tuskegee Machine" in his early career, along with philanthropic organizations such as the Carnegie Corporation and the Phelps-Stokes Fund. This realization, combined with his epiphany that the humanity of Black people could not be understood through facts and science alone, led him to leave Atlanta University, and thus the academic world, in 1910. In response to the real barriers that then existed in academia, Du Bois tried to create a counterdiscourse that would change what would be imagined, said, and thought about Black people in both America and the world.[33] Aware of the structural and historical constraints faced by Black artists, he states, "We have, to be sure, a few recognized and successful Negro artists; but they are not all those fit to survive or even a good minority. They are but the remnants of that ability and genius among us whom the accidents of education and opportunity have raised on the tidal waves of chance."[34]

Here Du Bois reiterates his philosophy of law and chance, articulated in his early essay "Sociology Hesitant," and posits the Black artist, the producer of cultural objects, as an actor imbued with generative possibilities. Seldom seen or recognized by the mainstream media, the Black artists had the ability to balance a vastly distorted historical record, a record that is not only one of text and fact but one of representation: of signs and symbols, and of flavor and feel. Du Bois goes on to state,

> Thus it is the bounden duty of black America to begin this great work of the creation of beauty, of the preservation of beauty, of the realization of beauty, and we must use in this work all the methods that men have used before. And what have been the tools of the artist in times gone by? First of all, he has used the truth—not for the sake of truth, not as a scientist seeking truth, but as one upon whom truth eternally thrusts itself as the highest hand-maid of imagination.[35]

Du Bois believed that Black artists were conscripted into this New Negro agenda because slavery and racist ideology continued to deny their humanity, and he viewed the role of the Black artist as that of truth teller and incisive social critic. This line of thinking was deeply rooted in the New Negro Movement ideology that promoted racial uplift through Black respectability and the linked fate of representing one's race. He asserted,

Slavery only dogs him when he is denied the right to tell the truth or recognize an ideal of justice. Thus all art is propaganda and ever must be, despite the wailing of the purists. I stand in utter shamelessness and say that whatever art I have for writing has been used always for propaganda for gaining the right of black folk to love and enjoy. I do not care a damn for any art that is not used for propaganda. But I do care when propaganda is confined to one side while the other is stripped and silent.[36]

It is this unbalanced history, the erasure of nonwhites from the narratives of society and nation, the villainization of Blackness, and the downright lies of which Du Bois speaks. What Du Bois understood, and was trying to evoke in his listeners' consciousness, was that history is not neutral; it is a construct. Therefore, for Du Bois, the pen, his artistic instrument, was always political.

Publishers stand as the gatekeepers who determine how and which forms of knowledge are publicly disseminated and as such play a consequential role in legitimating what the public comes to know as true through reinforcing master narratives. Du Bois himself acknowledged that "the white public today demands from its artists, literary and pictorial, racial pre-judgment which deliberately distorts truth and justice, as far as colored races are concerned, and it will pay for no other."[37] However, the dilemma of the Black artists was not merely an issue of access, but one of being able to speak with their own voice, as these artists faced not only the external dilemma of fighting the very real market forces that silenced and whitewashed Black expression but also the internal battle of grappling with double consciousness—in other words, the sensation of "constantly seeing oneself through the eyes of the other," the internal feeling of living in a house of mirrors. In this case, the house of mirrors was white society, whose members regarded Black people, and therefore their art, as inferior. As Du Bois put it in "The Criteria of Negro Art,"

As it is now we are handing everything over to a white jury. If a colored man wants to publish a book, he has got to get a white publisher and a white newspaper to say it is great; and then you and I say so. We must come to the place where the work of art when it appears is reviewed and acclaimed by our own free and unfettered judgment. And we are going to have a real and valuable and eternal judgment only as we make ourselves free of mind, proud of body and just of soul to all men.[38]

Nowhere do we see Du Bois railing against this barrier in his own profession more clearly than in *Black Reconstruction*, a work in which he reinterprets the history of the Reconstruction era through the perspective of the efforts and experiences of Black people. With this text Du Bois aimed not only to produce a work of history but also to redress what he viewed as a deliberate historical erasure on the part of his fellow historians on the topic of Reconstruction. He takes up this issue in the last chapter of the book, titled "The Propaganda of History," in which he asserts,

> Herein lies more than mere omission and difference of emphasis. The treatment of the period of Reconstruction reflects small credit upon American historians as scientists. We have too often a deliberate attempt so to change the facts of history that the story will make pleasant reading for Americans. . . .
>
> But are these reasons of courtesy and philanthropy sufficient for denying Truth? If history is going to be scientific, if the record of human action is going to be set down with that accuracy and faithfulness of detail which will allow its use as a measuring rod and guidepost for the future nations, there must be set some standards of ethics in research and interpretation. If on the other hand, we are going to use history for our pleasure and amusement, for inflating our national ego, and giving us a false but pleasurable sense of accomplishment, then we must give up the idea of history either as a science or as an art using the results of science, and admit frankly that we are using a version of historic fact in order to influence and educate the new generation along the way we wish.[39]

What Du Bois experienced in his initial retelling of Reconstruction was an insistence by white publishers on excluding claims about the African American contribution to the era. He also received pushback against the assertion that slavery was the root cause of the American Civil War.[40] As we have seen, Du Bois was well aware of the ways prejudice and bias plagued social science research. And he warned his fellow scholars about the danger that continuing down a path of willful ignorance and bias posed to knowledge production writ large.

During his early years at Atlanta University, Du Bois believed that scientific fact was enough to dismantle the color line. However, he came to realize that the ideal of truth in social scientific inquiry alone would not suffice. As his program evolved, Du Bois understood that the knowledge could not be divorced from the political economy of its production. As a result, he relied on the scientific, political, and moral aims of his work. Where Du Bois intervenes in his revised approach is in the politics of sociologies both of knowledge and of knowledge production. However, he did not just make these interventions in the academic sphere. Du Bois rearticulated his sociological findings and presented his ideas in various mediums and forms so as to reach the public sphere.

The Crisis: Record of the Darker Races

Du Bois's primary focus at the beginning of his transition out of the academy was on establishing his new periodical, the *Crisis: Record of the Darker Races*. The *Crisis* was the official magazine of the newly founded NAACP, and Du Bois was its founding editor. Unlike with the *Horizon*, which was a collaborative endeavor, Du Bois maintained full editorial control of the *Crisis* and used it as a conduit to elevate the racial consciousness of a broad readership. Within its first eight years, the number of subscribers exploded from one thousand to one hundred thousand, making the *Crisis* one of the world's most widely circulated Black periodicals. But Du Bois did not enjoy success overnight, as the *Crisis* was his third attempt at editing a popular magazine. Unlike the *Moon* or the *Horizon*, the *Crisis* operated under the auspices of a well-run and sufficiently funded organization. Therefore it had the internal infrastructure, capacity, and reach to achieve Du Bois's original goal of creating a powerful organ that would incite a movement among the Black majority.

Du Bois made the mission of the *Crisis* clear from the start. In volume 1, issue 1, he announced,

The object of this publication is to set forth those facts and arguments which show the danger of race prejudice, particularly as manifested today toward colored people. It takes its name from the fact that the editors believe that this is a critical time in the history of the advancement of men. Catholicity and tolerance, reason and forbearance can today make the world-old dream of human brotherhood approach realization; while bigotry and prejudice, emphasized race consciousness and force can repeat the awful history of the contact of nations and groups in the past. We strive for this higher and broader vision of Peace and Good Will.

> The policy of THE CRISIS will be simple and well defined: It will first and foremost be a newspaper: it will record important happenings and movements in the world which bear on the great problem of inter-racial relations, and especially those which affect the Negro-American. Secondly, it will be a review of opinion and literature, recording briefly books, articles, and important expressions of opinion in the white and colored press on the race problem. Thirdly, it will publish a few short articles. Finally, its editorial page will stand for the rights of men, irrespective of color or race, for the highest ideals of American democracy, and for reasonable but earnest and persistent attempts to gain these rights and realize these ideals.
>
> The magazine will be the organ of no clique or party and will avoid personal rancor of all sorts. In the absence of proof to the contrary it will assume honesty of purpose on the part of all men, North and South, white and black.[41]

The aim of the *Crisis* was to focus on Black people and their experiences, and to situate them as agents of their social worlds and protagonists of history, not as an isolated subpopulation of American society but as global citizens. In the *Crisis*, Du Bois put his sociology into action by encouraging Black people to work through the issues affecting their own community. While the magazine centered on issues facing Black life, it was neither nationalistic nor monoracial. Du Bois and his editorial team showcased Black people and issues from around the world, and solicited contributions from intellectuals across the color line, including the American philosopher and NAACP board member John Dewey and the physicist Albert Einstein.

The magazine was organized in seven sections: Along the Color Line, Opinion, Editorial, The NAACP, Articles, The Burden, and What to Read. The opening section, Along the Color Line, provided readers with short bullet-style paragraphs about pressing issues and events of the day. The sections were organized topically around politics, education, the sciences, the arts, and so on. From the first page, the *Crisis* situated the reader as a political actor of great consequence to the world, and as a part of what Du Bois often referred to as the "human brotherhood." And significantly, Du Bois did not dumb down the language in the publication. He addressed his mostly Black audience with the assumption that they were capable and thinking people.

Of the various sections of the magazine, Editorial was where Du Bois engaged his readers with analyses of issues of importance to social and economic progress for Blacks, distilling the academic arguments that appeared in his books and articles into short, digestible pieces for everyday consumption. Du Bois's work as a public sociologist shines through in the *Crisis*. Through his editorial publications, Du Bois took the findings of his studies of "the Negro Problem" and disseminated them to the Black masses, engaging his readers in the process of making private problems public. The Editorial section of the first issue, in which Du Bois offers an analysis of the impending segregation of public schools in the North, is an example of this:

> SEGREGATION. Some people in Chicago, Philadelphia, Atlantic City, Columbus, OH., and other Northern cities are quietly trying to establish separate colored schools. This is wrong, and should be resisted by black men and white. Human contact, human acquaintanceship, human sympathy is the great solvent of human problems. Separate school children by wealth and the result is class misunderstanding and hatred. Separate them by race and the result is war. Separate them by color and they grow up without learning the tremendous truth that it is impossible to judge the mind of a man by the color of his face. Is there any truth that America needs to learn more? . . .
>
> The argument, then, for color discrimination in schools and in public institutions is an argument against democracy and an attempt to shift public responsibility from the shoulders of the public to the shoulders of some class who are unable to defend themselves.[42]

Du Bois made this argument as early as *Souls*, where in the chapter "Of Masters and Men" he discusses the negative effects of racial segregation on the social, economic, political, and psychological life of those on both sides of the color line. His main point is that racial segregation is the primary factor that helps promulgate racial inequality, prejudice, and racial hatred. In addition, he argued that segregation also meant that the best minds in the Black community—in other words, people like him—could not contribute to the solution of the social problems of the day, and that that represented a loss not only for the Black community but for American society—and humanity—as a whole. He also expounds on these arguments in other books, such as *The Philadelphia Negro* and *John Brown*, in which he elaborates on his key sociological ideas about the detrimental effects of racial segregation on society, and argues that the only redress is through human contact and fully incorporating Blacks into the national life. And the *Crisis* was just one of many platforms Du Bois used to transmit his message to the general public. While the magazine served as a vehicle to raise awareness about current issues facing Black Americans and people of color around the world, Du Bois used educational theater and performance to teach Black history and to affirm the intricacies of Black culture.

The Star of Ethiopia

In 1911, just one year into his new role as director of publications and research at the NAACP, Du Bois wrote a five-scene pageant, titled *The Star of Ethiopia*, that covered a thousand years of precolonial African and African American history.[43] Following the narrative arc of racial progress, the pageant celebrates the many contributions Black people have made to the modern world, ranging from innovations in iron making and the pyramids in Africa to George Washington Carver's contributions to agricultural science and Frederick Douglass's heroic efforts on behalf of abolitionism in America.

Du Bois initially pitched the idea to the NAACP board, but the idea did not generate sufficiently strong interest for Du Bois to move forward with the massive undertaking of staging the show. However, a year later, when New York governor William Sulzer appointed Du Bois to the organizing committee for the New York Emancipation Exposition, a statewide event to mark the fiftieth anniversary of the Emancipation Proclamation, Du Bois jumped on the opportunity to propose that *The Star of Ethiopia* be included as part of the program.[44] The committee promptly agreed.

The storyline of the pageant was carried out primarily by a dramatic musical score, written by Du Bois and J. Rosamond Johnson, and was performed by groups of mostly Black actors that ranged from 350 to 1200 per show. Du Bois enlisted a group of trusted friends and colleagues to bring the performance to life, specifically the composer Charles Burroughs, theatrical performer and director Dora Cole Norman, set designer Richard Brown, and his former student Augustus Granville Dill.

Du Bois's desire to present the pageant sprang from his deep conviction that aesthetics had the power to awaken the spirit and change hearts and minds. In his reporting of the pageant in the August 1916 issue of the *Crisis*, Du Bois reflected on what he regarded as the pageant's contribution to the workings of the spirit, heart, and mind: "It seemed to me that it might be possible with such a demonstration to get people interested in this development of Negro drama to teach on the one hand the colored people themselves the meaning of their history and their rich, emotional life through a new theatre, and on the other, to reveal the Negro to the white world as a human, feeling thing."[45]

The New York staging, the first of four productions, was a great success. It was performed by a cast of 350 actors and drew a large crowd. Over the next three years, *The Star of Ethiopia* was commissioned for three additional performances—in Philadelphia, Washington, DC, and Los Angeles—each time presented with more flair and grandeur. By the final show, the cast had swelled to twelve hundred actors. The productions themselves had grown so immense that they had to be performed in sports stadiums, and by the end of the final performance, the pageant had drawn a total of thirty-five thousand spectators.[46]

The Pan-African Congress, 1919–1927

By the third staging of *The Star of Ethiopia*, in October 1916, Europe was well into World War I. Du Bois did not venture abroad during wartime until December of 1918, when, at the very end of the war, he was sent on behalf of the NAACP to investigate the treatment of Black soldiers in the

United States Army. The anticipation of a return visit to Europe shook Du Bois to his core, and planted a seed that had lain dormant in his soul for nearly twenty years. Unbeknownst to his America-first colleagues at the NAACP, Du Bois had another goal in mind for his trip: He planned to convene what he called a Pan-African Congress.

Harkening back to the idea of "Pan-Africanism" introduced by the event's predecessor, Sylvester Williams's Pan-African Conference, the Pan-African Congress was Du Bois's renewed version of this failed organization. Along with studying the condition of African American soldiers in the war, he immediately began petitioning the leadership of the French and United States governments to support the convening of the congress.

He received a noncommittal response from President Woodrow Wilson, and a closed door from the French government. However, Du Bois convinced a Senegalese commissioner whom he knew in Paris to present the idea to a French official on his behalf, and the official approved his request. To the surprise of French and American government officials, the First Pan-African Congress was held on February 19, 1919, just three days before Du Bois's fifty-first birthday.

The congress was attended by fifty-seven delegates from the United States and fifteen countries in Africa and the West Indies. The low turnout was due in part to the fact that the United States and European colonial powers refused to issue special visas for those invited to travel to Paris. The participants were mostly people who already lived in France or were there because of the war. Nevertheless, the people attending that meeting were able to draft a petition to the Allied and Associated Powers by the end of the session. Their requests were threefold: (1) the establishment of an international code of law for the treatment of African natives, (2) the appointment by the League of Nations of a special bureau to enforce these protection laws, and (3) the transfer of power in Africa so that colonies there would have some say in the workings of their government.[47] It is unclear what level of lip service this petition garnered, although we can suspect not much. However, the idea of the Pan-African Congress was enough to inspire excitement and commitment among people of African descent around the world.

Three more Pan-African Congress meetings would be held in the United States and Europe during that decade: one in 1921, another in

1923, and a third in 1927. According to Du Bois, the organization faced debilitating stress as early as the second meeting. He attributed this to such external factors as intensified postwar colonial oppression of African colonies and peoples and Garveyism, a Black nationalist movement organized around the idea of self-repatriating back to Africa, noting that outsiders often conflated the aims of the Pan-African Congress with that of the Garvey movement, thus weakening the bargaining power of the former on the international stage.

Du Bois was hardly diplomatic in expressing his disdain for Marcus Garvey and his grassroots movement, once publicly referring to Garvey as "the man with the little hat." And in his assessment of the Garvey movement Du Bois wrote, "It represented a poorly conceived but intensely earnest determination to unite the Negroes of the world, more especially in commercial enterprise." Of Garvey's movement Du Bois contended, "It uses of all the nationalist and racial paraphernalia of popular agitation and its strength lay in its backing by the masses of West Indians and increasing numbers of American Negroes. Its weakness lay in its demagogic leadership, its intemperate propaganda, and the understandable fear which it provoked in the colonial powers."[48] Both movements attracted a frenzy of media attention, with most white news organizations lacing their reportage with expressions of fear of Black nationalism and retaliation.

Du Bois believed that the conflation of these two Black-led international movements hurt his own because the Pan-African Congress was trying very hard to work within the existing structures of racial colonial capitalism. Where the Garvey movement was nationalist and separatist, the Pan-African Congress was reformist at its core. While the concept of Pan-Africanism deeply influenced the African liberation movements of the 1940s, '50s, and '60s, the ideas that emerged from the first four meetings themselves worked within a colonial framework of liberal democracy. This is demonstrated by the way the organization sought recognition by and opportunities for negotiation with the existing power elite. It is also made apparent in a subtle way by the fact that, at the explicit insistence of colonial powers in Europe and of the United States, none of the meetings of the Pan-African Congress were ever held in Africa. During the 1920s, the Pan-African Congress continued to issue petitions to various heads of state and international bodies demanding immediate reform of governance and gradual release from colonial rule. It was not until 1945, with the end of the Second World War, that the Pan-African Congress would convene for the fifth time, this time to pose strong anticolonial demands.

What Du Bois's involvement in leading the Pan-African Congress shows is how World War I shaped his thinking and forever oriented him towards a Pan-African worldview. From this point on, Du Bois always theorized, organized, and acted from a diasporic perspective. Before this period, his goal was mainly to implement an interracial and America-centered program for Black freedom. His brief trip to wartime France changed that goal forever. Reflecting on this watershed moment, Du Bois wrote, "From 1910 to 1920, I had followed the path of sociology as an inseparable part of social reform, and social uplift as a method of scientific social investigation; then, in practice, I had conceived an interracial culture as superseding as our goal, a purely American culture; before I had conceived a program for this path, and after throes of bitter racial strife, I had emerged with a program of Pan-Africanism, as organized protection of the Negro world led by American Negroes."[49] This dramatic shift in perspective marked the beginning of Du Bois's decades-long friction with the NAACP. He was committed to a Pan-African vision of Black liberation, but, as he stated, "American Negroes were not interested."[50]

Back home in the United States, Du Bois continued to cultivate a sense of pride and racial consciousness among Black Americans. He also remained intent on bringing attention to actions that underscored the humanity of Black people—actions that could be understood across the color line—by highlighting the contributions of Black people to the history and culture of modern society. These twin aims were the focus of his program for Black freedom during this period of his career, marked by his break with the belief that whites would cease racial prejudice and oppression if presented with objective facts and science disproving inherent Black inferiority.

In this second era of the evolution of Du Bois's thought, he was convinced that facts and science had to be brought into the hearts and minds of society, across racial lines, through moral and political messaging— what he called propaganda. Further, he shifted his target audience from elite whites to Black intellectuals, artists, the broad Black middle class, and sympathizers across the color line. In short, during this period he believed that it was his job not only to present facts and truth to the public but also to make them *feel* these things. His main platforms during this period were based on his editorial stewardship, academic publication, and theater. While he is best known for his work with the *Crisis* during this era, he was also active in theater, literature, and poetry. For a short period of time, he even edited a magazine whose target audience was children of color.

Brownies' Book: A Monthly Magazine for the Children of the Sun

The Black public is a heterogeneous group, and the *Crisis* did a great deal of work to reach across class, regional, and gender differences within the group. However, there was a special subset of this group that constituted another public that Du Bois tried to engage—Black and brown children. In 1920, W. E. B. Du Bois founded a periodical called *Brownies' Book: A Monthly Magazine for Children of the Sun.* Issued as an offshoot of the *Crisis*, and sold for $1.50 for a six-month subscription or fifteen cents a copy, *Brownies' Book* remained in circulation for nearly two years.

Du Bois intended that this children's magazine serve as a much-needed medium through which children could learn about the many contributions of people of color around the world and as a public forum to discuss current issues facing Black and brown children and their families. In a call to elevate the consciousness and pride of "children of the sun" worldwide, Du Bois announced the aims of his as-yet-unnamed periodical in a 1919 issue of the *Crisis*:

1. To make colored children realize that being "colored" is a normal beautiful thing.
2. To make them familiar with the history and achievements of the Negro race.
3. To make them know that other colored children have grown into beautiful, useful and famous persons.
4. To teach them a delicate code of honor and action in their relations with white children.
5. To turn their little hurts and resentments into emulation, ambition, and love of their homes and companions.

6. To point out the best amusements and joys and worth-while things of life.

7. To inspire them to prepare for definite occupations and duties with a broad spirit of sacrifice.[51]

While the genre of "children's periodicals" occupied a thriving space in the magazine industry at the time, *Brownies' Book* was the first to target children of color as its primary audience. The magazine set out to do the work of counterrepresentation, providing positive alternatives to the otherwise derogatory popular representations of people of color in the media. Then and now, Black and brown children are either not represented in everyday products, imagery, and media, or they are subject to a deluge of negative representations of their race that present them as dangerous, foolish, or inconsequential to the world around them.[52] *Brownies' Book* was intended to redress these representational issues by centering children of color as matters of consequence to human history.

In the 1920s, whites were the only protagonists depicted in popular culture; they were its heroes, inventors, leaders, and winners. The dearth of positive representations of people of color in the public sphere had, and in many respects continues to have, grave effects on the consciousness and self-esteem of people of color. Du Bois articulated this idea at the turn of the twentieth century in his theory of double consciousness, and this problem has been repeatedly articulated, tested, and proven.[53] Such troubling images were everywhere for children to consume—from their textbooks to the radio, on television, in the news—and were invariably expressed by their elected officials and leaders. Du Bois very much understood the role of the visual in the emergence of double consciousness—the constant "sense of seeing oneself through the eyes of the other." He created *Brownies' Book* to intervene in this process.

A team of three ran the magazine. Du Bois was the editor-in-chief, Jessie Redmon Fauset was the literary editor, and Augustus Granville Dill served as the business manager. Fauset, who was an editor, novelist, educator, and scholar of the Black middle class, taught at the famous M Street School in Washington, DC, and later at the even more renowned DeWitt Clinton High in the Bronx, perhaps best known as the alma mater of the writer James Baldwin, the artist Romare Bearden, the physicist Robert Hofstadter, and the fashion designer Ralph Lauren. As the magazine's literary editor, Fauset was responsible for curating a varied selection of essays, poems, and short stories to incorporate in each issue and was also a frequent contributor to the magazine. The *Brownies' Book* business manager, Augustus Granville Dill, was a fellow African American sociologist and a former student of Du Bois at Atlanta University who had also received a second bachelor's and master's degree from Harvard. The background of Du Bois's colleagues in this endeavor makes clear that in undertaking such a project, Du Bois was working alongside members of the New Negro intelligentsia.[54]

He started this magazine with little to no money. However, as with his Atlanta University Studies program, this did not deter Du Bois from pursuing this effort. He reached out to a wide selection of artists, writers, and musicians to contribute to the magazine. In a vigorous letter-writing campaign, he shamelessly implored his contemporaries to consider contributing to *Brownies'*. On October 23, 1919, for example, he wrote to the classical composer Harry Burleigh, saying, "In speaking with Mr. George Crawford the other night, he told me that you had a collection of children's songs for which you had not found a publisher. I am writing to ask if you would not let us publish some of these songs in the *Brownies' Book* from month to month and, perhaps, afterward collect them in a book."[55] In that same year he also wrote separately to the fine artists Laura Wheeler and William Edward Scott, saying, "I want very much that you should give us some of your best artistic work. Eventually, we shall pay for all your contributions, but we may not be able to give you any actual cash during the first year."[56] Du Bois was unabashed about the fact that although he could not pay, he wanted their best work, and he was willing to expend his social capital in an effort to ensure the magazine's success. *Brownies' Book* was no pastime for Du Bois, as he believed that it contributed greatly to the work of undoing the psychological damage of double consciousness. The inside cover of each issue contained the same declaration: "DESIGNED FOR ALL CHILDREN BUT ESPECIALLY FOR OURS. It aims to be a thing of Joy and Beauty, dealing in Happiness, Laughter and Emulation, and designed especially for Kiddies from Six to Sixteen. It will seek to teach Universal Love and Brotherhood for all little folk—black and brown and yellow and white. Of course, pictures, stories, letters from little ones, games and oh—everything!"[57]

The periodical represented a call and response to the community. In addition to vividly illustrated children's stories, songs, and poems, each issue featured distinct sections for children, parents, and the editor, Du Bois, to describe their experiences and voice their concerns. The editors strongly encouraged parental involvement, and therefore reserved the Grown-Ups Corner section for parents to articulate their concerns and requests.

Consider the March 1920 edition of the Grown-Ups Corner: "The editors of the Brownies' Book would like pictures, and accounts of the deeds of colored children. If parents are going to the trouble and expense of having new pictures made, we should like to inform them, that a black and white, shiny print reproduces best. And letters! Do have your children write and tell us about their schools, their ambitions, their views of life, in general. A great deal of wisdom comes from the mouth of babes." In addition to sending in photographs and notes to praise their children's accomplishments, parents wrote in to express their concerns regarding their children's development and racial consciousness. Bella Seymour, a concerned mother in New York, wrote,

I have been waiting with some interest for the appearance of *The Brownies' Book*, but I understand the printer's strike has delayed it. I am sure you have many good plans in mind for our children; but I do hope you are going to write a good deal about colored men and women of achievement. My little girl has been studying about Betsey Ross and George Washington and the others, and she says: "Mamma, didn't colored folks do anything?" When I tell her as much as I know about our folks, she says: "Well, that's just stories. Didn't they ever do anything in a book?"

I have not had much schooling, and I am a busy woman with my sewing and housekeeping, so I don't get much time to read and I can't tell my little girl where to find these things. But I am sure you know and that now you will tell her.

My husband worked in a munitions plant during the war and there were a few foreigners there. He said they often spoke of some big man in their country, but didn't seem to know about any big colored men here. And he said that when he came to think of it, he didn't know much about anybody but Booker T. Washington and you and Frederick Douglass. Our

little girl is dark brown, and we want her to be proud of her color and to know that it isn't the kind of skin people have that makes them great.[58]
—Bella Seymour, New York City

Each issue featured a handful of notes like Mrs. Seymour's, highlighting issues that their children encountered as they came to experience the intangible contours of the color line for themselves, seeking recommendations for information and resources to enlighten their children about Black contributions to society, and offering recommendations for future issues. Aware of the ways in which gender, skin tone, age, perceived attractiveness, and locale intersect and bear upon the experiences of their children, parents almost always specified these particularities in their letters in hopes that in their responses the editorial team would attend to these very real nuances. This letter represents just one example of how pressing the problem of double consciousness was for the Black population. As the excerpts show, Du Bois addressed his audience as a public of "knowing subjects" because they were. The parents and children made clear through their letters that they had a structural understanding of their condition; in Mrs. Seymour's case, it was clear that she realized how race, class, gender, *and* skin color would shape the experiences and opportunities that her daughter could expect during her life.

While the Grown-ups Corner provided a small space for adults to participate in the *Brownies'* community, the magazine truly centered on children: their interests, their issues, and their voices. The Jury, for example, was the standing section of the magazine that published excerpts of letters sent in by children. They wrote in to tell Dr. Du Bois about their neighborhoods in this or that city, which story they liked best from past issues, their aspirations, and their awareness of the limits that the color of their skin placed on their chances of attaining their dreams.

George Max Simpson wrote from Toronto,

Could you take time to suggest a small library for me? Or if you couldn't, do you know anybody who could? I want to know a great deal about colored people. I think when I finish school I shall go to Africa, and work there in some way. If I decide to do this I ought to know a great deal about our people and all the places where they live, all over the world, don't you think so? My father is always saying that a great many wonderful things are going to happen to Negroes within the next twenty-five years, and I want to be able to understand and appreciate them.[59]

Often, children would write to ask Du Bois if they should hold onto their dreams or resign themselves to accepting the distorted image that the color line imposed upon them, even if they did not use or were not familiar with that particular term. Augustus Hill from Albany wrote,

I wish you would tell me what to do. I am fifteen years old, and I want to study music. My mother and father object to it very much. They say no colored people can succeed entirely as musicians, that they have to do other things to help make their living, and that I might just as well start doing this first as last. Of course, I say that just because things have been this way, that's no sign they'll be like that forever. But they talk me down. Won't you tell me what you think about this? And tell me, too, about colored musicians who have made their living by sticking to the thing they love best? Of course, I know about Coleridge-Taylor and Mr. Burleigh.[60]

The section called "The Jury" reflected the hopes, aspirations, and anxieties of post–World War I Black youth. Their place in the world was uncertain, and they looked to Du Bois and the *Brownies' Book* to calibrate their expectations in life. The section titled "As the Crow Flies" featured writing by Du Bois himself, often presented via short but serious bullet points, about world affairs, similar to the style of the section titled "On the Color Line" that opened the *Crisis* magazine. In the first issue Du Bois apprises his readers of the emergence of new global organizations and political formations after World War I, such as the League of Nations. He also offered an intellectual framework through which they could think about how the fallout from the war would affect them personally: "Always after a great war there is much unrest, suffering and poverty. This is because war kills human beings, leaves widows and orphans, destroys vast amounts of wealth, and destroys the organization of industry. The war of 1914–1918 was the greatest of human wars, and we hope it is the last. It destroyed untold wealth and turned men from their usual work. The result is great unrest and dissatisfaction throughout the world. People are thinking, they are hungry, and everything costs more."[61]

He would take his readers around the world via a series of a few dozen bullet points and situate their biographies within history. Through the *Brownies' Book*, Du Bois animated their sociological imaginations.

The KRIGWA Players

In 1927, W. E. B. Du Bois and the playwright and librarian Regina Anderson cofounded a Black theater company known as the KRIGWA Players Little Theatre, which was housed in the basement of the Harlem Branch of the New York Public Library on East 135th Street (currently known as the Schomburg Center for Black History and Culture). KRIGWA, an acronym that stands for the Crisis Guild of Writers and Artists, was hardly the first Black theater, but it was the first to focus on specifically Black dramaturgy, meaning not simply offering performances but presenting plays grounded in the cultural lifeworlds of its subjects.

Du Bois was incensed by the way Black people were typecast by way of menial, one-dimensional, and often derogatory roles in American theater. He understood the power of drama, and viewed even the most ostensibly benign roles, such as Black women constantly playing the domestic "mammy," as harmful to Black progress. Du Bois was very vocal about this issue, leading the national protest against D. W. Griffith's infamous *Birth of a Nation*, the racist movie released in 1915 depicting Black men as sexual predators towards white women and white Klansmen as protective heroes, which turned out to be a blockbuster event in the United States. He also complained to the power elite of Broadway, arguing that the way Black people were represented in American theater was harmful to the promise of earnest racial integration. However, at the height of the Harlem Renaissance, with the concentration in New York City of a cadre of brilliant Black artists, writers, singers, and scholars, whose work focused with laser-sharp intensity on issues involving race, Du Bois saw a window of opportunity:

> Today, as the renaissance of art comes among American Negroes, the theatre calls for new birth. But most people do not realize just where the novelty must come in. The Negro is already in the theatre and has been

there for a long time; but his presence there is not yet thoroughly normal. His audience is mainly a white audience and the Negro actor has, for a long time, been asked to entertain this more or less alien group. The demands and ideals of the white group, and their conception of Negroes, have set the norm for the black actor. He has been a minstrel, comedian, singer and lay figure of all sorts. Only recently has he begun tentatively to emerge as an ordinary human being with everyday reactions.[62]

Steeped in what was known as the New Negro ideology, the KRIGWA Players Theater was based on a philosophy known as "FUBU," Black vernacular for "for us, by us."

Unlike existing Black playhouses, KRIGWA staged original plays written for, by, and about Black life and culture. The playhouse drew an audience representing all races and ethnicities, as did most of the Harlem hotspots during the Renaissance; it did not cater to the desires of the white gaze that Du Bois so keenly described in the quotation above. In this way, he tried to create a "single-consciousness" Black performance space, one in which Black people would always see themselves through the eyes of themselves:

> The movement which has begun this year in Harlem, New York City, lays down four fundamental principles. The plays of a real Negro theatre must be: *One: About Us.* That is, they must have plots which reveal Negro life as it is. *Two: By Us.* That is, they must be written by Negro authors who understand from birth and continual association just what it means to be a Negro today. *Three: For Us.* That is, the theatre must cater primarily to Negro audiences and be supported and sustained by their entertainment and approval. *Four: Near Us.* The theatre must be in a Negro neighborhood near the mass of ordinary Negro people.[63]

As with most of Du Bois's public endeavors, he did not create KRIGWA alone. Along with working with his cofounder, Regina Anderson, to establish the organization, the pair appointed an all-star board of directors, including Harlem Renaissance figures such as the writer and anthropologist Zora Neale Hurston, the fine artist Aaron Douglas, and the vaudeville actress Minnie Brown. The board selected plays from a pool of original manuscripts submitted to the *Crisis* for the annual literary prize award.

KRIGWA staged six plays between 1924 and 1927, the last of which went on to win first place for "Best Unpublished Play" at the Fifth Annual National Theatre Tournament. Unfortunately, that win was a source of irreparable injury for the KRIGWA theater company, as the group split up over disagreement about Du Bois's use of the two-hundred-dollar cash award. He claimed to have used the money to cover production costs, leaving nothing to pay the writer or performers. Shortly thereafter, the group of performers split, and the KRIGWA Theatre closed.

This era of Du Bois's thinking, shaped by the pragmatics of propaganda, spanned nearly twenty years, during which time he founded several platforms and organizations for Black people to control the production of their own knowledge and cultural expression, such as the *Crisis*, the *Brownies' Book*, the Pan-African Congress, and the KRIGWA Players. By the end of the 1920s, however, all of these endeavors had died or were near collapse.

Financial crises, suppression imposed by external entities, and interpersonal disagreements all helped explain why they did not last. The one thing that did remain consistent was Du Bois's commitment to trying to enact social change through engaged scholarly, artistic, and cultural expression. He repeatedly plunged into new ventures, corralled strong partners to lead and support them, and put up his own money to get them off the ground. Remarkably, he kept up his scholarly work during this time, producing new books on Black life and communities, including *Darkwater: Voices from within the Veil*, *The Negro*, and *The Gift of Black Folk: The Negroes in the Making of America*, along with two novels, *The Quest of the Silver Fleece* and *Dark Princess*. Du Bois celebrated his sixtieth birthday in 1928; ahead of him would lie nearly thirty years of organizing, activism, and scholarly production.

Era III: Return to Atlanta and Building a Black Cooperative Economy (1928–1944)

In 1928, Du Bois accepted an invitation to visit Russia to assess the country's social and economic conditions. During that trip, Du Bois took the opportunity to visit Germany, Turkey, and Italy, and according to him, the visit "marked another change in my thought and action."[64] He had long had sympathy for socialism, and had briefly been a member of the

Socialist Party between 1910 and 1912, although he left the organization because he felt that it did not offer an answer to the needs and demands of Black people. The Russian Revolution of 1917 and the subsequent rise of the Soviet Union, however, captured Du Bois's imagination. At this moment, he recalled, he "began to read Karl Marx," adding, "I was astounded and wondered what other lands of learning had been roped off from my mind in the days of my 'broad' education."[65]

As he reflected in "My Evolving Program for Negro Freedom" in 1944, it was at this time that he understood the importance of building a community economic base.

> I saw clearly, when I left Russia, that our American Negro belief that the right to vote would give us work and decent wage; would abolish our illiteracy and decrease our sickness and crime, was justified only in part; that on the contrary, until we were able to earn a decent, independent living, we would never be allowed to cast a free ballot; that poverty caused our ignorance, sickness and crime; and that poverty was not our fault but our misfortune, the result and aim of our segregation and color caste; that the solution of letting a few of our capitalists share with whites in the exploitation of our masses, would never be a solution of our problem, but the forging of eternal chains, as Modern India knows to its sorrow.[66]

While Du Bois's sociological analyses had always pointed to the economic factors that affected the African American community, this statement signals the first time that he gave primacy to the economic aspects of the struggle as an organizing strategy to set his people free. At this time in his life, Du Bois believed that without a solid economic base to stand on, Black people could not win political and civil rights. Similarly to his insistence on controlling the production of intellectual and cultural expression that was the hallmark of the second wave of his program, with his insistence on creating media outlets and platforms by and for Black people, in this 1928 moment he came to the conclusion that Black people must also control their own economic destiny. While inspired by what he witnessed in Russia and learned from Marxist analysis, Du Bois did not think that communism offered a feasible or desirable strategy for Black people in the United States. He instead believed in a slow and steady strategy, based on self-reliance and community-based wealth accumulation. As he wrote in "My Evolving Program for Negro Freedom," "I believed that revolution in the production and distribution of wealth could be a slow, reasoned development and not necessarily a blood bath. I believed that 13 millions of people, increasing, albeit slowly in intelligence, could so concentrate their thought and action on the abolition of their poverty, as to work in conjunction with the most intelligent body of American thought; and that in the future as in the past, out of the mass of American Negroes would arise a far-seeing leadership in lines of economic reform."[67]

Du Bois became convinced that building an economic base preceded civil rights in terms of achieving the essential elements for Black freedom. This thinking was antithetical to the NAACP's view, which was that civil rights would eventually lead to economic mobility. Given his Pan-Africanist worldview and seemingly segregationist economic strategy, Du Bois began to realize that his days at the NAACP were numbered.

His plan was to continue to use the *Crisis* as a bullhorn to spread his new ideas to the masses, at least for as long as the NAACP let him maintain control of the magazine's editorship. However, before Du Bois had the chance to implement this strategy, as in eras past, a world crisis intervened. The stock market crash of 1929 shocked the US economy to its core. The Great Depression brought the *Crisis* to near bankruptcy. The loss of the *Crisis*'s economic autonomy threatened Du Bois's editorial control.

In 1934, Du Bois parted ways with the NAACP and returned to Atlanta University upon the invitation of the institution's president, John Hope. With conviction similar to the one he carried in his soul when he was in the sordid steerage deck of the ship returning to the United States from Germany nearly forty years earlier, Du Bois was on a mission. His goals were threefold: "First with leisure to write, I wanted to fill in the background of certain historical studies concerning the Negro race; secondly I wanted to establish at Atlanta University a scholarly journal of comment and research on race problems; finally, I wanted to restore in some form at Atlanta, the systematic study of the Negro problems."[68]

In this second go-around, Du Bois worked at Atlanta University for the next ten years, from 1934 to 1944, a period in which he did exactly what he set out to do. First, he did "fill in the background of certain historical studies concerning the Negro race," publishing three new books of sociology: *Black Reconstruction in America: Toward a History of the*

Part Which Black Folk Played in the Attempt to Reconstruct Democracy in America, 1860–1880; Black Folks Then and Now: An Essay in the History and Sociology of the Negro Race; and *Dusk of Dawn: An Essay toward an Autobiography of Race Concept.* These three books reflect Du Bois's new approach to Black emancipation.

In *Black Reconstruction in America*, he argues that it was the failure of enacting land reform in the South that doomed the prospects of democracy in the United States. He argued that it was the lack of an independent economic base that put the Black population in the South at the mercy of the dominant white hegemonic bloc at the end of Reconstruction, and made it possible to reverse the political and social gains of the Reconstruction period.

In *Dusk of Dawn*, Du Bois both reflects on his own life to make sense of what race meant in his times and developed his approach to the Black struggle for freedom. At that point in time Du Bois believed that segregation was too entrenched in American society to be eradicated through sheer racial incorporation and that the integrationist policy of the NAACP was not working. He realized that Black people needed to develop their own institutions for the advancement of the community. The NAACP and a large part of the "Talented Tenth," those members of the Black middle class and elite who were supposedly responsible for uplifting the Black masses, criticized Du Bois for embracing a segregationist policy. But *Dusk* makes clear that he did not advocate self-segregation on the grounds of Black nationalism, as Garvey had done. For Du Bois, integration was still the ultimate goal; he simply believed that it was not achievable at that time. He argued that until such time as the color line could be undone, the Black community had to rely on itself. Furthermore, he believed that it was impossible to achieve political and social rights without first building an economic base for Black people. He identified health, education, and employment as the three most urgent goals for Black communities in the United States, the latter being the most important. And he wrote, "We believe that the labor force and intelligence of twenty million people is more than sufficient to supply their own wants and make their advancement secure. Therefore we believe that, if carefully and intelligently planned, a co-operative Negro industrial system in America can be established in the midst of and in conjunction with the surrounding national industrial organization and in intelligent accord with that reconstruction of the economic basis of the nation which sooner or later must be accomplished."[69]

Du Bois's second goal in returning to Atlanta University was to "establish at Atlanta University a scholarly journal of comment and research on race problems."[70] And indeed, by 1940, he established the journal *Phylon: A Journal of Race and Culture*, a peer-reviewed publication that is still being published today by Clark Atlanta University.[71] As was eminently clear throughout his life, Du Bois was always a scholar, and those who argue otherwise are unaware of the facts of his life. But his scholarship was always closely linked with his activism.

The link between Du Bois's scholarship and his program for Black freedom can be seen again in his third goal, restoring the Atlanta University Studies in some form. He had returned to academic life some twenty years later to discover that several institutions of higher education, both white and Black and in the North and the South, were seriously studying what they defined as "the Negro Problem." He saw no value in reinventing the wheel, but he did take the advice of W. R. Banks, a former student who was then president of Prairie View State, a historically Black college in Texas, to "unite the seventeen Negro Land-Grant colleges in the South in a joint co-operative study, to be carried on continuously." Du Bois thought this a magnificent idea. As he wrote, "I laid before the annual meeting of the presidents of these colleges in 1941, such a plan. I proposed the strengthening of their departments of the social sciences; that each institution take its own state as its field of study; that an annual conference be held where representatives of the colleges come into consultation with the best sociologists of the land, and decide on methods of work and subjects of study." All seventeen colleges agreed, and in April of 1943 the twenty-sixth Atlanta Conference met at Morehouse College. The goal was to plan and coordinate a program of cooperative social studies.[72] To Du Bois's great pleasure, "After a quarter century, the Atlanta conferences live again."

The relaunching of the empirical research program, however, was not simply for scientific purposes. In Du Bois's mind, this program was designed to address the pressing needs of the Black community, in particular the issue of employment. Elaborating on the purpose of his research program, Du Bois asserted, "But of all these efforts, the college and community should concentrate their first and chief attention upon

the problems of earning a living among Negroes, since these are fundamental to practically all other efforts. Attention should be paid specially
to work now available, and for general economic reorganization, such as
is involved in consumers' and producers' cooperation, whereby not only
intelligent saving can be made in the expenditure of income, but that
new occupations, especially in home industries and small manufactur-
ers, can be established among Negroes."[73]

Du Bois also articulated this idea in an article that was published in
the *American Journal of Sociology* in March of 1944. The paper, titled
"Prospect of a World without Race Conflict," is an analysis of the state
of racial and colonial capitalism from a global perspective as America
started to anticipate the end of World War II and the likely victory of the
Allies.[74] In this paper, still one of the very few articles published in that
journal on racial and colonial capitalism, Du Bois expressed his pessimism regarding the likelihood that the war's end would bring an end to
racial conflict, such conflict being the product of racism and colonialism. But, always invested in the undoing of the color line, Du Bois also
proposed viable ways to reduce racial conflict.

His recommendations are worth quoting at length because they
describe well his program for freedom at this time and reveal how
he viewed the relation between science and emancipation. The first
thing needed, he asserted in the article, was to disseminate scientific
knowledge:

> What now can be done by intelligent men who are aware of the continu-
> ing danger of present racial attitudes in the world? We may appeal to two
> groups of men: first, to those leaders of white culture who are willing
> to take action and, second, to the leaders of races which are victims of
> present conditions. White leaders and thinkers have a duty to perform
> in making known the conclusions of science on the subject of biological
> race. It takes science long to percolate to the mass unless definite effort
> is made.[75]

White leaders needed to counter in public the discourse of biological
racism. But this was not enough. It was also necessary to address race
conflict through political action by people of color and colonized people. But what type of political action? Du Bois offered a clear proposal:

Next we need organized effort to release the colored laborer from the domination of the investor. This can best be accomplished by the organization of the labor of the world as consumers, replacing the producer attitude by knowledge of consumer needs. Here the victims of race prejudice can play their great role. They need no longer be confined to two paths: appeal to a white world ruled by investors in colored degradation or war and revolt. There is a third path: the extrication of the poverty-stricken, ignorant laborer and consumer from his bondage by his own efforts as a worker and consumer, united to increase the price of his toil and reduce the cost of the necessities of life.[76]

In addition to dispelling racial discourses that promoted biological racism and inherent racial inferiority, it was necessary to empower racialized and colonized workers. This the workers themselves could achieve through their own organized action as producers and consumers, in order to create a different form of economic relations. This was Du Bois's plan for an autonomous cooperative economy for both Black workers in the United States and colonized workers worldwide. But in order to act, people had to have knowledge about economic organization. They could not reorganize their economic life without understanding how the economy works. As Du Bois asserted, "Here colored leaders must act; but, before they act, they must know. Today, naturally, they are for the most part as economically illiterate as their masters."[77]

Du Bois's recommendations were not just the usual policy proposals that one sees in articles in sociological journals today. On the contrary, he offered actionable political recommendations to counter structural and ideological racism and provided economic strategies for the sustained political organization of workers of color. All that emerged from an analysis of global forms of racialized and colonial power and the particular form that racial and colonial capitalism assumed at that time—and it was all articulated in the pages of the *American Journal of Sociology*. It is hard to imagine that such a publication would allow that kind of sociological thinking today.

Du Bois saw the newly reestablished Atlanta Conference as the tool to generate social scientific knowledge that would allow workers of color in the United States to reorganize their economic life. He believed that the conference would be a key tool to gather information to address the pressing problems of the Black community at a time of rebuilding of the national economy. In the relaunching of the Atlanta Conference, Du Bois's empirical research plans and his plans for emancipation of Black people came together as never before or after. And indeed, the relaunching of the Atlanta Conference generated in Du Bois a sense of excitement.

A second conference was scheduled for 1944. But the sense of excitement was quickly extinguished when, that year, Du Bois at the age of seventy-five was arbitrarily retired by the university. According to the administration, he had aged out. For Du Bois, this move represented a lost opportunity to use social science research to empower Black people. But it was also a major loss for the discipline of sociology. Reflecting in his autobiography on the failure of his efforts to relaunch his community research program, Du Bois asserted,

> There was another loss in the giving up of this plan, which I have never mentioned. Here was an unprecedented chance for an experiment in sociology; for measuring and classifying human action, on a scale never before attempted; it would be reasonably sure of adequate funds and the best of trained cooperation and nationwide if not worldwide criticism. On such a base a real science of sociology could have been built.
>
> The opportunity was surrendered and the whole science of sociology has suffered. I even had projected a path of scientific approach: I was going to plot out beside the world of physical law, a science of sociology which measured "the limits of chance in human action." If this field proved narrow or non-existent, world law was proven. If not, the resultant "chance" was what men had always regarded as "free will."[78]

At the end of his life—Du Bois was in his nineties when he wrote his autobiography—as he reflected on the failure of his second Atlanta Studies effort, Du Bois returned to the sociology program he articulated in 1905 in "Sociology Hesitant." Du Bois was always a scholar, always a sociologist, but his sociology and his scholarship were always closely linked to his program for freedom. His sociological and political bet was that there is room for chance in this world, that is, for organized action by people who suffer under the yoke of racism and colonialism to emancipate themselves and humanity as a whole.

Era IV: Pan-Africanism and Socialism

After being retired from Atlanta University in 1944, Du Bois returned to work at the NAACP. His intentions were to "revive the Pan African movement and give general attention to the foreign aspects of the race problem."[79] Du Bois's second stint at the NAACP lasted four years and was marked by constant conflict with Walter White, the organization's executive secretary, until Du Bois was dismissed from the organization at the end of 1948. Yet, neither forced retirement, dismissal, nor age prevented him from continuing his activism, his organizing, and his scholarship for the rest of his life.

Throughout Du Bois's last years in the United States, from 1944 until his departure to Ghana in 1961 at the age of ninety-three, his focus became increasingly global. Both his work and his thought came to focus on a critique of racial and colonial capitalism, and the promotion of anticolonial Pan-Africanism and socialism. Indeed, in 1945, after nearly twenty years of dormancy, a Pan-African Congress convened once again in Manchester, England—this time with young African liberation movement leaders such as Kwame Nkrumah of Ghana and George Padmore of Trinidad in leadership roles. With more than two hundred delegates representing Black-led organizations from around the world, this was the best attended of the five Pan-African convenings that Du Bois participated in.[80] It is also historically distinct from the previous four because the stated plan was not to lobby for reform but to advocate for an end to colonialism.

Recognizing Du Bois's vision and commitment to Pan-Africanism, the delegates unanimously elected him the congress's international president. Of Du Bois, the Fifth Congress's press secretary, Peter Abrahams, said, "He can, justly, be called the 'Father' of the Pan-African movement, motivated by the inspiration of contacts with Negroes of different origins and nationalities."[81] Yet by this point, Du Bois had begun to realize that the leadership of the Pan-African movement was moving from the United States—and from the Africana diaspora in general, the place from which Du Bois initially thought the movement's leadership would come—to the growing anticolonial movement in Africa.

During this period Du Bois wrote two important books that present his anticolonial and Pan African thinking: *Color and Democracy*, written in 1945, and *The World and Africa*, written in 1947. The first book was written to intervene in the debate on dismantling colonialism after World War II. The second one was written to correct the historical record as to the place of Africa and African people in world history—much as *Black Reconstruction* was written to correct the historical record about the role of Black enslaved people in their own emancipation and the historical memory of the Reconstruction period. These two books, much like *Black Reconstruction*, develop Du Bois's theory of racial and colonial capitalism. In writing them, Du Bois advanced his role as both public intellectual and social theorist.

The start of the Cold War and the Red Scare that followed it brought turbulent years to Du Bois's life. In March of 1949 he attended the Cultural and Scientific Conference for World Peace that gathered at New York City's Waldorf Astoria. This was a politically contentious event, as it not only supported global denuclearization but was also antiwar and largely anticapitalist. The US government opposed the conference's goals, and many of those invited, such as the renowned artist Pablo Picasso, were denied visas.[82]

Yet in the peace movement Du Bois found a community wherein he could roll up his sleeves and work towards his ultimate goal—human emancipation. In 1948 and 1949, Du Bois attended peace congresses and conferences in Paris and Moscow—he was the only American to attend the Moscow meeting, even though twenty-five people from the United States were invited. There he addressed an audience of an estimated six thousand people,[83] opening with these words:

> I represent millions of citizens of the United States who are just as opposed to war as you are. But it is not easy for American citizens either to know the truth about the world or to express it. This is true despite the intelligence and wealth and energy of the United States. Perhaps I can best perform my duty to my country and to the cause of world peace by taking a short time to explain the historic reasons for the part which the United States is playing in the world today.[84]

Du Bois then launched into an impassioned analysis of the roots of war, suffering, and global inequality—his tried and true analysis of racialized modernity. Citing capitalism, imperialism, and the enduring structure of the global color line, Du Bois urged his Soviet audience to awaken their second sight and recognize the connections between the systems of oppression that kept them all unfree. Thanks to his expression of these opinions, Du Bois quickly became a persona non grata with the United States government.

Soon after his return to America, Du Bois became an officer of the Peace Information Center, a US-based organization dedicated to lobbying for international denuclearization. Part of Du Bois's role was to help disseminate what were called "Peacegrams" to the world's citizens. In 1950 he helped distribute the "Stockholm Appeal" to individuals and social reform organizations across the country. This concise, eighty-word statement read, "We demand the absolute banning of the atomic weapon, an arm of terror and of mass extermination of populations. We demand the establishment of strict international control to ensure the implementation of this ban. We consider that the first government henceforth to use the atomic weapon against any country whatsoever will be committing a crime against humanity and should be treated as a war criminal. We call on all people of good will throughout the world to sign this appeal."[85] The appeal went viral, garnering an estimated 2.5 million signatures from people of all backgrounds in the United States alone.

At a moment when McCarthyism was peaking, the Peace Information Center not surprisingly caught the attention of the Department of Justice, which demanded that the organization register as an agent of a foreign principal. The Department of Justice contended that the center was acting on behalf of the Soviet Union. The group's leaders countered by claiming that the center was an American organization accountable only to itself. When the Department of Justice insisted that its demand be met, the center's board of advisors decided to dissolve the organization. It was active only from April to October of 1950. Yet, in February of 1951, the Department of Justice decided to indict Du Bois and four other former officers of the organization for failure to register as agents of a foreign principal.

The trial took place that November 1951, and after hearing testimony the judge dismissed the charges. Reflecting on the trial in his posthumously published *Autobiography* Du Bois wrote,

But of course this unjustified effort to make five persons register as the source of foreign propaganda for peace and particularly to scare 15 million Negroes from complaint was not the real object of this long and relentless persecution. The real object was to prevent American citizens of any sort from daring to think or talk against the determination of big business to reduce Asia to colonial subserviency to American industry; to reweld the chains of Africa; to consolidate United States control of the Caribbean and South America; and above all to crush socialism in the Soviet Union and China.[86]

Although all the charges against him were dismissed, Du Bois was never the same after the trial. His reputation among his peers had been sullied, and, even worse, he had to experience the gut-wrenching sensation of becoming a pariah to the Talented Tenth, whom he thought would have his back. Du Bois was bitter about the way his people turned on him. At the same time, he adopted a new perspective that would guide him in the last decade of his life, a perspective that was increasingly global, anticolonial, and socialist. Of the painstaking days of the trial he wrote,

It was a bitter experience and I bowed before the storm. But I did not break. I continued to speak and write when and where I could. I faced my lowered income and lived within it. I found new friends and lived in a wider world than ever before—a world with no color line. I lost my leadership of my race. It was a dilemma for the mass of Negroes; either they joined the current beliefs and actions of most whites or they could not make a living or hope for preferment. Preferment was possible. The color line was beginning to break. Negroes were getting recognition as never before. Was not the sacrifice of one man, small payment for this? Even those who disagreed with this judgment at least kept quiet. The colored children ceased to hear my name.[87]

Despite his bitterness, Du Bois continued throughout the 1950s to participate in American politics that were associated with the causes of the political Left, publishing articles on the pressing issues of the day in a variety of left-wing periodicals, notably the *National Guardian*, where his work appeared regularly from the late 1940s until he left the United States for good.[88]

And between 1957 and 1961, Du Bois published a trio of historical novels, known as *The Black Flame Trilogy*, that presented in fictional form his ideas about the historical experience of African Americans. These novels did not receive literary acclaim, but they reveal Du Bois's attempt to use different media, in this case narrative fiction, to convey his political and sociological ideas. But as he himself recognized, he had lost his leadership position among African Americans. His voice, powerful as it was, did not reverberate as it had before.

Yet, as his local reputation declined, his international reputation increased. During the 1950s, Du Bois was a global voice for Pan-Africanism and anticolonialism. But he encountered a new problem in trying to implement his new global agenda. Even though Du Bois was absolved in his trial, the United States revoked his passport and did not issue him a new one until 1958, when the United States Supreme Court ruled that American citizens have a right to travel, and the government does not have the authority to deny passports—and therefore deny the right to travel—to people suspected of being communists, as was common throughout the 1950s.[89]

The denial of a passport prevented Du Bois from participating in important international events. For example, he was invited to address the 1955 Bandung conference, in which Asian and African states met to discuss cooperation and to oppose colonialism.[90] Cooperation between Asia and Africa was always central to Du Bois's vision of the possibility of undoing the color line, and he wrote a memo to the conference, addressing it in the name of "the twenty five million colored people of America" and urging the participants to stand for "an Africa and Asia equal with and independent of Europe and America, standing on its own feet, governing themselves as they decide . . . and conducting their own industrial systems as they see fit and not as British and Americans command."[91]

If the color line was global, the undoing of the color line also required global action. At this stage in Du Bois's life, that meant Pan-Africanism, socialism, and cooperation between Africa and Asia—in particular between the newly independent African states and China.

He articulated his vision for a postcolonial Africa in a letter to Kwame Nkrumah in February of 1957. Excusing himself for not being able to attend the celebration marking Ghana's independence and Nkrumah's inauguration—the reason being that the government was still refusing to issue him a passport—Du Bois proposed to Nkrumah his vision for the future of Africa, stating that

> the consequent Pan Africa, working together through its independent units, should seek to develop a new African economy and cultural center standing between Europe and Asia, taking from and contributing to both. It should stress peace and join no military alliance and refuse to fight for settling European quarrels. It should avoid subjection to and ownership by foreign capitalists who seek to get rich on African labor and raw material, and should try to build a socialism founded on old African communal life, rejecting the exaggerated private initiative of the West, and seeking to ally itself with the social program of the Progressive nations; with British and Scandinavian Socialism, with the progress toward the Welfare State in India, Germany, France and the United States, and with the Communist States like the Soviet Union and China, in peaceful cooperation and without presuming to dictate as to how Socialism must or can be attained at particular times and places.[92]

This is an important statement when it comes to understanding Du Bois's late attitudes about socialism. Since his 1928 trip to the Soviet Union, he sympathized with communism but always kept his distance. Du Bois thought that the Soviet model, with its revolutionary violence and its authoritarian government, was not a model for political action for Black people in the United States. But after World War II he openly expressed sympathy for Soviet and, later, Chinese socialism, even though the political tide in the United States was moving in the opposite direction. Once his passport was restored in 1958, he embarked on a trip to the socialist countries, where he was received by Nikita Khrushchev, then the leader of the Soviet Union, and Mao Zedong, then the leader of communist China.

From very early on, Du Bois regarded the common action of Africa and Asia as crucial in undoing the color line.[93] In his late years he was particularly fond of China. He was in Beijing for his ninety-first birthday, and at this occasion he gave a speech that was broadcast to the world, in which he pleaded for the unity of Africa and Asia. In this speech he advised the peoples of Africa that "China is flesh of your flesh, and blood of your blood. China is colored and knows to what a colored skin in this modern world subjects its owner. But China knows more, much more than this: she knows what to do about it. She can take the insults of the United States and still hold her head high. She can make her own machines, when America refuses to sell her American manufactures, even though it hurts American industry, and throws her workers out of jobs."[94]

Du Bois's sympathy for the communist countries, particularly China, increased in his last years. And indeed, before leaving the United States he joined the Communist Party—after arguing all his life that Soviet communism was not a valid path for addressing the problems of America and criticizing multiple times the policies of the Communist Party of the United States because it failed to understand the race question. Did he change his mind about those questions, or did he join the Communist Party out of spite and frustration? We don't know. Clearly this late sympathy for communism was problematic because it ignored or was blind to the violence exercised by the Soviet and Chinese regimes against their own people. But from Du Bois's perspective, the Soviet Union and particularly China were Africa's allies in the anticolonial struggle and thus should be allies in building Africa's postcolonial states.

At the same time, it is clear that Du Bois's understanding of socialism was not similar to the form of socialism practiced by the Soviet or the Chinese regimes. Ever independent minded, Du Bois envisioned a form of socialism rooted in African communal traditions and geared towards the democratic and methodical development of the economy. How exactly he thought that this form of socialism would work he did not explain. But, as he asserted in his letter to Nkrumah, he believed that Africa should look for its future in its own traditions, drawing also from the best that existing historical experiences had to offer (and that included learning from the Western welfare states), without copying any other system or accepting any impositions. When Du Bois looked for reservoirs of alternatives to the existing world, he looked for them in the cultural traditions of Black people, whether in spirituals, as he wrote in

1903 in *Souls*, or in the communal traditions of Africa, as he contended in his old age.

In 1961, tired of American racism and ignored by Black Americans, Du Bois accepted Nkrumah's invitation to move to Ghana to direct the project of writing an Encyclopedia Africana. In a farewell note to a friend, sent before his expatriation to Ghana, Du Bois wrote, "I just cannot take any more of this country's treatment. We leave for Ghana October 5th and I set no date for return. Chin up, and fight on, but realize that the American Negroes can't win."[95]

Du Bois first conceived of the Encyclopedia project in 1909 and tried to bring it to fruition again in the 1930s, but to no avail. Yet, ever the optimist, ever the activist, and ever the scholar, at the age of ninety-three, Du Bois uprooted himself and migrated to a new country to work on a long-deferred intellectual and political dream: that of recording true and undistorted knowledge about Africa, Black people, and their histories. In a statement he wrote in 1962, as he was working on the Encyclopedia project, he articulated his vision this way:

> My idea is to prepare and publish an Encyclopedia not on the vague subject of race, but on the peoples inhabiting the continent of Africa. I propose an Encyclopedia edited mainly by African scholars. I am anxious that it be a scientific production and not a matter of propaganda. While there should be included among its writers the best students of Africa in the world, I want the proposed Encyclopedia to be written mainly from the African point of view by people who know and understand the history and culture of Africans.[96]

The Encyclopedia was Du Bois's last project, and it combined his roles as a scholar and a public intellectual. But this long-dreamed-of project, like many other of his projects, did not come to fruition.[97] Old age finally caught up with him, his health deteriorated, and he died two years later in Accra, at the age of ninety-five, on the eve of the 1963 March on Washington, a protest in which a quarter of a million people gathered at the Lincoln Memorial and heard the Reverend Martin Luther King Jr. deliver his now-legendary "I Have a Dream" speech.

Conclusion

Clearly, the breadth of Du Bois's public sociologies was enormous, and they were complemented by his enduring commitment to enacting social change. His approach evolved over time; he started out as an objective empiricist who maintained a certain disdain for mixing scientific inquiry with social reform. It was not that he did not want his research to effect change. It was that he believed that science alone would loosen people from the racial prejudice that seemed to bind their thoughts and actions. He learned through experience that science, facts, and truth alone would never be enough to undo the color line. Racism is in part irrational, and it is deeply rooted in unconscious biases and all sorts of everyday privilege. Du Bois never veered from his mission to dismantle the color line, but his belief about how to do so continued to evolve, and the bright boundaries between his sociology, his activism, and his organizing blurred.

As Martin Luther King Jr. stated in his 1968 speech at Carnegie Hall celebrating Du Bois's one hundredth birthday, "Above all he did not content himself with hurling invectives for emotional release and then to retire into smug, passive satisfaction. History had taught him it is not enough for people to be angry—the supreme task is to organize and unite people so that their anger becomes a transforming force. It was never possible to know where the scholar Du Bois ended and the organizer Du Bois began. The two qualities in him were a single, unified force."[98]

Du Bois did not jump in and out of his roles as a sociologist, an activist, an organizer, or a public intellectual. Rather, he was always a sociologist, always an activist and an organizer, and always an intellectual. For this reason, no single academic discipline is capacious enough to hold him and his work. That is acceptable. However, it is disingenuous to assert, as many sociologists continue to do, that he was not really one of our own. He was a sociologist and thought about himself as a sociologist, although never only a sociologist. And although his underlying philosophies and his program for action changed over time, Du Bois never abandoned sociology.

Quite the contrary. He continued to expand the capacity of the discipline by directing and twenty years later resuscitating one of the oldest empirical research programs of the early twentieth century, by creating an academic journal focused on social scientific inquiry on the race question, and by training and working alongside a generation of young sociologists—all the while producing his own magnificent body of sociological research.

What is sometimes distracting when it comes to evaluating Du Bois's contributions as a sociologist is his increasingly visible commitment to organizing and activism outside of the ivory towers of academia. Over the long arc of his career, his path appears less and less like what present-day academics consider that of a "true" sociologist. However, the narrative about Du Bois's departure from sociology after he first left Atlanta University is inaccurate. Du Bois was a sociologist par excellence, and he and his work are central to our field.

There is another issue that comes into play when evaluating Du Bois's contribution as a sociologist. Was W. E. B. Du Bois a scholar of the African American experience, of the Black diaspora, or did his concerns and interests extend to non-Black people who also lived on both sides of the color line? His record shows that all three issues preoccupied him and that none was antithetical to the others. W. E. B. Du Bois was a proud African American man, and theorized first and foremost from the lived experiences of the millions of Black Americans with whom he shared a common history and experience. His commitment to the rigorous scientific study of the phenomenological, social, and economic conditions of African Americans—what he referred to as "the study of Negro problems"—was motivated by his sincere belief that this research would have a positive impact on the liberation of Black people in America, extinguish the "psychological wages of whiteness" that burdened those who occupied that social position, and advance science as a whole.

However, from very early on Du Bois was also a Pan-Africanist, firmly believing that Black people across the diaspora shared a linked fate and a common struggle against both anti-Black racial oppression and colonialism. He also wrote, organized, and struggled for the liberation of all people of color. As the research of the sociologist Katrina Quisumbing King reminds us, the "color line" is not and never has been solely a Black-white construct. Rather, it is a macro-level structure that reproduces the racial world order between whites and nonwhites, or "the darker races," as Du Bois often called them. Du Bois was the first to assert this argument in the early 1900s, and he was deeply concerned with the living conditions of people of color around the world. This is shown by his longstanding involvement with anticolonial struggles. He was concerned with the predicament of all colonized people, and saw in the unity of what we call today the Global South the path to undoing the color line.

The source of this unfortunate tension between a local, a diasporic, and a global understanding of Du Bois's work is multifold. Sometimes it springs from the reality that scholars of color are so marginalized in the academy that there is an unnecessary impulse to claim Du Bois solely for one's own. A second source of misunderstanding lies in the compartmentalized way in which his work is read and assigned in academic settings. For example, most sociologists are only familiar with his earlier works, such as *The Philadelphia Negro* and *Souls of Black Folk*, which do center African Americans. This focus on two early texts contributes to the inaccurate narrative that Du Bois was purely a race scholar who focused on the sociology of the African American experience. This narrative can be seen across disciplines, where a selection of Du Bois's works are cherry-picked as exemplary and repeatedly assigned to the exclusion of his vast body of work.

An additional point about Du Bois's work is that he did not work in isolation. Lionizing historical figures too often renders their network of collaborators, supporters, and peers invisible and reinforces a liberal narrative of the rugged individual: the genius, the hero, the leader. However the truth of the matter is that Du Bois worked with a legion of people in and out of the academy. Works by the sociologists Cheryl Thompson Gilkes, Aldon Morris, and Earl Wright II contribute enormously to the excavation of the roles of these hidden figures. Du Bois not only worked and struggled in solidarity with other academics; he was also deeply embedded in the Harlem Renaissance movement, working alongside a host of poets, artists, composers, and writers such as Aaron Douglas, Langston Hughes, and Lorraine Hansberry. He was also part of global Pan-African networks of intellectuals and activists. In this way, a Du Boisian sociology is clearly a collaborative endeavor.

* * *

Most sociologists hope that their research will have an influence in the public sphere. Whether in politics, policy, social movements, or formal or informal organizations, sociology generally has something of importance to contribute to the conversation. However, there is little agreement about where the boundaries separating the scholar from the public intellectual, the activist, and the organizer should be drawn. Du Bois was clear as to where he stood on this issue, and he provides an example of a path that can be followed.

A contemporary Du Boisian sociology still aims to undo the color line and destroy all forms of oppression. A contemporary Du Boisian sociology would seek not only to insert sociological insights and perspectives into the public sphere but also, and even more importantly, to engage the public when it comes to working through these pressing issues. It is a sociology that is unapologetic in its emancipatory aim. For Du Bois, that aim was directed towards eradicating the global problem of the color line. For another scholar, the aim might be something different. Nevertheless, what a Du Boisian sociology offers is a path to address the long-held tension between what it means to be a serious sociologist and what it means to work in and with communities and the lay public.

Du Bois's life shows that it is possible to do both. It also shows that public engagement does not diminish sociological insights. To the contrary. It sharpens these insights and makes them more relevant and enduring.

5

A Manifesto for a Contemporary Du Boisian Sociology

When we started this project, we believed that we were familiar with W. E. B. Du Bois's work. After all, we have read it and taught it more than most sociologists. Yet, as we read his work closely to write this book, we realized that it was much richer, more complex, and more powerful than we had previously thought. In Du Bois, we encountered a scholar and intellectual who changed his way of looking at things as he confronted new situations, who incorporated new perspectives into his thinking, and who was remarkably self-reflexive about his changing approach. We also encountered strong continuities in his thinking. The global nature of the color line, the pervasiveness of racialization, and the centrality of colonialism and coloniality in historical capitalism were constant themes in his work, themes that he developed and that evolved through his life, but were never abandoned. In Du Bois we encountered a scholar activist who was always a scholar and always an activist, a scholar activist whose work was deeply rooted in the African American experience but also addressed the whole world.

This chapter is our manifesto for a contemporary Du Boisian sociology, our vision of how sociology can and ought to be different. Our goal was never limited to bringing Du Bois to the attention of our colleagues, nor simply to add his name to an already existing canon. We have always had a more ambitious goal: to contribute to building a new Du Boisian sociology for our times. Ours is certainly not a call to a new Du Boisian orthodoxy. We believe that the construction of a contemporary Du Boisian sociology is an aspirational and collective endeavor, and we present this concluding chapter not as a set of definitive remarks but as our contribution to opening a conversation with our Du Boisian colleagues. With them we want to consider certain questions: What would a contemporary Du Boisian sociology look like? If Du Bois's sociology truly was a "path not taken," what lies in store for those of us who want to adopt a Du Boisian approach to sociological analysis?

We suspect that many sociologists do not see themselves as Du Boisians and yet would agree with different parts of our proposal. These could be postcolonial sociologists, world-systems analysts, or other postpositivist sociologists. We hope to engage them in a conversation about working together to expand and diversify the practice of the discipline. We also want to address our fellow mainstream sociologists and talk with them about how the practice of sociology must change in order to be more inclusive. To be sure, we are not asking of all sociologists to change the way they practice their trade. But we do ask our colleagues to be reflective about the exclusionary practices of the discipline, both historical and in our present day, and to have an open mind about sociological approaches that differ from theirs.

This request is the result of observing the experiences of so many as-yet "scholars denied." These are those graduate students, mainly students of color, who are repeatedly told that the questions they want to ask are not "sociological" enough, that their methods and analytical frames are merely descriptive, or that their research is more appropriate for the humanities and that perhaps they should pursue their interests in an ethnic studies department. Sometimes these encounters are that forthright; at other times they are cloaked in politeness. Nonetheless, many young scholars find themselves confronting the same question as Du Bois did so long ago: "How does it feel to be a problem?" These scholars denied are also the undergraduate students who seek a critical intellectual space and find a home in departments of comparative literature, ethnic studies, or history rather than in sociology. They are also the junior scholars who feel compelled to disguise their true research interests until they get tenure, only to realize that their interests still encounter a hostile reception in the discipline, or find themselves pulled into departments outside of sociology.

We believe that taking seriously the full scope of Du Bois's sociology will create the space to take inventory of "who we are" as a discipline, reevaluate our ideals of who we strive to be, and help us build a critical and inclusive sociology. We aim to build on the work of Du Bois, and other anticolonial and antiracist thinkers, to expand the sociological imagination and the range of accepted sociological thought and practices. We are not alone in our sentiments. This book is part of a long and ongoing conversation among generations of scholars and activists about what constitutes sociological theory and the purpose of sociological practice.[1] And we invite our readers to envision with us a Du Boisian sociology for the twenty-first century.

Du Bois's Sociology

We have shown that Du Bois was a social theorist who theorized modernity in a unique and original way that is still relevant today, and that he was also one of the founders of empirical sociology. We described his theoretical approach as a critique of racialized modernity—that is, the idea that racialization, racism, colonialism, and coloniality are structuring elements of the modern world. Du Bois argued that colonialism and racism were intrinsic to capitalism, a historical system that perpetually reproduces global inequalities along a multitude of axes, particularly race, class, and gender. For Du Bois, race was the product of European expansion, slavery, and colonialism; there was no concept of "race" as we understand it today before the European colonial expansion. That is not to say that people didn't construct different regimes of difference prior to European colonialism, but it is to say that there was no institutionalized global system constituted to maintain and reproduce white supremacy in perpetuity. The color line is what marks modernity as a singular epoch in the annals of history.

Through the systematic dehumanization of Black people and people of color around the globe, whole swaths of the world population became commodities in the service of racial and colonial capitalism. But race is not only a product of historical capitalism; it is also a structuring principle of social relations and inequalities within this historical system. Du Bois developed this understanding in the 1930s, after his creative engagement with the work of Karl Marx. But the premise that the color line was the structuring force and *the* defining global problem of his century was present in his early writings.

Du Bois also developed an analysis of the intersections of race and class. He argued that the racial and colonial character of capitalism leads to very different experiences for different segments of the working class, fracturing both labor movements and workers' solidarity. He also pointed out that racial and colonial capitalism is based on the actions of the racial state—the organization of political power along racial lines—as it sustains the pervasiveness of racial inequalities and imposes severe limits to democracy. The racial state, in turn, is sustained by an alliance between white workers and different factions of the white bourgeoisie, based on support for racial and colonial privilege.

A hallmark of Du Bois's sociology was his ability to seamlessly link the macro historical analysis of racial and colonial capitalism to the phenomenological analysis of the lived experience of racialized people. His theory of double consciousness was an analysis of the phenomenology of racialized subjectivity—the veil, twoness, and second sight—and the different ways in which racialized peoples encounter and respond to the color line.[2] He also showed how the color line articulated the subjectivities not only of people of color but also of those who are socially categorized as white. To that end, Du Bois also applied his phenomenology of the veil to the analysis of the formation of white subjectivity, showing that it was based on willful ignorance toward life behind the veil. Du Bois described the fragmented way in which the colonial world appears to the colonizer, showing how the colonizer does not see—and *actively chooses* not to see when challenged—the brutality and cruelty that lies behind the colonial commodities they consume. Furthermore, Du Bois shows how the sciences were mobilized to justify colonialism and racism and further render invisible the experience of the colonial and racialized subjects.

A key concern for Du Bois was the possibilities and limits of human action. For him, this was an overarching theoretical issue, which he formulated as the study of the scope and limits of "Law" and "Chance." "Chance" for Du Bois meant the possibilities of agency and free will, while "Law" meant the regularities and structures of social life that are impervious to human conscious action. Du Bois embraced the idea that people have the ability to shape their own reality. In doing so he borrowed the language of chance from William James's pragmatism. But Du Bois's belief in the ability of people to change their circumstances emerged mainly from his own experience and the experience of struggle of African Americans and the Africana diaspora. But that ability was and is limited by the presence of a concrete structural barrier: the color line that limited the freedom of people of color and colonized people, limits that Du Bois dedicated his entire life to undoing.

The overwhelming presence of the color line did not mean that people living behind the veil lacked agency. They always organized to reclaim a measure of humanity and dignity and to demand equality and freedom. Also whites, as shown by John Brown, the abolitionist and antiracist activist, can also choose to drop the veil of ignorance and act against the system. However, to do that they must renounce their privilege, something they are reluctant to do because doing so goes against their interests and because, as John Brown's example shows, they are likely to pay a personal cost for their actions. Ultimately, the color line is the product of the agency of whites.

Du Bois was not only a social theorist; he was also the founder of American empirical sociology, and he conducted important empirical urban and community studies as early as the 1890s. He aimed to develop an empirically based scientific sociology through the study of the structure, experiences, and lives of Black communities. However, Du Bois's sociology was different from the one that later developed in Chicago and became one of the foundations of mainstream sociology. Du Bois's empirical program and that of Chicago are different in three main ways.

First, Du Bois's mixed-methods methodology for community and urban studies combined deep historical analysis, descriptive statistical analysis, and sociological interpretation. Second, Du Bois's urban and community studies were rooted in his theoretical understanding of racialized modernity as a power-laden structure. Finally, Du Bois's urban and community studies, as opposed to Chicago's sociology, did not search for universal patterns and generalizable concepts. Rather, they were geared to develop in-depth analyses of community lives rooted in their specific social and historical contexts, recognizing the multiplicity of experiences of urban and rural African American communities. This does not mean that Du Bois's sociology did not seek to develop generalizable concepts. It certainly did. But generalizations for Du Bois had to be the result of a careful and painstaking contrast between the multiple different situations that Black communities encountered. Through the detailed study of communities and their embeddedness in their historical contexts, Du Bois's analyses seamlessly brought together the local in all its richness and detail and the global historical trends.

Du Bois innovated methodologically by using his own experience to reflect on the structural conditions of racialized modernity. In many of his works, he used autobiographical reflections to provide a structural analysis of regimes of power and exclusion. He referred to his life not for the sake of describing his own experiences (or "me-search," as some pejoratively call it today) but as a source to reflect on the world in which he lived. Many contemporary sociologists might argue that this puts Du Bois closer to the humanities than the social sciences or makes him a public intellectual rather than a social scientist. We believe, however, that Du Bois's self-reflective methodology carries great promise for expanding our sociological understanding of racialized subjectivity and the mechanisms of racial, gender, and class exclusion in the present.

Du Bois was a public intellectual and an activist who was deeply engaged in public sociology, meaning the type of sociological work produced to bring sociological insights and findings to the public sphere. His activism was informed by his sociological understanding, and vice versa. He reflected on the dialectical relationship between the two in his several autobiographical works, including his essay "My Evolving Program of Negro Freedom" and his books *Darkwater*, *Dusk of Dawn*, and *The Autobiography of W. E. B. Du Bois*. Du Bois's public sociology and activism presented itself through a wide range of mediums. He spoke through the public arts by curating a selection of photographs and graphical representations to convey the predicament of Black people in America at the Paris world exhibition in 1900, an event that drew more than fifty million visitors. He wrote across literary genres, including pure fiction, traditional academic writing, and a genre that he called "historical fiction," with the specific aim of delivering his theoretical points to a broad audience.

For example, he used his novels to discuss the way race, class, and gender structure the lives of racialized and colonized people and their forms of resistance to colonialism and the color line; *Dark Princess* and the *Black Flame Trilogy* are examples of this type of writing. He also used allegorical narrative to illustrate his theory of double consciousness, as in "The Coming of John" in *Souls* and in *Dusk of Dawn*. He even published a children's magazine to reach young minds with his ideas. He was an organizer of several organizations and movements, including several Pan-African Congresses, which advocated against racism and colonialism globally, and the Niagara Movement, which led to the formation of the NAACP, one of the main civil rights organizations in the United States. Du Bois's life and actions blurred the line between scholar, public intellectual, and activist; his scholarship was central to his activism, his activism was central to his scholarship, and he was ever the intellectual.

Du Bois's sociology sought equality and freedom for people of color in the United States and around the world. His understanding of how this was to take place changed throughout his life, as did his understanding of the relationship between the practice of science and emancipation. At first his program was one of uplifting, which was an early statement of modernization and incorporation theories. He contended that it was the duty of the "talented tenth," the elite of the group, to lead the backward masses into what he then termed "modern civilization." Du Bois has been rightly criticized for his early elitist position vis-à-vis the Black masses. It is important to note, however, that he regarded backwardness as a consequence of slavery and racism, not the result of any innate biological or cultural characteristic, and he always emphasized the agency of people of color in the uplift process. The later Du Bois emphasized the role of the self-activity of the masses in their own emancipation and paid careful attention to the economic structures that kept the Black masses in poverty.[3]

To sum up, Du Bois was an original social theorist, an innovative empirical researcher, and a public sociologist committed to the global antiracist and anticolonial struggle. He fervently wrote, organized, produced, and spoke on these issues throughout his ninety-five years of life. His sociology emerged from his own experience of racialization and was aimed at undoing the color line. We find in his work a firm base upon which to build our reflections about a different way to practice sociology. And we invite you to imagine a contemporary Du Boisian sociology with us.

Envisioning a Contemporary Du Boisian Sociology

In envisioning a contemporary Du Boisian sociology, we must be careful not to regard Du Bois's sociology as a panacea, as a one-size-fits-all solution to all social problems. In fact, we find it useful to disaggregate Du Bois the man from both Du Bois's sociology (his own scholarly endeavors) and a contemporary Du Boisian sociology, a term we use to refer to a sociological approach, a mode of inquiry, and a disposition toward the aims and practice of knowledge production. A contemporary Du Boisian sociology is a critical project that takes a strong position against racism, against colonialism in all its past and present forms, and against all forms of oppression and exclusion. A contemporary Du Boisian sociology is an activist project in that it aims to use knowledge to make this world better for the oppressed and for those who are written off as expendable. At the same time, it is a quintessential sociological approach in that it bases its critique in systematic and detailed empirical research of social practices, institutions, and structures.

The Du Boisian sociology we propose here begins with Du Bois's work but ultimately transcends it. It transcends Du Bois's work first by incorporating the work of other scholars denied. We want to bring back not only Du Bois but also his fellow outcasts, who have been exiled from the realm of mainstream social theory and sociology, scholar activists such as Ida B. Wells, Anna Julia Cooper, Pauli Murray, C. L. R. James, Frantz Fanon, and others who helped build a tradition of anticolonial and antiracist social theory. The contemporary Du Boisian sociology we envision also transcends Du Bois's work in that it incorporates issues and ideas he did not sufficiently address. Du Bois's sociology had important blind spots, and we should not hide them.

For example, Du Bois identifies racial slavery as the starting point for racial colonial capitalism. This is an important contribution to the analysis of modernity, but at the same time it ignores questions of indigeneity and settler colonialism. Further, although Du Bois acknowledged the intersections of race and gender in a few of his writings, issues involving gender and patriarchy were often overlooked and undertheorized in many of his analyses. Nor did he acknowledge the work of several women of color who were his intellectual contemporaries and often his interlocutors. Furthermore, contemporary issues involving sexuality and the environment were not part of the critical discourse of his time.[4] We believe these are issues that a new Du Boisian sociology must incorporate, and it can do so in a Du Boisian spirit, by incorporating new issues, ideas, and approaches to his critical thinking.

A contemporary Du Boisian sociology, as a critical project that aims to change how we practice the discipline, is a collective *project-in-the-making*. One or two isolated scholars cannot accomplish this feat alone, nor should they want to do so. Therefore, this book aims to contribute to a collective intellectual challenge of disciplinary practice. In the following sections, we present our ideas and suggestions concerning the theoretical orientation of a contemporary Du Boisian sociology, its methodological approach, and the ways to train graduate students. These suggestions are the product of our own conversations on Du Bois's work and its implications for the future of the discipline. We offer them as our contribution to the collective conversation about the building of a contemporary Du Boisian sociology and the future of the discipline.

A Critique of Racialized Modernity

We imagine that a contemporary Du Boisian sociology would build on Du Bois's critique of racialized modernity. Modernity is a vague concept that refers to the historical moment in which we live today. It has been characterized in many different ways: as being based on the rise of science and the implementation of technology, the emergence of capitalism, the prevalence of bureaucracy and instrumental rationality, the growth of cities and industrialization, the deepening of specialization and the division of labor, the year 1492 and the European encounter with the Americas, the rise of individualism, and other social processes that took place in past centuries. For many, modernity is synonymous with progress and a desired social order. Du Bois had a much more critical view. He argued that the main problem of his time was the color line. Du Bois did not use the word "modernity"—the early Du Bois wrote about "modern culture" and "civilization," the late Du Bois about colonialism, imperialism, racism, and capitalism—but he clearly asserted that the main characteristic of our times is the color line.

Du Bois made clear from the very beginning that he understood the color line as a global structure. For him, the color line created the conditions under which a historically new human classification system would form, in which race would order and overdetermine social relations. This new structure emerged along with a specific historical political and economic system: racial and colonial capitalism. By this Du Bois meant a global system oriented to the production of commodities based on the hyper-exploitation and dispossession of workers of color, the oppression and general denial of humanity of people of color, white supremacy, and the prevalence of colonial forms of political organization. Race and racism are the products of the slave trade and colonialism, but they became in turn central organizational principles in historical capitalism for classifying people and their access to rights and opportunities. That is, they became structuring forces on their own—hence modernity was from the beginning racialized modernity.

We understand racialized modernity to be the historical period that began with the European expansion into the Americas in what the late world systems theorist Immanuel Wallerstein describes as the long sixteenth century. It is with the European expansion into the Americas that the main historical forms of racial classification and exclusion emerged: slavery and the plantation economy on the one hand, and settler colonialism and the dispossession of Native Americans on the other. And it is with the European expansion into the Americas that one of the paramount developments of racialized modernity took place: the invention of whiteness. It was not until this period of imperial expansion that people of European descent began to organize and accumulate resources around a consolidated racial identity.

The world has changed since Du Bois wrote his work, spanning from the late 1800s to the early 1960s. Colonial empires have largely though not completely disappeared. Settler colonialism, on the other hand, is still a feature of our world, and neocolonial structures of power continue to reproduce many of the former colonial forms of inequality and exclusion. Also, the global and local forms of the color lines have changed. Today racism is less overt and more difficult to pinpoint, and racial boundaries are ostensibly more porous. But racial inequalities and exclusions still help define social relations and structures. Du Bois anticipated the rise of neocolonial forms of political domination, and also pointed to the pervasiveness of the cultural and knowledge forms generated by colonialism and racism—the kind of cultural critique that now informs the postcolonial and decolonial approaches.

In keeping with this first-order critique of racialized modernity, we believe that a contemporary Du Boisian sociology will take on the study of how various forms of historical and present colonialism and regimes of coloniality, and the subsequent color lines that emerge from them, shape our present-day social and political debates.[5] These debates focus on issues of immigration and movement of refugees and asylum seekers from the periphery to the core; mass incarceration; economic exploitation through new forms of organizing work; and the racialization of religion, to name a few. Some questions to examine in these discrete yet interrelated contexts: How are social categories constructed by different racial states? How is state and group power exerted, and in whose interests? What types of subjects and subjectivities emerge? And how, and in what modes, does the subaltern speak, organize, and resist?

It cannot be emphasized enough that colonialism does not refer to a past historical structure. Classic colonialism may have largely ended, but the inequalities and exclusions it created continue in the present through unequal power relations and the persistence of colonial categories and modes of understanding the world.[6] Furthermore, by addressing settler colonialism and the dispossession of indigenous peoples, a contemporary Du Boisian sociology will go beyond Du Bois's own analysis and address one of his glaring omissions. A contemporary Du Boisian sociology will investigate these and other contemporary and historical structures of oppression, exploitation, displacement, dispossession, and erasure.

Furthermore, the contemporary Du Boisian sociology we imagine will go beyond Du Bois by fully incorporating analyses of patriarchy, gender, sexuality, ableism, and religion as central to its endeavor. Du Bois went beyond other male social theorists of his time in starting to address questions of gender. However, he failed to fully incorporate and learn from the work of his contemporary Black feminist colleagues, a fact that considerably diluted the analytical power of some of his arguments. A contemporary Du Boisian sociology will study the local and global forms of intersectional exclusion, oppression, and exploitation, along with the construction of intersectional solidarity and collective action. By doing so, Du Boisian scholars of the twenty-first century will go beyond the concepts and categories that Du Bois left for us, and incorporate the necessary words, concepts, visions, and vocabularies necessary to explain our current world, in all of its complexity. A contemporary Du Boisian sociology will seek to enter into dialogue with other existing (and many longstanding) critical sociologies that are building from queer, indigenous, or intersectional perspectives to develop a more comprehensive critique.[7]

In addition, a contemporary Du Boisian sociology will focus on the analysis of the lived experiences of racialized people, which was a key and unique feature of Du Bois's own sociology. The phenomenology of the racialized self is the linchpin that links the structures of racial and colonial capitalism and the agency of racialized and racializing subjects. In a Du Boisian mode, subjectivity is analyzed in the context of power relations. However, forms of subjectivity, while formed within the constraints of power relations and social positions, are not fully determined by or derivative of those constraining structures. A contemporary Du Boisian sociology sees human agency as emerging out of historical contexts characterized by pervasive patterns of power differentials and historically prevalent ideas about human beings and cultural understandings about the social order. But it also presupposes the ability of the oppressed to see beyond the existing order and to act in search of equality, dignity, emancipation, and the assertion of humanity.

These two elements, the global and structural character of the color line and the focus on the possibilities of human action, may seem to be in tension with each other and allow different readings of Du Bois's sociology: a structuralist reading on the one hand and a pragmatist reading on the other. In our reading, though, the combination of structural analysis and the analysis of subjectivity and action is a hallmark of Du Bois's sociology and is central to a contemporary Du Boisian sociology. Du Bois positioned the unresolved tension between "Law" (social regularities and constraints) and "Chance" (the presence of alternatives and the possibilities of social action) as a central element of his reflection and analysis. The main goal of sociology, for him, was to investigate this tension empirically. The answer to this question was not metaphysical and abstract but historical and on the ground. A contemporary Du Boisian sociology should continue this endeavor.

We also suggest that a contemporary Du Boisian analysis of racialized modernity should recognize that unobservable and persistent forms of social relations and patterns of inequality and exclusion, such as the color line and colonialism in all their historical and present forms, constrain and condition the actions, thoughts, and aspirations of individuals who live within those structures. Yet the contemporary Du Boisian sociology we propose does not see those constraining structures as external to social action. They are, in fact, the *crystallization* of historical social action. Racism and colonialism are historical social formations and the product of the agency of individuals and groups. However, once institutionalized, they impinge on the lives of people as external forces. Yet those external forces are potentially subject to modification or even disruption and transformation through social action. The linking of subjectivity and the structures of power, the analysis of the lived experience of the dominant and the dominated, the critique of the structures of knowledge, and the emphasis on the ability of the oppressed to see beyond the present, to imagine change, and to assert their own humanity are pillars of Du Bois's sociology and of the Du Boisian sociology we envision.

Contextualization, Relationality, Historicity

Contextualization, relationality, and historicity are, we argue, three of the four core pillars of a Du Boisian methodology. The fourth core element is a subaltern standpoint. We chose to discuss this in a separate section because it is perhaps the most controversial of the elements that constitute the core of a contemporary Du Boisian methodology. By "contextualization" we mean that theorization and analysis are rooted in local histories and conditions. In his empirical studies Du Bois emphasized the need to take into account the diversity of experiences of the Black communities in the United States and in the world as a whole, a diversity of experience that emerged from different local histories and configurations of power. He further emphasized the need to study in detail these different experiences. Du Bois himself did this through his advocacy of the social study, what he defined as bounded studies that examined "exhaustively, the conditions of life and action in certain localities" with the purpose of providing a deep dive into social problems.

A contemporary empirical Du Boisian sociology must start by acknowledging the plurality of places and experiences through the detailed study of local institutional contexts and the different intersections of local histories, power, and agency. For example, the color line works differently in José's place of birth in Buenos Aires, Argentina (yes, the color line does exist in Latin America!) than it does in Karida's hometown of Long Island, New York, in the United States. Yet the color line and settler colonialism are present and at work in Argentina as they are in the United States. Like a matryoshka doll, these contexts are hyper-embedded from the localest of the local out to the broadest conceptions of the global. The onus is on us, fellow Du Boisian scholars, to attend to the particular, just as we are trained as social scientists to do for the universal.

The second pillar of a Du Boisian methodology is relationality. Du Boisian sociology emphasizes the specificity of local contexts and histories, but it sees the development of institutions, forms of action, and ideas as taking place in relational, not isolated, contexts. Whether we are looking at community institutions or the economic and political trajectories of countries or regions, our analysis must address the networks of institutional and power relations in which they are embedded. While we need to pay attention to local specificities and contexts, in order to understand them we must look at them in relation to other specific contexts and to the broader contexts of power.

As Du Bois shows in *The Philadelphia Negro*, the Black community of Philadelphia has a specific history, organization, and set of problems, but we cannot understand them without looking at the actions of white Philadelphians who hold political and economic power in the city. And as he shows in *The World and Africa*, we cannot understand the historical trajectory of the different regions of the African continent without seeing them in relation to other regions and to the historical processes in Europe and Asia. In short, a contemporary Du Boisian sociology will follow sociologist Julian Go's call for relationality in global analysis. This approach is important in order to transcend the methodological nationalism and analytical bifurcation that characterize mainstream sociology. Different local, specific histories are linked to one another, and the Du Boisian methodological approach proposed here emphasizes the search for those links.[8]

Historicity is the third methodological principle of a Du Boisian sociology. Local contexts are not only analyzed in their specificity and relational embeddedness; they are also situated in their historical contexts, that is, in relation to the specific form in which racial colonial capitalism and the color line materialize, in specific historical moments and geographical regions. Du Bois proposed that the tension between social constraints and the possibility of agency was *the* empirical question for sociology. He regarded the tension between the global and the local the same way. The color line and racialized modernity are global and historical structures. These global structures condition and affect local histories. Racialized modernity operates as a landscape of meaning for social action in local contexts, but within this broad landscape of meaning there is room for multiple experiences of oppression, exclusion, and resistance.[9] To what extent the local is influenced by the global and vice versa is an empirical question that differs geographically and historically.

The emphasis on contextualization and historicity naturally leads to questions of generalizability. Like other sociological approaches, a contemporary Du Boisian sociology aims to generalize its concepts and arguments, but generalization would be the result of carefully exploring the historical and contextual applicability of concepts.[10] Let us, for example, consider Du Bois's theory of double consciousness. This is a theory that emerges out of his analysis of the lived experiences of African Americans in the American South. As it is a theory that addresses the construction of subjectivity under conditions of racial oppression, it can be extended to similar situations of racialization, colonialism, and othering in other settings. Du Bois extends the theorization of racialized subjectivity in *Dusk*, and there are numerous parallels between Du Bois's phenomenology and Fanon's theorization of racial subjectivity in *Black Skin, White Masks*. As a theory of the formation of subjectivity under oppression, the theory can potentially travel and be applied to other situations of racialization and coloniality. However, we caution against applying these theoretical concepts in a way that is unreflexive or unmoored from historical context.[11] Du Boisian sociology studies concrete historical social formations and does not assume generalizability across historical periods or from one marginalized group to another.[12]

Du Boisian sociology is a critical approach that is rooted in the sociological traditions of empirical studies. A distinctive mark of Du Boisian sociology is its commitment to careful and thorough empirical research. After all, Du Bois was, among many other things, the founder of American empirical sociology, and he himself was a meticulous and systematic empirical researcher. In his many writings, Du Bois employed a variety of methods. In his community studies, he employed a mixed-methods approach that included historical, statistical, and interpretative analysis. For the study of subjectivity, he used phenomenological analysis. And in his historical sociology, he employed a global and relational approach. A contemporary Du Boisian sociology would draw from Du Bois's combination of methodological techniques, privileging those that are most suitable to the questions at hand or the primary matters of concern of the study.

We are not being prescriptive as to which methods one must use in order to be regarded as a Du Boisian sociologist. The Du Boisian difference in empirical research methods, we believe, is twofold. First, it embraces a wider set of empirical methods, some of which are part of the tool kit of every sociologist, and others of which are shunned by the mainstream of the discipline. Second, the difference in approach lies in the methodology, that is, the emphasis on contextualization, historicity, and relationality. Quantitative analysis, for example, is the most common method used by the discipline today. Du Bois used statistics for descriptive purposes and made statistical analysis part of his mixed-methods approach. Today, statistical techniques are much more advanced than in Du Bois's times, and there is no reason for Du Boisian sociologists not to avail themselves of advanced statistical methods. At the same time, the unreflective use of statistical methods can be misleading and even harmful, especially when explaining the social problems facing subaltern or otherwise othered communities.

Quantitative research often does not recognize the historical structures of power in which those studies take place or the historical and geographical contextual limits of their data and findings. Further, quantitative data itself is too often regarded as neutral and detached from any historical-political context. This has been a particular problem in the sociology of race. As sociologist and demographer Tukufu Zuberi pointed out, the causal analysis of the "effects" of race tends to regard race as an individual attribute rather than as a historical social relation. As a result, the effects found in regressions are often attributed to the characteristics of individuals rather than to the prevalence of systemic racism and racialization.[13] This mode of reasoning naturalizes racial inequalities and categories. Zuberi's critique points to the problems of fetishizing methods at the expense of critical sociological reasoning. As he points out, the effects of racial variables should be interpreted as effects of the different forms and practices of racism. For that, however, we need a theoretical account of the contemporary work of racial and colonial capitalism. The contextual, historical, and relational analysis must be carried through the whole analysis, not just stated as an analytical framework at the beginning.

A contemporary Du Boisian sociology will also make use of ethnography, archival methods, oral history, and other qualitative techniques. It would embrace the use of a variety of techniques to achieve a comprehensive understanding of the details of community life, its forms of organization, and the meanings of community practices. Qualitative analysis tells us about agency, the hopes and plans of people, the barriers they encounter, their failures, and their sources of pride, joy, and dignity—the subjectivity of social life. Contemporary Du Boisian sociologists can use qualitative methods as part of mixed-methods studies, as Du Bois did, or as stand-alone ethnographies, as is common in the discipline today. Our argument is that Du Boisian qualitative studies—as with quantitative studies—must be rooted in the context of power relations and the complexity of local communities, in their specific history, and in their relationship to racialized modernity as a global historical formation.[14]

For example, many contemporary ethnographies are ahistorical in the sense that they fail to address the historical trajectories and power relations that construct communities; this is very much an offshoot of the model of ethnographic work developed at Chicago.[15] As Alford A. Young Jr. has pointed out, much of contemporary urban ethnography has focused on the question of the similarities or differences between mainstream culture and the culture of the minority poor. Some ethnographers have tried to establish the deviant character of minority cultures, while others have replied that minority poor people are just like mainstream middle-class Americans, but living under more dreadful circumstances.[16]

A qualitative Du Boisian sociology would focus instead on highlighting and documenting the ways in which intersecting axes of power impinge on people's lives and on communities. Du Boisian qualitative analysis would not necessarily focus on the poor, and certainly not on deviance and social disorganization. These may be topics of interest but not the sole interest, as seems to be the case with much contemporary urban ethnography. This relentless focus on disorganization and deviance is a testimony to the power that the Chicago School still holds on the sociological imagination. By contrast, Du Boisian sociology aims to understand the self and subjectivity in their historical context of power, and to analyze the ways people act, based on that subjectivity, to change their situation and/or reclaim their dignity and humanity. A Du Boisian qualitative approach helps us understand people within the context of their institutions, history, and power. It takes account of local cultural practices and expressions of agency without stigmatizing them.

A contemporary Du Boisian sociology will also practice its own historical sociology, focusing on the different forms of racialization and organization of colonialism and coloniality, and the particular groups that benefit from or struggle against the global racial and colonial order in different times and places. A Du Boisian sociology would investigate the continuities and rearticulations of the broad forms of power and exclusion under racial and colonial capitalism. It would also analyze local historical social formations in their specificity, always keeping a lens in the relationality between different local histories and the overlaps and tensions between local contexts and racialized modernity as a landscape of meaning.[17] The main model for a Du Boisian historical sociology is Du Bois's work itself. In *Black Reconstruction* and *The World and Africa*, Du Bois presents a model of how to combine local and global relational analysis and how to look at racial and colonial capitalism as a global structure while accounting for its historical and geographic specificities.[18]

A contemporary Du Boisian sociology also opens the door to research that is descriptive and noncausal, research that addresses the questions of *how* rather than *why*. Du Bois's phenomenology excelled in studying subjectivity and lived experience. A contemporary Du Boisian sociology would still try to answer Du Bois's question—"How does it feel to be a problem?"—in its many manifestations. The answer to the question of the experience of being a "problem" is a description of racialized people's ways of being, their ways of reacting to the multiple denials of their own humanity, and their many ways of reclaiming the humanity and mutual recognition that are systematically denied them. The uniqueness of a Du Boisian phenomenology is that it takes into account context and history, as something is a problem only in a certain historical context that defines it as a problem, and only in a certain configuration of power and exclusion that sets the form of the problem.

Du Boisian sociology brings to fruition C. Wright Mills's assertion of the sociological imagination: the combination of biography, structure, and history.[19] Du Boisian sociology invites us to rethink the place of personal experience in sociological analysis, as it recognizes the importance of theorizing from lived experience. Racism and colonialism are not theoretical abstractions constructed from observation and theoretical discussion. They are real and a part of many people's everyday lived experiences. For Du Boisian sociologists, the concepts of racialized modernity and racial colonial capitalism emerge from everyday lived experience and social practice.

Yes, experiences are personal and individual, but the point is not just to narrate one's life. It is to use one's lived experience as a starting point to examine the contours and mechanisms of exclusion and domination. Du Bois did this often, but the main model for this analytical approach is *Dusk of Dawn*, appropriately subtitled *An Autobiography of the Concept of Race*. In the opening section, the "Apology," Du Bois argues that his life had significance only *"because it was part of a Problem"* that is the central problem of our times. This is a method that has been widely accepted for some time in interdisciplinary fields, such as gender and ethnic studies. Some sociologists employ this approach, often working within the subfield of auto-ethnography. A Du Boisian sociology will expand the use of this method in sociological research.

Finally, Du Bois also engaged in the use of fiction to develop his social analysis. In this way, he was free to bring together analysis, critique, and normative statements and—he hoped—to reach a wider public with his sociological and political concerns. While we are not suggesting that to be a Du Boisian sociologist one must start writing novels, we do believe that a serious reflection on Du Bois's use of fiction invites us to consider the role of form, voice, and medium in our scholarly work. It would be difficult to convince the mainstream of sociology, which aims to bolster the scientific credentials of the discipline, to accept this mode of theorizing and arguing. A contemporary Du Boisian sociology, however, is also a public sociology, a sociology committed to an emancipatory—anticolonial and antiracist—project, and as a result, committed to bringing its ideas, analyses, and concerns to a broad audience. And public sociology can certainly benefit from the use of the narrative imagination of sociologists for the purpose of influencing the public sphere and public debate.[20]

A Subaltern Standpoint

A fourth pillar of a Du Boisian methodology is the taking of a subaltern standpoint. Standpoint theory is rooted in the sociological insight that our social position and experience condition, although they do not determine, what we can see of the world and how we see it. Du Bois's sociology was not a neutral sociology, but a sociology that privileged the subaltern standpoint in theorizing racialized modernity, with the expressed aim of dismantling those racial and colonial structures of oppression that he was critiquing. Standpoint theory has been subjected to two related types of critiques. One is that of essentialism, that is, that it reifies and homogenizes the identities of those whose position it takes, and the other one is that of epistemological privilege, suggesting that the subaltern necessarily has a better understanding of social life than the dominant group.[21]

We believe that Du Bois's analysis of double consciousness addresses these two critiques. The theory of double consciousness argues that the perception of the world of the dominant groups is determined by the fact that they are mostly ignorant of life behind the veil. On the other hand, those who live behind the veil, the racialized and the colonized, know of racism and coloniality through its direct impact on their lives. However, the views from both sides of the veil are the result of historical processes of subjectivity formation, and they are not essential or primordial. Furthermore, there is not one but many positions and worldviews behind the veil. Du Bois showed how living behind the veil does not mean unity or homogeneity of worldviews. There is no one true and authentic subaltern standpoint, but rather many positions that deal with the shared experience of oppression and exclusion.

Du Bois's analysis also answers the question of epistemic privilege. As Du Bois points out, the racialized subject can develop parochial outlooks or may seek to imitate the dominant group. Not everyone living behind the veil will develop a second sight. And even if the racialized subject develops a critical consciousness, different people will not necessary develop the same critical analysis of the structures of oppression. What a subaltern standpoint means is that people living behind the veil have a set of shared experiences that can lead to the emergence of different forms of critical analysis of the structures of racial and colonial oppression. For those sociologists who live behind the veil, theories of racialization, power, and domination are not abstract ideas; they are a very real fact of everyday life. Yet this does not mean that they will develop a unified worldview. It just means that all of them have to deal with racialization and racism. This common experience may (or may not) lead them to develop a sharper and more critical view of the work of the color line. Furthermore, as Du Bois shows in his biography of John Brown, those living outside the veil can also develop a critical consciousness, pierce the veil, and understand the nature of domination. But this implies that they need to become conscious of their own dominant positionality and try to see the world through the eyes of the racialized, something that is difficult to do for the dominant group, and usually also implies paying a personal cost.

Sociologist Julian Go's recent argument for a postcolonial sociology proposes a perspectival realism as an alternative to the universal abstract standpoint that is hegemonic in sociology. By this Go means that no theory can claim to obtain full knowledge of social reality, and that looking at the world from different perspectives allows us to see different aspects of it, thus enriching our sociological understanding of social life. Go urges sociology to embrace a pluri-perspectival approach instead of its current neutral-universal one. We join Go's call for a multiplicity of standpoints in the discipline, as this indeed would improve sociological analysis.

A contemporary Du Boisian sociology accepts, of course, that other approaches and standpoints can generate useful and interesting knowledge. There is no doubt that the mainstream standpoint is not universal. William James understood the formation of the self from the perspective of white middle-class Americans and failed to consider the self-formation experiences of Blacks, women, immigrants, or poor people. Marx looked at capitalism from the perspective of the Western European intellectuals and workers and failed to see the centrality of racism and colonialism for historical capitalism. Yet, Du Bois was able to build on both of them to construct his analysis of racial and colonial capitalism and racialized subjectivity. Similarly, world-system analysis is a critical perspective that looks at the world from the perspective of the history of expansion of the core and the social dynamics of the world-system as a whole. Subaltern perspectives are often lost in this analysis, but the knowledge generated by it can be useful for people trying to understand historical and global racial and colonial structures of domination.

Furthermore, other forms of sociological analysis, such as analyses of state institutions or studies of the work of organizations such as schools or hospitals, can generate knowledge about the work of different forms of power, which can be used in the analysis of historically embedded forms of domination, exclusion, and subaltern agency. To that extent, the perspectival realism advocated by Go would indeed make for a more diverse and vibrant sociology. The specific contribution of a contemporary Du Boisian sociology to this pluri-perspectival approach, however, would be to embrace a subaltern standpoint, as this is the imperative of a critical and emancipatory sociology.

Decolonizing the Sociological Imagination

Embracing a contemporary Du Boisian sociology would also entail changes in the training of graduate students. Most of the emphasis in training in sociology graduate programs is on teaching methodological skills, particularly quantitative skills. Many departments also have qualitative or ethnography courses, and most departments have a research design course geared to teach the design of research projects. Most of these courses teach a version of the positivist hypotheses testing research design. Most sociology departments also have a theory course or two in which they survey a variety of canonical theorist, theories, and systems of thought. While the aim is to introduce graduate students to those regarded as the greatest thinkers known to our discipline, theory courses usually teach a Eurocentric canon that includes Marx, Weber, Durkheim, and Bourdieu, to which sometimes are added Simmel, Goffman, Gramsci, Habermas, or Foucault. This creates the illusion that the only sociologists who have ever generated important theory were white and nearly always men. Increasingly, Du Bois is also added to this list. Theory instructors often feel the pressure from graduate students to include his work, but the general knowledge of it is limited, and it is typically taught as an add-on at the end of the syllabus. There are of course great differences and variation among graduate programs, but we believe that a survey of graduate programs would offer a picture not too different from the one we paint here.

A contemporary Du Boisian sociology would adopt a different training model. To begin with, as a critical approach, Du Boisian sociology emphasizes the development of critical theorizing skills. For this purpose, a contemporary Du Boisian sociology would advocate the teaching of a set of theorists that come from the racialized and colonized peripheries, beyond the Eurocentric canon. We believe that Du Boisian sociologists, as well as mainstream sociologists, should read and be familiar with the work of antiracist and anticolonial thinkers and scholars such as Ida B. Wells, Anna Julia Cooper, C. L. R. James, Aimé Cesairé, Walter Rodney, Audre Lorde, and Frantz Fanon, as well as with the work of contemporary decolonial and postcolonial theorists such as Dipesh Chakrabarty, Glenn Sean Coulthard, Sylvia Winter, Gurminder K. Bhambra, Julian Go, and Manuela Boatcă. In developing a Du Boisian sociology, we are not urging that Du Bois be canonized alongside the existing "founding fathers of the discipline." We are calling for something much more transformational: to introduce into the discipline an alternative epistemological genealogy of the modern world, a genealogy that emerged from its peripheries and exclusions. Learning this alternative lineage of theorists will begin the process of decolonization of the sociological imagination—the process of bringing the histories, experiences, and ideas of modernity's outcasts into the center of sociological thinking.

A contemporary Du Boisian sociology is not only a theoretical enterprise. As in Du Bois's own work, a Du Boisian sociology would put strong emphasis on thorough and systematic empirical research. To that extent, Du Boisian sociologists should receive training in qualitative and quantitative methods, the discipline's current tools of the trade. But the focus of the training of Du Boisian sociologists should emphasize the rooting of empirical studies in history and in particular social contexts, along with the importance of linking empirical investigation to an overall theoretical framework. This means training students in historical methods and historical reasoning, and expanding the definition of mixed-methods research to include historical analysis, as Du Bois did in his many community studies. Furthermore, students should also be trained in phenomenological analysis.

As we mentioned, a contemporary Du Boisian sociology would insist on a different approach to generalization. Rather than seeking abstraction and generalization from a case or set of cases, a contemporary Du Boisian sociology would emphasize historical context and would proceed to generalize through cautious induction. This means that rather than be trained to seek decontextualized generalizable concepts or patterns, students would be taught to situate concepts and theories in space and time. A contemporary Du Boisian sociology would not oppose generalization, but it would emphasize that generalization should emerge from the careful contrast and comparison of local and historical contexts and that, although concepts travel, when they do so they require translation and adaptation.

The goal of this program of training is to decolonize the sociological imagination—to train sociologists to have a critical mind, to understand the roots and characteristics of their time, and to be committed to producing emancipatory knowledge. Of course, changing graduate programs of training in this direction will not be easy. But there is a rising wave of young scholars and graduate students who are seeking alternative ways of practicing the discipline, which is currently perceived as stale. A contemporary Du Boisian sociology is an alternative for these young scholars.

An Emancipatory Sociology

In the words of Martin Luther King Jr., "It was never possible to know where the scholar Du Bois ended and the organizer Du Bois began. The two qualities in him were a single, unified force."[22] Du Bois was all his life a scholar, a public intellectual, and an organizer. There was no line separating these three areas of practice. His scholarship was rooted in his experience as an individual and in his practice as an organizer, and his activities as an organizer and public intellectual were informed and guided by his scholarship. For Du Bois, scholarship was at the service of emancipation, which for him meant undoing the color line, racism, and colonialism. We envision a contemporary Du Boisian sociology that is at the service of emancipation. Identifying the political and organizational forms of an emancipated society goes beyond the scope of this book. This is a question for which there may be many answers, but in a very broad sense, it means recognizing everyone's humanity while recognizing the right to difference, and being committed to making the world more equal and more habitable for everybody. This in turn implies dismantling the color line, along with all oppressions based on gender, class, and sexuality.

An emancipatory sociology implies a commitment to public sociology. Du Bois showed us that there are so many ways to do this—from being a public intellectual and intervening in public debates through media such as opinion pieces or blogs to engaging in organizing, working with grassroots or rights organizations, and intervening as experts in public disputes. Currently, the mainstream of the discipline does not value this kind of sociological practice. Although we hold "policy relevance" in high regard, this notion is very narrowly and technocratically conceived and seen as worthy only when these contributions directly impact the process of policy making.[23] Furthermore, mainstream sociology detaches policy making from the political process that makes policy making possible. A contemporary Du Boisian sociology will embrace sociologists' participation in the policy and public sphere as advocates, organizers, or policy advisors. And it will also recognize that the notion of the "public" extends far beyond policymakers.

The prevalent ideas and theories of social scientists can permeate the public sphere, from which consensuses and common sense emerge. Du Bois understood this well, and he always repackaged the knowledge he generated through his research and translated it to lay audiences. Du Boisian sociologists should follow this example, and seek to get the hard-earned knowledge that they produce into the hands of the people who can use it in their own efforts to get free. Sociologists can contribute a great deal to public discussions through the arts, K–12 educational programming, and other approaches that reach a broad range of people. Until these activities are more substantially recognized and counted by the discipline, Du Boisian sociologists will have to support one another in this endeavor.

An emancipatory sociology, however, implies more than a public sociology. It implies a critical scholarly practice, an understanding that the sphere of ideas can in itself be a sphere of emancipatory praxis aimed toward sharpening our understanding of the mechanisms of oppression and imagining a more humane world. An emancipatory sociology also implies a commitment to teaching, to education, and to the formation of critical consciousness among our students. This does not mean proselytizing or spreading a Du Boisian orthodoxy. An emancipatory sociology offers a genuine invitation to be reflexive and critical, to question established knowledge, and to ask the hard questions of ourselves as an intellectual community about how to make our discipline more inclusive. It also implies a commitment to mentoring and supporting students, particularly students of color and first-generation students, those for whom the university is a potentially hostile environment. An emancipatory sociology involves working to make sure that those who usually lack access to our institutions and professional positions can finally acquire that access. This is a call for reflecting about the everyday practices of teaching, mentoring, hiring, and promotion within the academy. This is a call to work for change in the one area in which we can have a strong impact—our professional world.

Finally, an emancipatory sociology implies a commitment to the development of a professional ethic of cooperation and solidarity. Professionalization is often understood as embracing the values of extreme individualism and competition. The model of professional success is one of concern with individual achievement, where anything that distracts from that goal is seen as detrimental. An emancipatory sociology puts a greater emphasis on the value and importance of collaborating, sharing, mentoring, doing things for others, and also—no small issue—being kind and supportive towards one another. To be sure, we are not against individuals striving to develop their own careers. But we believe that the exclusive focus on individual striving creates a professional milieu that is costly for individuals and reproduces within the academy the very inequalities and exclusions that we study. Moreover, and importantly, this approach imposes a cost when it comes to the progress of research and ideas. Progress in our fields of study emerges from exchange and cooperation rather than from isolated work. An ethics of solidarity and cooperation would allow us to build a more inclusive academy and to produce much livelier debates and greater scientific progress.

Taking the Path Not Taken

In writing this book we had two goals. The first was to define the tenets of Du Bois's theoretical and empirical sociology. We joined the company of the generations of Du Boisian scholars who have long argued that his was a unique and original approach and that he is one of the founders of the discipline. For us, writing the book involved an awe-inspiring journey of discovery of the depth and sophistication of Du Bois's research and activism. We hope that we have convincingly demonstrated the contemporary relevance of engaging with the full body of his work. We realize that not every Du Boisian would agree with our reading of it, but we hope that at the least this book generates lively debate.

Our second goal was to explore ways to bring Du Bois's work to bear on our practice as sociologists—in other words, to propose the outlines of a contemporary Du Boisian sociology. A contemporary Du Boisian sociology is a reflexive endeavor that is rooted in the origins of the discipline and aims to expand the boundaries of sociological practice in the present. The contemporary Du Boisian sociology that we advocate draws from Du Bois's work and other critical traditions within and outside sociology to build a sociological practice that is rooted in a critical understanding of our historical present and provides tools for the empirical research of forms of oppression and resistance to them.

It is worth repeating: A contemporary Du Boisian sociology is not a sociology of race. Rather, it is a sociological approach that puts racism and colonialism in all their forms at the center of sociological analysis. Furthermore, a contemporary Du Boisian sociology is guided by a commitment to undoing the present forms of the color line and all forms of oppression, patriarchy, and exclusion. We believe that the time has come to bring Du Bois to the center of sociology. Creating a Du Boisian sociology equipped to handle the problems of the twenty-first century, however, is a collective endeavor. We hope, dear reader, that you will accept our invitation to think about how we can take today the path the discipline rejected a century ago.

ACKNOWLEDGMENTS

Writing this book took four long years of work. Analyzing the broad corpus of Du Bois's work to understand his sociology and its implications for the present is not something that either of us could have done alone. This book is the product of a true collaboration between two people who think alike on most issues but don't always agree. But working through our differences made our book richer and better.

Throughout the process we enjoyed the collaboration and support of many people whom we want to acknowledge. First, we want to acknowledge a group of people at Brown University who, for José, were at first students and, for Karida, were at first fellow graduate students. Now, some of them are also our colleagues. These young scholars created a Du Boisian Collective that served as an incredible source of ideas, support, friendship, and comradeship. They were our fiercest critics. But their fierce critique was born of support for the project. Our book would not be what it is without their input. These young Du Boisians are Michael Rodriguez Muñiz (now at Northwestern), Michael Murphy (now at the University of Pittsburgh), Marcelo Bohrt (now at American University), Ricarda Hammer, Tina Park, Syeda Masood, Maria Ortega, Amy Chin, Prahb Kehal, and Laura Garbes. We are forever indebted to them for being our primary intellectual community throughout this journey. We are grateful that we can continue to count on them to push forward the Du Boisian agenda.

At Brown we also enjoyed the feedback and friendship of Michael Kennedy and Paget Henry, who supported our endeavor and were there for us in moments of doubt as colleagues, mentors, and friends. We also want to thank Dan Hirschman and Tina Park, who read an early version of the manuscript. Their generosity is only matched by the thoughtfulness of their comments. Other friends and colleagues provided us with feedback and have rooted for the project as we went through the writing. We want to thank Orly Clergé, Trina Vithayathil, Zophia Edwards, Cedric de Leon, and Jennifer Mueller for reading and commenting on parts of the manuscript and for their continuous encouragement of our work. Our thanks also to Earl Wright II, Aldon Morris, Cheryl Townsend Gilkes, Dee Royster, and Marcus Anthony Hunter for their continuous encouragement and support of our work.

Several colleagues invited us to present our work or organized panels in which we could discuss our ideas at different fora. Indeed, we greatly benefited from the feedback we received in presenting this work at different instances, including the 2017 Social Theory Forum, the American Sociological Association, the Eastern Sociological Society, the Departments of Sociology at U Mass–Amherst, the University of Georgia, and the W. E. B. Du Bois Symposium at Harvard University. We want to thank Diana Graizboard, Saida Grundi, Moon-Kie Jung, Patricio Korzeniewicz, and Julian Go for creating opportunities for us to present our work

While this was a collaborative work through and through, we also have people who have been important to each of us separately.

I, Karida, would like to offer my deepest gratitude to my family for their unconditional love and support. My parents, Richard Climber Brown and Arnita Davis Brown, are my foundation. They simultaneously keep me lifted up and grounded as I navigate the tumults of academic life. My big brother, Richard Charu Brown, my sister-in-law, Latobia Brown, and my beautiful nieces and nephew, Chania, Sy'rai, Eisele, and Chazz (rest-in-heaven), are my inspiration. I love you all. I also thank my beloved partner, Charly Palmer. Thank you for keeping me draped in a regal cloak of love.

I also want to thank the motley crew of friends and family who continually hold me down: Marcus Anthony Hunter, Danté Maurice Taylor, Zandria Robinson, Courtney Patterson-Faye, Nicole Truesdell, Kimberly Kay Hoang, Abigail Sewell, Saida Grundy, Larry Wade, Alicia and Kola Jegede, Vanessa Hunter, Chantal Spencer, Nicole Gray, Kara Pierre, and Tabatha Pirtle. Y'all my tribe.

Last, but certainly not least, I want to thank you, José. It has been such an honor and a joy to work with you on bringing this book to fruition. You are my mentor, colleague, friend, and as far as the Browns are concerned, a part of our family. Thank you for giving me a mic, even before I knew I had anything of import to say in this world.

I, José, would like to start by thanking you, Karida, for our shared work on this book. This book is the most meaningful project I have been a part of in my academic career, and it would not have happened without you and without the two of us working together. Working on this book with you showed me that a different academic life is possible.

I want to acknowledge friends and colleagues in Argentina. I made it my mission to introduce Du Bois's work into my country of birth. This is a challenge because his work is not known there, and the idea of a world structured around the color line is not widely accepted in the Argentine academic world. I was fortunate to find there colleagues who immediately saw the importance of this work and want to see it in Spanish together with Du Bois's own writings. My thanks to Juan Francisco Martinez Pería, Federico Pita, Pablo Sebastian Gomez, and Menara Guizardi for their enthusiastic support of this project. Other colleagues invited me to present my work, engaged with my arguments, challenged me, and helped me clarify and improve my thinking. For creating opportunities to discuss Du Bois's work and for engaging with this book, my thanks go to Luis Donatello, Alejandro Grimson, Fortunato Mallimaci, Silvina Merenson, and Marisa Pineau.

I also want to acknowledge my parents, Jose Alberto Itzigsohn and Sara Dina Minuchin Itzigsohn. In their nineties, they read all the drafts of the chapters that I produced, engaged with them, learned from them, and constantly encouraged me to finish the book. They very much wanted to see it in print. In this moment of happiness, as the book is going into production, I lament that time caught up with them and they are not with us to see it. May their memory be a blessing.

Finally, we both want to thank Ilene Kalish and NYU Press. Ilene heard about our interest in Du Bois and contacted us at the precise moment in which we decided to write this book. She was supportive of the project from the beginning and throughout the writing process and bore with us through all our delays in meeting deadlines. It was great to work with such a supportive and visionary editor. Last but not least, we want to acknowledge Constance Rosenblum, who edited the text and forced us to make it much better and much more readable.

GLOSSARY OF KEY CONCEPTS

This glossary aims to make it easier for the reader to understand how we use certain key theoretical concepts in the analysis of Du Bois's work. We discuss and define these concepts throughout the book, but we offer this glossary as a resource where the reader can easily look for explanation of our use and understanding of them.

AGENCY
Agency refers to the capacity of human beings to act and shape the world in which they live. To what extent people have the ability to consciously shape their lives or are subject to the structures of power of the world in which they live is one of the central questions of the social sciences.

BLACK
Black refers to people of African descent, living in the continent or in diaspora. Black people share an imposed racial categorization and, in most cases, a voluntary identification as a member of this global racial group. While black, the color, is written in lower case, Black, the group of people, is capitalized throughout this text.

CAPITALISM
By *capitalism* we refer to a historical social system based on the global production of commodities for markets through the exploitation of labor. For Du Bois, colonial and neocolonial forms of political organization are central to *historical capitalism*, that is, the concrete historical form in which capitalism unfolded (as opposed to abstract, stylized ideas about capitalism). Race and racism are both a consequence and a structuring principle of historical capitalism. Hence, we speak of *racial and colonial capitalism*.

Coloniality

Coloniality refers to the ways of knowing the world and power structures characteristics of colonialism that continued after the formal fall of colonial empires. That is, the new independent nations emerging from decolonization rest upon the *racialized* and neocolonial structures of domination created by colonialism. Colonial empires may have disappeared, but the legacies of empires still affect our lives.

Color Line

For Du Bois, the central social structure of his time was the *color line*, that is, the division of people into racialized groups. For Du Bois the *color line* was the product of colonialism and the transatlantic slave trade that led to the invention of whiteness, and the denial of humanity of racialized groups and the multiple forms of exclusion, oppression, exploitation, and inequality constructed along racial lines. Although the *color line* is historically the product of slavery and colonialism, it became a force of its own in shaping our world. Du Bois saw the *color line* as global, but taking different forms in different places and at different times.

Double Consciousness

By *double consciousness* Du Bois refers to the construction of the *racialized self* and *racialized subjectivity*. Du Bois describes *double consciousness* as a feeling of twoness, of belonging to two different social worlds—on the one hand, the Black world that is humanity affirming, and on the other one, the white world that denies the humanity of the racialized person. This construction of the self is structured around the *veil*, which is Du Bois's metaphor to describe how the *color line* appears in interpersonal relations. In addition to a sense of twoness, *double consciousness* generates in the racialized person the possibility of *second sight*, that is, the possibility of seeing and criticizing the world behind the *veil*, the world of whiteness. On the other hand, the *veil* makes it impossible for whites to see and recognize the humanity of racialized people (unless they recognize white supremacy and consciously act to dismantle it).

INTERSECTIONALITY

Intersectionality refers to the ways in which the interconnected effects of different dimensions of power and inequality create different social positions and experiences. *Intersectional analysis* is rooted in Black feminism and was first articulated in the late nineteenth century by intellectuals and activists such as Anna Julia Cooper, who argued for the specificity of Black women's experience vis-à-vis Black men and white women. Du Bois developed the analysis of the *intersectionality* of class and race and also a limited analysis of the *intersections* of race and gender.

INTERSUBJECTIVITY

Intersubjectivity means that our understanding and experience of the world is social, that is, shared with other people. What we see as we go about our lives and how we interpret our encounters with others and the world are shaped in our interactions with other people and are shared with people with whom we interact.

LAW AND CHANCE

For Du Bois *chance* refers to the ability of people to make undetermined choices, that is, Du Bois asserts that there is a space for free will in human action. For Du Bois, the multiple forms of individual and collective action of the racialized could challenge the *color line*. The ability of the racialized and the colonized to imagine change is rooted in *second sight*, an element of *double consciousness* that potentially allows racialized people to see beyond their dehumanizing present. But the action of the racialized takes place within the constraints imposed by the historical power structures and social relations of *racial and colonial capitalism*, that is, by what he refers to as *law*. For him *law* refers to the historical and structural limits to the ability of individuals to make free choices and shape their world. For Du Bois the goal of sociology is to determine empirically the scope of *chance* and the limits of *law* in social action.

PHENOMENOLOGY

Phenomenology in sociology is the study of how we experience the world in our everyday lives. It is the examination and description of the structures of our *intersubjective* worlds that are constructed through social interaction.

RACIALIZATION

Racialization is the social process through which different groups of people are assigned *racial* labels and characteristics. *Racialization*, the social construction and reconstruction of race, is a politically and culturally contentious process through which the world of *racialized modernity* is reproduced. For Du Bois *racialization* was the product of the emergence of *racial and colonial capitalism*, but it became the structuring force of *subjectivity* and the social order in *racialized modernity*.

RACIALIZED MODERNITY

Modernity refers to our contemporary historical period. It is defined by reference to various social processes, including urbanization and industrialization, the rise of bureaucracy, the application of science and technology to production, the deepening of the division of labor, and the spread of secularization and democracy. It is usually seen as the image of a successful present or a desirable future. But modernity was always entangled with colonialism and racism. For Du Bois, the defining characteristic of modernity was the *color line*: the invention of whiteness, and the multiple forms of exclusion, oppression, exploitation, and inequality constructed along colonial and racial lines. For Du Bois *modernity* is *racialized modernity* from its inception.

RACIAL STATE

The concept of the *racial state* points to the fact that in *racialized modernity*, politics and political power are organized along *racial lines*. That is, the state—the governing institutions that organize our social and political lives—is not a neutral organization but it reflects and reproduces the social power of white people. For Du Bois the *racial state* is based on a broad class alliance of white elites and the white working class. Similarly, for Du Bois, the *colonial state* was the product of an alliance between the colonial bourgeoisie and the white working class of colonial powers.

Self-formation

Self-formation is the process through which we come to understand who we are. This process develops through the internalization of the views of people who are important to us and of society in general. It takes place through interaction and communication. Du Bois's theory of *double consciousness* shows how the color line skews communication and interaction, and as a result, the *self* that emerges from these processes is a *racialized self.*

Social construction

Social construction refers to the idea that the institutions and understandings of our social world are the product of historical processes of social interaction and communication. Du Boisian sociology argues that *racialized modernity* is a historical *social construction.* That is, we need to understand how past *social constructions* shape our contemporary social world.

Standpoint theory

Standpoint theory is based in the sociological insight that our social position and experience affect, although they do not determine, what we can see of the world and how we see it. In other words, our knowledge of the world is rooted in our social experience. Du Boisian sociology privileges the *subaltern standpoint* in theorizing *racialized modernity.* By *subaltern standpoint,* we mean the standpoint of groups that are oppressed, dispossessed, marginalized, and exploited. Taking a *subaltern standpoint* means a critique of the *abstract universalism* that is widespread in the social sciences. *Abstract universalism* argues that the scientist can look at reality as a neutral observer and analyst.

Subjectivity

Subjectivity refers to how we understand, think, and feel about ourselves, other people, and the world we live in. Our understanding of social reality is formed through our interpretations of our everyday encounters with others and with the world. In a society organized around the color line, our understandings and feelings are shaped by *racialization.* Hence, we speak of *racialized subjec-*

tivity. Although our experiences are personal and individual, the understandings of the social world that emerge from interaction are shared with other members of society (otherwise we could not interact or communicate). We refer to these shared understandings as *intersubjectivity,* the shared construction of the social world.

NOTES

PREFACE

1 For the acknowledgment of Du Bois's work during the early twentieth century, see Robert W. Williams, "The Early Social Science of W. E. B. Du Bois," *Du Bois Review* 3, no. 2 (2006): 365– 94.

INTRODUCTION

1 We highlight here key moments of Du Bois's career as a sociologist. For a full biography of Du Bois, see Lewis, *W. E. B. Du Bois: Biography*; Du Bois, *Autobiography of W. E. B. Du Bois*; Lewis, *W. E. B. Du Bois, 1919–1963*.

2 King, *Honoring Dr. Du Bois*. Speech delivered at Carnegie Hall in New York City, February 23, 1968, on the one hundredth birthday of W. E. B. Du Bois.

3 Du Bois, *Dusk*, 10.

4 Shamoon Zamir argues that Hegel's *Phenomenology of the Spirit*, which Du Bois learned about from George Santayana, was a stronger influence on Du Bois's thought than James's pragmatism. Zamir's book makes a compelling case for this argument, but Du Bois acknowledged James's influence on him, and, as we argue in this book, there are strong elements of pragmatism in Du Bois's work. See Zamir, *Dark Voices*; West, *The American Evasion of Philosophy*.

5 Du Bois, *Autobiography of W. E. B. Du Bois*, 155.

6 Zimmerman, *Alabama in Africa*.

7 See Wright, *The First American School of Sociology*.

8 Du Bois, *Black Folk Then and Now*; Du Bois, *The World and Africa*.

9 Du Bois, "My Evolving Program for Negro Freedom," 47–48.

10 King, *Honoring Dr. Du Bois*.

11 George Padmore (1903–1959) was a leading Pan-African thinker, journalist, and organizer. He was born in Trinidad and moved to the United States, where he studied medicine. At the beginning of his political career, he joined the communist movement and spent time in the Soviet Union and in Europe organizing for the communist cause. In 1935 he broke with communism and became fully engaged with Pan-Africanism. Padmore was the main organizer of the fifth Pan-African Congress that took place in Manchester in 1945. During the last years of his life, he moved to Ghana and worked closely with Kwame Nkrumah.

12 Morris, "Sociology of Race."

13 Morris, *The Scholar Denied*. Morris establishes clearly that Du Bois created a school of sociology, traces its origins, and describes its relations with other contemporaries. Morris argues that it was Du Bois who influenced Weber's thought, and not the other way around as is usually argued. He additionally shows how Park and the Chicago school ignored Du Bois's scholarship even though they were aware and cognizant of it.

14 Wright, *The First American School of Sociology*. Wright brings the Atlanta studies to the center and front of the attention of the discipline, emphasizing how they are the precursors of contemporary sociology, and again, how they were ignored by the discipline.

15 Rabaka, *Against Epistemic Apartheid*. Rabaka argues that Du Bois developed a unique brand of sociology characterized by a focus on the specific problems of American society and presents a detailed description of the contributions of Du Bois to several areas of sociology. We disagree, though, with the claim that Du Bois's sociology was specific to America. Instead, we argue that Du Bois was a global theorist.

16 Emirbayer and Desmond, *The Racial Order*, 1.

17 "Coloniality" refers to the ways of knowing the world that emerge under colonialism and continue to structure the postcolonial world. Quijano, "Coloniality of Power."

18 Emirbayer and Desmond state that their book is not only about the racial order—that "at the highest levels of analysis, there is nothing so special or unique about race, and believing otherwise only reifies and calcifies that which, like class or gender, is but a well-founded fiction"; Du Bois, *The Autobiography of W. E. B. Du Bois*, 155.

19 "Racialized modernity" is our concept, which we use to describe Du Bois's sociology. It was not a term used by Du Bois.

20 Du Bois, *Autobiography of W. E. B. Du Bois*, 155.

21 Du Bois, *Autobiography of W. E. B. Du Bois*, 155.

22 For the forms of racism prevalent in the early-twentieth-century social sciences, see McKee, *Sociology and the Race Problem*.

23 In this definition of subjectivity, we are following the definition proposed by anthropologist Sherry Ortner. See Ortner, "Subjectivity and Cultural Critique."

24 Referring to Du Bois's work as addressing the phenomenology of racialized subjectivity is our reading of his work. These are not Du Bois's words. The concept is based on our reading of *Souls of Black Folk*, *Dusk of Dawn*, and other texts. Yet, if Zamoon Shamir is right and Du Bois was influenced by Hegel's *Phenomenology of Spirit* in writing *Souls of Black Folk*, then Du Bois was intentionally conducting phenomenological analysis without calling it that. See Shamir, *Dark Voices*. For another text linking *Souls* to the Hegel's *Phenomenology* see Shaw, *W. E. B. Du Bois*.

25 See James's 1884 lecture *The Dilemma of Determinism*.

26 For Du Bois's differentiation between race as a category of exclusion and Blackness as a basis for group formation, see Chandler, "The Figure of W. E. B.

Du Bois." For the global dimensions of Du Bois's thought see Chandler, *Toward an African Future*.

27 Du Bois, "The Conservation of Races," in Chandler, ed., *The Problem of the Color Line*, 54.

28 Du Bois, "The Conservation of Races," in Chandler, ed., *The Problem of the Color Line*, 54.

29 For thorough discussions of "The Conservation of Races" see Appiah, *Lines of Descent*; Chandler, "On Paragraph Four of 'The Conservation of Races.'"

30 Du Bois, "The Conservation of Races," in Chandler, ed., *The Problem of the Color Line*, 54.

31 In *Lines of Descent* Appiah emphasizes the Herderian roots of Du Bois's understanding of race in "Conservation" and of the concept of striving that is so central in his early works. Appiah also argues that although the Herderian paradigm emphasizes the uniqueness of cultural groups, it also asserts the equality between the groups.

32 Du Bois, "The Study of Negro Problems."

33 See Du Bois, *The Health and Physique of the Negro American*.

34 Du Bois believed that the racial understanding of Darwinism, which emphasized the survival of the fittest, created harmful barriers between peoples, impeding the contact between the elites of different groups and in this way hampering human progress, which, following pragmatism, he understood as a process of adaptation to the surrounding context. The early Du Bois embraced an alternative understanding of Darwinism. In *John Brown* he states, "Freedom of development and equality of opportunity is the demand of Darwinism and this calls for the abolition of hard and fast lines between races, just as it called for the breaking down of barriers between classes. Only in this way can the best in humanity be discovered and conserved, and only thus can mankind live in peace and progress." Du Bois, *John Brown*, 295.

35 Du Bois, *Dusk*, 137–38.

36 Du Bois, *Dusk*, 153.

37 Du Bois, *Dusk*, 133.

38 For Du Bois's own description of his evolving thought, see his 1944 essay "My Evolving Program for Negro Freedom." He also describes and analyzes the evolution of his thought in *Dusk of Dawn* and his posthumously published *Autobiography of W. E. B. Du Bois*.

39 Chandler, ed., *The Problem of the Color Line*, 54.

40 Gooding-Williams asserts that Du Bois's early theories were theories of leadership. See Gooding-Williams, *In the Shadow of Du Bois*.

41 See his early essays such as "The Relation of the Negroes to the Whites in the South" (1901), "The Talented Tenth" (1903), and "The Development of a People." The three essays are included in Chandler, ed., *The Problem of the Color Line*.

42 Du Bois, *John Brown*. In that book Du Bois summarizes his changing position on the question of the uplifting of the masses, asserting that

the freedmen did not, as the philanthropists of the sixties apparently expected, step in forty years from slavery to nineteenth century civilization.
Neither, on the other hand, did they, as the ex-masters confidently predicted,
retrograde and die. Contrary to both views, they chose a third and apparently quite unabated way. From the great, sluggish, almost imperceptibly
moving mass, they sent larger and larger numbers of faithful workmen and
artisans, some merchants and professional men, and even men of educational ability and discernment. They developed no world geniuses, no mil-
lionaires, no great captains of industry, no artists of the first rank; but they
did in forty years get rid of the greater part of their total illiteracy, accumulate a half-billion dollars of property in homesteads, and gain now and then
respectful attention in the world's ears and eyes.

Du Bois, *John Brown*, 282–83.

43 Du Bois never got completely rid of his elitism. See, for example, his 1941 address to the presidents of Black land-grant colleges urging them to join a new
cycle of Atlanta studies. There he states that if the lives of the Black poor were
improved, "the group will become nearer to actual equality with their fellow Americans and to civilized people the world over, and will thus remove
from color prejudice a very real reason for its perpetuation." *Autobiography of
W. E. B. Du Bois*, 312. Still, after his first tenure in Atlanta, in most of his work
he develops a different take on the Black masses, one that values more their
capacity for agency.

44 We believe that it is important to address the biographical contexts of all social
theorists. If we did this we would realize how much theory is rooted in lived
experience and how much the supposedly universal works of European and
North American theorists are in fact provincial accounts rooted in their place and
time. As Julian Go put it in his presentation at the W. E. B. Du Bois Symposium at
Harvard University (October 25–27, 2018), Marx, Weber, and Durkheim engaged
in fact in "me-search."

CHAPTER 1. DOUBLE CONSCIOUSNESS

1 Phenomenology in sociology is the analysis of how we experience the world in
everyday life. Du Bois does not call his analysis phenomenology, but that is what
he does in his analysis of double consciousness. Zamir Shamoon argues in *Dark
Voices* that Du Bois's analysis of double consciousness was influenced by Hegel's
analysis of the dialectic of the consciousness of master and slave in the *Phenomenology of Spirit*. This is a plausible argument. We argue that Du Bois's analysis
was also influenced by William James's pragmatism.

2 Double consciousness has long been part of debates among Africana and African
American studies scholars. See Paul Gilroy, *The Black Atlantic*; Gooding-Williams,
In the Shadow of Du Bois; Gordon, *Existentia Africana*; Rampersad, "The Art and
Imagination of W. E. B. Du Bois"; A. L. Reed et al., *W. E. B. Du Bois and American
Political Thought*; Smith, *Photography on the Color Line*; Zamir, *Dark Voices*.

3 Lemert, "A Classic from the Other Side of the Veil," 389.

4 For the concept of ontological myopia see Rodríguez-Muñiz, "Intellectual Inheritances."

5 Du Bois, *The Souls of Black Folk*, 2.

6 Critics of the theory of double consciousness assert that it just expressed common ideas about twoness and alienation present in Du Bois's time. Furthermore, they argue that the theory was just articulated by Du Bois in *Souls* and never taken up again. See, for example, Dennis, "Continuities and Discontinuities"; Dennis, "Du Bois's Concept of Double Consciousness." It is indeed true that the idea of twoness was present in the thinking of Du Bois's contemporaries, but Du Bois gave it a different and particular meaning. It is also true that Du Bois only laid out the conceptual framework for the theory of double consciousness in "Of Our Spiritual Strivings." Yet those concepts sketched in *Souls* informed his vast analysis of the lived experiences of Blacks and whites.

7 Du Bois, *The Souls of Black Folk*; Du Bois, *Dusk*.

8 There are, however, a few sociological works that engage seriously with *Souls* and the theory of double consciousness. See Blau and Brown, "Du Bois and Diasporic Identity"; Lemert, "A Classic from the Other Side of the Veil"; Rabaka, *Against Epistemic Apartheid*; Rawls, "'Race' as an Interaction Order Phenomenon"; Winant, *The World Is a Ghetto*; Wortham, *The Sociological Souls of Black Folk*.

9 Lemert, "A Classic from the Other Side of the Veil."

10 Du Bois had previously hinted at his differences with Booker T. Washington in a review of the latter's biography published in the *Dial* in July of 1901. But the essay in *Souls* develops a much more confrontational critique of Washington's positions. See "The Evolution of Negro Leadership," in Wortham, *The Sociological Souls of Black Folk*, 55–57.

11 Du Bois, *Dusk*, 221.

12 Du Bois, *Dusk*, 133.

13 Du Bois, *Souls*, xx. He articulated this idea for the first time in the "Address to the Nations of the World" of the First Pan-African Conference.

14 Quisumbing King, "Recentering US Empire."

15 Du Bois, "Apology," in *Dusk*, xl.

16 Du Bois's theorization of racialization and double consciousness anticipates Bourdieu's much later theorization of symbolic violence. See Bourdieu, *Language and Symbolic Power*.

17 James, *The Principles of Psychology*.

18 James, *The Principles of Psychology*, 293.

19 James, *The Principles of Psychology*, 294.

20 Mead, *On Social Psychology*, 200.

21 Mead, *On Social Psychology*, 208.

22 Mead, *On Social Psychology*, 219.

23 Mead, *On Social Psychology*, 278.

24 Mead, *On Social Psychology*, 272.

25 Cooley, *Human Nature and the Social Order*.
26 Cooley, *Human Nature and the Social Order*, 261.
27 Cooley, *Human Nature and the Social Order*, 262.
28 Alfred Schutz, *The Phenomenology of the Social World*.
29 Rawls, "'Race' as an Interaction Order Phenomenon," 244.
30 Du Bois, *Dusk*, 27.
31 Du Bois, *Dusk*, 130–31.
32 Du Bois, *Dusk*, 131.
33 Smith, *Photography on the Color Line*, 29.
34 Du Bois, *Dusk*, 135–36.
35 Du Bois, *Dusk*, 173.
36 . Wortham, "W. E. B. Du Bois," 144–72.
37 Du Bois, *The Souls of Black Folk*, 123.
38 Du Bois, *The Souls of Black Folk*, 123.
39 Du Bois, *The Souls of Black Folk*, 122.
40 Du Bois, *The Souls of Black Folk*, 30.
41 Du Bois, *Dusk*, 186.
42 Du Bois, *Dusk*, 187.
43 Du Bois, *Dusk*, 131.
44 Du Bois, *Dusk*, 187.
45 Du Bois, *Dusk*, 187.
46 Du Bois, *The Souls of Black Folk*, 2.
47 Du Bois, *The Souls of Black Folk*, 43.
48 Du Bois, *The Souls of Black Folk*, 148.
49 Du Bois, *The Souls of Black Folk*, 149.
50 Du Bois, *Dusk*, 58.
51 Du Bois, *Dusk*, 67.
52 Du Bois, *Dusk*, 140.
53 Blau and Brown, "Du Bois and Diasporic Identity," 221.
54 Du Bois, *Dusk*, 153.
55 Du Bois, *Dusk*, 171–72.
56 Bonilla Silva and his collaborators expand the work of French sociologist Pierre Bourdieu, who coined the concept of habitus. But the notion of racialized habitus was already present in Du Bois's analysis of racialized subjectivity. See Bonilla-Silva, Goar, and Embrick, "When Whites Flock Together"; Bourdieu, *The Logic of Practice*.
57 Chandler, "The Souls of an Ex-White Man."
58 Du Bois's biography of John Brown is also a superb analysis of collective action. The analysis of Brown's raid on Harpers Ferry is based on a combination of what today we would recognize as the political opportunity model, on the one hand, and the interpretative approach to social movements, on the other.
59 Du Bois, *The Autobiography of W. E. B. Du Bois*.
60 Chandler, ed., *The Problem of the Color Line*, 276.

61 See Du Bois, "Sociology Hesitant," in Chandler, ed., *The Problem of the Color Line*.

62 Chandler, ed., *The Problem of the Color Line*, 277.

63 In *Sociology Hesitant*, Du Bois brings to sociology the questions that William James addressed in his 1884 lecture titled "The Dilemma of Determinism." In that lecture, James accepts that there are contexts that constrain the choices of human action but argues that within those constraints there is always the possibility of choice and free will, emphasizing the importance of the question of the ethics of action.

64 Chandler, ed., *The Problem of the Color Line*, 278.

65 Du Bois, Letter from W. E. B. Du Bois to Kwame Nkrumah, February 7, 1957.

66 Du Bois, *Dusk*, 7.

67 Du Bois, *The Autobiography of W. E. B. Du Bois*, 324. In this book, written when Du Bois was in his nineties, he is reflecting on his sociological research program, emphasizing the point that he was a sociologist his entire life.

68 We thank Paget Henry for pointing out the normative attitude of hesitancy implied in Du Bois's argument.

69 Goffman, *The Presentation of Self in Everyday Life*.

70 Goffman, *Asylums*.

71 Goffman, *Stigma*.

72 Bourdieu, *Outline of a Theory of Practice*.

73 Sewell, *Logics of History*.

74 Sewell, *Logics of History*, 114.

75 A partial exception to this lack of attention to structural constraints was Herbert Blumer, the founder of symbolic interactionism—one of the sociological approaches derivative of pragmatism and one of the traditions that emerged from Chicago. Blumer did theorize how whiteness and racial inequality work, coining the concept of sense of group position and showing how the civil right movement only made dents on the color line. Blumer, *Selected Works of Herbert Blumer*.

76 Du Bois, *Dusk*, 30.

77 Du Bois, *The Souls of Black Folk*, 29.

78 Du Bois's work anticipates later critiques of colonialism such as Memmi, *The Colonizer and the Colonized*; Fanon, *Black Skin, White Masks*; Coulthard, *Red Skin, White Masks*.

79 Du Bois, "The Races in Conference." *Crisis* 1, no. 2 (December 1910): 17.

80 This is the problem that affected Marxist predictions concerning the development of working-class consciousness: They did not take into account the intersectionalities that shape the working class's experiences.

81 See Fanon, *Black Skin, White Masks*.

82 An example of a contemporary Du Boisian study of racialized subjectivity and agency is Karida Brown's *Gone Home*. This book examines the changing subjectivities of an African American mining community in eastern Kentucky as it goes through the transformations of the twentieth century. The book bridges the micro study of identity and subjectivity and the study of macro-level structural change.

It describes the encounters of the Black miners of Appalachia with different institutional forms of racism, their changing identities, and the construction of ideas of "home" across generations and structural transformations—particularly the Great Migration, school desegregation, and the civil rights movement. Brown uses life histories and historical sources in this study, and her research also involved the creation, along with members of the community, of a participatory digital archive and a public exhibit telling their story.

CHAPTER 2. RACIAL AND COLONIAL CAPITALISM

1 Kwame Nkrumah (1909–1972) was the leader of Ghana's independence and its first prime minister.

2 George Padmore (1903–1959), born Malcolm Nurse, was a Trinidadian activist, organizer, and intellectual who became one of the main figures of Pan-Africanism in the first half of the twentieth century. In the later years of his life he became one of Kwame Nkrumah's close advisers.

3 In this he anticipated today's rising postcolonial sociology. See Go, *Postcolonial Thought and Social Theory.*

4 Du Bois, *The Souls of Black Folk,* 9.

5 For a contemporary analysis, see Quisumbing King, "Recentering US Empire."

6 Du Bois, *The Souls of Black Folk,* 9.

7 Du Bois, "The Present Outlook for the Dark Races of Mankind," in Chandler, ed., *The Problem of the Color Line,* 111–37.

8 In "The Present Outlook for the Dark Races of Mankind," Du Bois criticizes colonialism, but has kind words for the ways in which England treated its colonial subjects. He even had positive words for Leopold II's Congo Free State. It is important to remember that the full extent of Leopold's crimes in Congo were not publicly known at the time of publication of this essay.

9 Du Bois, "The African Roots of War," in Du Bois, *W. E. B. Du Bois: A Reader,* 642–51.

10 Du Bois, *Darkwater.*

11 The text of the conference's address, "To the Nations of the World," asserts the following: "The problem of the twentieth century is the problem of the colour-line, the question as to how far differences of race—which show themselves chiefly in the colour of the skin and the texture of the hair—will hereafter be made the basis of denying to over half the world the right of sharing to their utmost ability the opportunities and privileges of modern civilization." Special Collections and University Archives, University of Massachusetts Amherst Libraries, http://credo.library.umass.edu.

12 The Bandung conference met in 1955 and brought together delegations from Asia and Africa. The conference is considered an important milestone in the formation of the Non-Aligned Movement, a movement of states, most of them from the Global South, that saw themselves as nonaligned with any of the major powers of the Cold War.

13 See Kenneth Mostern, "Bandung Conference," in Horne and Young, *W. E. B. Du Bois*, 23–24.

14 Martin Luther King delivered his speech "Honoring Dr. Du Bois" in February 1968, on the one hundredth anniversary of Du Bois's birth. The speech was delivered at Carnegie Hall, in New York City.

15 Robinson, *Black Marxism*, 195.

16 The previous books were *The Negro*, published in 1915, and *Black Folk Then and Now*, published in 1939.

17 We emphasize the theoretical importance of *Color and Democracy* and *The World and Africa*. The empirical claims of the books were based on the time's secondary literature and on Du Bois's own engagement with the anticolonial movement. Those claims may have been superseded by newer scholarship. This is certainly the case of the differences in the empirical claims of these three books. Du Bois always tried to rely on the most updated literature available to him. Yet this should not constitute an impediment for our theoretical engagement with these books. After all, there is a whole literature that discusses the empirical validity of Weber's *Protestant Ethic and the Spirit of Capitalism*, and nobody today will vouch for the empirical accuracy of Durkheim's major works, and yet, sociologists keep reading them for their theoretical arguments.

18 Du Bois, *Dusk*, 303. At the same time that he emphasized the importance of Marx's work, Du Bois asserted that he was not a communist and did not "believe in the dogma of inevitable revolution to right economic wrong" (202).

19 James, "Lectures on *The Black Jacobins*," 91.

20 Kenneth Pomeranz, one of the most important global historians, like Marx, emphasizes colonial extraction as the origin story of capitalism, but not as a continuous process. Rosa Luxemburg, a Marxist thinker, did see the colonies as central to capital accumulation beyond the origin point of capitalism, but she focused on its economic aspects, not on the racialization of labor and social relations. See Luxemburg, *The Accumulation of Capital*; Pomeranz, *The Great Divergence*.

21 When we say that historical capitalism is structured around racial and colonial differences, what we mean is that the dominant groups in the colonial centers, in their search for profits and domination, divided the population into different racial groups, and assigned them different positions in the division of labor, different bundles of rights, and different cultural meanings. These systems of racial classification became, in turn, a structuring force of the global social, cultural, and economic order.

22 For contemporary work on whiteness as willful ignorance, see Mueller, "Producing Colorblindness."

23 Du Bois's work is different from the subaltern school of thought in that he does not tell the stories of groups silenced in national histories. His analysis is also different from vindicatory histories that want to emphasize that Africa and African people had grandeur, culture, and development. What Du Bois aims to do is bring Africa and the African peoples to the center of world history.

24 Du Bois, *"The World and Africa,"* 47.
25 Du Bois, *"The World and Africa,"* 144.
26 Du Bois, *"The World and Africa,"* 270.
27 Du Bois, *"The World and Africa,"* 253.
28 Du Bois, *"The World and Africa,"* 23.
29 Du Bois, *"The World and Africa,"* 41.
30 Du Bois, *"The World and Africa,"* 22.
31 Du Bois, *"The World and Africa,"* 15.
32 Du Bois, *"The World and Africa,"* 310.
33 Du Bois, *"The World and Africa,"* 305.
34 Du Bois, *"The World and Africa,"* 284.
35 Du Bois, *Autobiography*, 403. He urged the newly independent African states to find a different path of development rooted in their own traditions and in friendship with the socialist bloc, particularly with China. From very early on, Du Bois saw in the rise of Asia the possibility of the emergence of an alternative world order to that of racialized modernity. He showed accurate foresight in understanding that the rise of Asia could pose a challenge to Western hegemony, but he was also blind to the problems involved in the rise of Asia. For example, he wrote approvingly of Japanese imperialism after his visit to Manchuria in 1936 and was blind to the destruction caused by the Great Leap Forward during his visit to China in 1959. He could not have predicted, though, the current relation between China and Africa, which for many analysts takes a neocolonial form. For a discussion of Du Bois's writings on Asia see Chandler, "A Persistent Parallax"; Mullen and Watson, *W. E. B. Du Bois on Asia*.
36 Du Bois, *"The World and Africa,"* 285.
37 Du Bois, *"The World and Africa,"* 285.
38 Du Bois, *"The World and Africa,"* 61.
39 Du Bois, *"The World and Africa,"* 270.
40 Du Bois, *"The World and Africa,"* 13.
41 Du Bois, *"The World and Africa,"* 103.
42 Du Bois, *"The World and Africa,"* 23.
43 Du Bois's analysis of lived experience started even before *Souls*. Shamoon Zamir discusses a short, unpublished story that Du Bois wrote at Harvard that is based on changing positions between a Black and a white student. Zamir, *Dark Voices*.
44 Du Bois, *"The World and Africa,"* 23.
45 Du Bois, *"The World and Africa,"* 38.
46 Du Bois's analysis is a form of radical humanism. He not only takes the standpoint of the oppressed but also asserts their humanity. Du Bois uses the human as the ontological category of analysis, not races. In that way he always puts racial groups in their historical context. It's not that that's who they are; it's who they've been historically made to be. Much like Fanon, he believed that the possibility of asserting our common humanity lay in the emancipation of the racialized and the colonial subjects and in the end of whiteness as a category of domination.

47 Du Bois, *Black Reconstruction in America*, 87.
48 James, "Lectures on *The Black Jacobins*," 93. James argues in his lectures that if he were to write *The Black Jacobins* again, he would take Du Bois's analysis in *Black Reconstruction* as a model.
49 Thompson, *The Making of the English Working Class*.
50 Du Bois, *Black Reconstruction in America*, 67.
51 Du Bois, *Black Reconstruction in America*, 121.
52 Du Bois, *Black Reconstruction in America*, 700–701.
53 Du Bois, "*The World and Africa*", 309. As we saw in the previous chapter, Du Bois makes a similar point in *Dusk*, where he argues that white people cannot remain true to their ideals or to the golden rule because they consistently choose white privilege over their ideals of justice and equality.
54 Du Bois, "*The World and Africa*", 309.
55 For another analysis of the fetishism of the colonial commodity see Lowe, *The Intimacies of Four Continents*.
56 Du Bois, "*The World and Africa*", 26.
57 Du Bois, "*The World and Africa*", 26.
58 Benjamin, *Illuminations*, 253–64.
59 Du Bois's work combines the analysis of the political economy of colonialism and neocolonialism with the analysis of the colonial and postcolonial cultural structures of domination and knowledge formation. The latter has been the area of postcolonial and decolonial analysis. See Bhambra, *Rethinking Modernity*; Go, *Postcolonial Thought and Social Theory*; Quijano, "Coloniality of Power and Euro-centrism in Latin America."
60 For an analysis of the structure of *Black Reconstruction* see Lemert, *Dark Thoughts*.
61 Du Bois anticipates the analysis of split labor markets developed in the 1970s by sociologist Edna Bonacich. See Bonacich, "A Theory of Ethnic Antagonism."
62 Du Bois, *Black Reconstruction in America*, 22.
63 Du Bois, *Black Reconstruction in America*, 12.
64 Du Bois, *Black Reconstruction in America*, 700.
65 Du Bois, "*The World and Africa*," 300.
66 Du Bois, "*The World and Africa*," 276.
67 Du Bois, "The Damnation of Women," in *Darkwater*, 105. *Darkwater* is a book of essays and poetry, texts criticizing and denouncing global racism and social injustice, and celebration of the Africana diaspora, its culture, and its struggles.
68 James, "The Profeminist Politics of W. E. B. Du Bois," 147.
69 James, "The Profeminist Politics of W. E. B. Du Bois," 157.
70 Du Bois, *Darkwater*, 96.
71 Cheryl Townsend Gilkes argues that it is this suffering that informs the unique standpoint of African American women. See Gilkes, "The Margin as the Center of a Theory of History."
72 Du Bois, *Darkwater*, 100.

73 Du Bois, *Darkwater*, 104.

74 Du Bois, *Darkwater*, 107.

75 The Moynihan Report, titled "The Negro Family: A Case for National Action," was a policy document written by then assistant secretary of labor and later senator Daniel Patrick Moynihan. The report argued that the structure and culture of Black families were responsible for Black poverty. Moynihan, "The Negro Family"; Wilson, *The Truly Disadvantaged*.

76 Du Bois, *The Gift of Black Folk*, 120. "The Freedom of Womanhood" is a difficult text. On the one hand, it shows Du Bois at his sharpest in arguing that Black women's experience prefigures the modern industrial order and also arguing that Black women are ahead of white women in the fight for women's rights in that they don't bow to men's leadership or opinion. At the same time, this text shows Du Bois at his worst in his analysis of the Black concubine as bringing together two human races. Perhaps because of this, this text is not addressed in discussions of Du Bois's thought. For an analysis of this text see Gilkes, "The Margin as the Center of a Theory of History."

77 Du Bois, *Darkwater*, 96.

78 Anna Julia Cooper's famous phrase states that "only the black woman can say 'when and where I enter, in the quiet, undisputed dignity of my womanhood, without violence and without suing or special patronage, then and there the whole Negro race enters with me.'" Cooper, *The Voice of Anna Julia Cooper*, 63.

79 Du Bois, *Darkwater*, 100–101; Cooper, *The Voice of Anna Julia Cooper*, 63.

80 For an analysis of Du Bois's erasure of the work of Anna Julia Cooper and Ida B. Wells, see James, "The Profeminist Politics of W. E. B. Du Bois."

81 Cooper, *The Voice of Anna Julia Cooper*.

82 There has been some work in sociology on the racial state since Du Bois, but not much. Omi and Winant make the racial state the locus of their analysis of racial politics. But their focus is on discourses and projects more than on institutions and politics. Of late, Glenn Bracey and Moon-Kie Jung have addressed the analysis of the racial state. Bracey, "Toward a Critical Race Theory of State"; Jung, *Beneath the Surface of White Supremacy*; Omi and Winant, *Racial Formation in the United States*.

83 In putting the question of democracy in these terms, Du Bois challenges the formal and procedural understanding of democracy that prevailed and still prevails in the United States, an understanding of democracy that ignores the limits to substantive democratic participation of minorities and the poor.

84 Du Bois, *Black Reconstruction in America*, 184.

85 Du Bois, *Black Reconstruction in America*, 67.

86 Rueschemeyer, Huber, and Stephens, *Capitalist Development and Democracy*.

87 Du Bois, *Black Reconstruction in America*, 212.

88 Du Bois, *Black Reconstruction in America*, 625–26.

89 Du Bois, *Black Reconstruction in America*, 626.

90 Woodward, *The Strange Career of Jim Crow*.

91 Du Bois, *Black Reconstruction in America*, 625–26.

92 Du Bois, *Black Reconstruction in America*, 631.

93 These developments can be clearly understood using the theoretical frame of the racial state proposed by Du Bois.

94 Du Bois, *Black Reconstruction in America*, 631.

95 Du Bois, "The World and Africa," 288.

96 Du Bois, "The World and Africa," 282.

97 In *Color and Democracy* Du Bois articulates the dilemma of the relationship between economic planning and democracy in the following terms: "It may well be that the real fight which is dividing the world today is the question as to how much of human action must by the laws of science be subject to scientific control; and on the other hand, can be reserved as the area of human freedom for individual action, creative thought, and artistic taste" (293). Du Bois thought that productive activities and, to some extent, the distribution of goods, imposed constraints that made them subject to the rule of managers. But he asserts that what is produced and how it is produced and distributed among nations and classes is a matter for democratic decision making. Here Du Bois reformulates the dilemma between law and chance in human action that he posed in his 1905 unpublished text "Sociology Hesitant," a theme that is recurrent in Du Bois's writings.

98 For a contemporary example of this discussion, see the exchange between Howard Winant and Andreas Wimmer in *Ethnic and Racial Studies*. Winant, "Response to Andreas Wimmer"; Ray and Seamster, "Rethinking Racial Progress"; Wimmer, "Race-Centrism."

99 A Du Boisian historical sociology has an affinity with world-systems analysis in that both emphasize the interconnectedness of global economic and political processes. But whereas world-systems analysis follows mainly a deductive strategy that focuses on the global systemic determinations, Du Boisian sociology focuses on the concrete local forms of racial and colonial capitalism and argues that the specific relations between the local and the global need to be investigated empirically. If we take the three modes of historical comparative work proposed by Theda Skocpol and Margaret Sommers in their by-now-classic article—hypothesis testing, demonstration of theory, and contrast of contexts—a Du Boisian historical sociology would operate mostly in the space between the contrast of contexts and the demonstration of theory modes. A Du Boisian historical sociology will also use single case studies to illuminate, discuss, and reformulate theory. Finally, a Du Boisian historical sociology has a strong affinity with Bhambra's contemporary connected sociologies. See Itzigsohn, "Class, Race, and Emancipation"; Skocpol and Somers, "The Uses of Comparative History"; Bhambra, *Connected Sociologies*.

100 Go, *Postcolonial Thought and Social Theory*.

CHAPTER 3. DU BOIS'S URBAN AND COMMUNITY
RESEARCH PROGRAM

1 Wilberforce University, "Letter from Wilberforce University to W. E. B. Du Bois."
2 Du Bois, "My Evolving Program for Negro Freedom," 37.
3 Du Bois, *The Philadelphia Negro.*
4 Hunter and Robinson, *Chocolate Cities.*
5 Young, "W. E. B. Du Bois and the Sociological Canon."
6 Du Bois, "The Study of Negro Problems," in Chandler, ed., *The Problem of the Color Line,* 78.
7 Du Bois, "The Study of Negro Problems," in Chandler, ed., *The Problem of the Color Line,* 78.
8 Du Bois, "The Study of Negro Problems," in Green and Driver, eds., *W. E. B. Du Bois on Sociology and the Black Community,* 72.
9 Du Bois, "The Study of Negro Problems," in Green and Driver, eds., *W. E. B. Du Bois on Sociology and the Black Community,* 73.
10 King, "'I Have a Dream' Speech."
11 Du Bois, "The Study of Negro Problems," in Green and Driver, eds., *W. E. B. Du Bois on Sociology and the Black Community,* 71.
12 Du Bois, "The Study of Negro Problems," in Green and Driver, eds., *W. E. B. Du Bois on Sociology and the Black Community,* 78.
13 Du Bois, "The Study of Negro Problems," in Green and Driver, eds., *W. E. B. Du Bois on Sociology and the Black Community,* 76.
14 Du Bois, "The Atlanta Conferences," 53.
15 Du Bois, "The Atlanta Conferences," 53.
16 See chapter 2 for a discussion of Du Bois's theory of agency.
17 Du Bois, "The Atlanta Conferences," 55.
18 Du Bois, "The Study of Negro Problems," in Green and Driver, eds., *W. E. B. Du Bois on Sociology and the Black Community,* 79.
19 Du Bois, "The Atlanta Conferences," 56.
20 Du Bois, "The Study of Negro Problems," in Green and Driver, eds., *W. E. B. Du Bois on Sociology and the Black Community,* 79.
21 Du Bois, "The Atlanta Conferences," 57.
22 Du Bois, "The Negro Race in the United States of America," 105.
23 Du Bois, "The Negro Race in the United States of America," 111.
24 Du Bois, "The Twelfth Census and the Negro Problems," 67.
25 Du Bois, "The Twelfth Census and the Negro Problems," 66.
26 Du Bois, "The Twelfth Census and the Negro Problems," 66.
27 Du Bois, "The Atlanta Conferences," 58.
28 Green and Driver, *W. E. B. Du Bois on Sociology and the Black Community,* 14.
29 Du Bois, "The Study of the Negro Problems," *Annals of the American Academy of Political and Social Science.*

30 Du Bois, "The Study of Negro Problems," in Green and Driver, eds., *W. E. B. Du Bois on Sociology and the Black Community*.

31 Du Bois, "The Study of Negro Problems," in Green and Driver, eds., *W. E. B. Du Bois on Sociology and the Black Community*, 81.

32 Du Bois, "The Study of Negro Problems," in Green and Driver, eds., *W. E. B. Du Bois on Sociology and the Black Community*, 82.

33 Du Bois, "The Study of Negro Problems," in Green and Driver, eds., *W. E. B. Du Bois on Sociology and the Black Community*, 82.

34 Du Bois, "The Study of Negro Problems," in Green and Driver, eds., *W. E. B. Du Bois on Sociology and the Black Community*, 82.

35 Du Bois, "The Study of Negro Problems," in Green and Driver, eds., *W. E. B. Du Bois on Sociology and the Black Community*, 83.

36 Du Bois, "The Study of Negro Problems," in Green and Driver, eds., *W. E. B. Du Bois on Sociology and the Black Community*, 81.

37 Du Bois, "The Study of Negro Problems," in Green and Driver, eds., *W. E. B. Du Bois on Sociology and the Black Community*, 75.

38 Du Bois, *Some Notes on Negro Crime*, 4.

39 For some of the most important sociological works on *The Philadelphia Negro* see Elijah Anderson, "Introduction," in Du Bois, *The Philadelphia Negro*, ix–xxvi, and Anderson, "The Emerging Philadelphia African American Class Structure"; Hunter, "W. E. B. Du Bois and Black Heterogeneity"; Hunter, "A Bridge over Troubled Urban Waters"; Loughran, "*The Philadelphia Negro* and the Canon of Classical Urban Theory"; Zuberi, "W. E. B. Du Bois's Sociology."

40 Du Bois, *The Philadelphia Negro*, 44.

41 Du Bois, *Some Notes on Negro Crime*, 4.

42 Split labor market theory describes situations in which the labor market is divided along ethnoracial lines as a result of the actions of workers from a dominant ethnoracial group who monopolize certain occupational niches and exclude workers from subaltern ethnoracial groups from those occupations. See Bonacich, "A Theory of Ethnic Antagonism."

43 Du Bois, *The Philadelphia Negro*, 129.

44 Hunter, "W. E. B. Du Bois and Black Heterogeneity."

45 Du Bois, *The Philadelphia Negro*, 207.

46 Du Bois, *The Philadelphia Negro*, 233.

47 Du Bois, *The Philadelphia Negro*, 259.

48 Du Bois, *The Philadelphia Negro*, 249.

49 Du Bois, *Some Notes on Negro Crime*, 56.

50 Du Bois, *Some Notes on Negro Crime*, 56–57.

51 Du Bois, *Some Notes on Negro Crime*, 64.

52 Du Bois, *The Philadelphia Negro*, 385.

53 Du Bois, *The Philadelphia Negro*, 385.

54 Du Bois, *The Philadelphia Negro*, 385.

55 Du Bois, *The Philadelphia Negro*, 388.

56 Du Bois, *The Philadelphia Negro*, 392.

57 Du Bois, *The Philadelphia Negro*, 394.

58 For in-depth analyses of *The Philadelphia Negro* and its contributions to urban sociology, see Hunter, "W. E. B. Du Bois and Black Heterogeneity"; Hunter, "A Bridge over Troubled Urban Waters"; Du Bois, *The Philadelphia Negro*.

59 Morris, "Sociology of Race and W. E. B. Du Bois."

60 In their *Introduction to the Science of Sociology* textbook, sociologists Robert Park and Ernest Burgess provide selected bibliographies for the many different topics covered by the text. In these bibliographies, which are quite extensive, Park and Burgess mention three of Du Bois's works. The bibliographies are organized in topical sections and subsections. *Souls* is mentioned twice. The first time is in the bibliographies for the second chapter, which is titled "Human Nature," in a subsection on "Materials for the Study of the Person," within a section on "Personality." The second time is in chapter 11, which is titled "Assimilation." Here *Souls* is mentioned in a subsection titled "Personal Documents" within a section on literature on "Immigration and Americanization." *Darkwater* is also listed in that section (but the book is listed under its subtitle: *Voices from within the Veil*). The third of Du Bois's works mentioned is the 1908 Atlanta University Study on *The Negro American Family*. This study is mentioned in the selected bibliography for the third chapter, titled "Society and the Group." The study is mentioned in a subsection on "Studies in Family Organization" within a section on the "Sociology of the Family." The places in which Du Bois's works are or are not mentioned are telling. Park and Burgess's massive *Introduction* has also suggested literatures on topics such as "Studies of Communities," "Race Conflict," and "Slavery," among others in which Du Bois's work is relevant but not mentioned. In the "Studies of Communities" section, for example, Charles Booth's classic studies of London are mentioned, but *The Philadelphia Negro* is not. The *Introduction*'s bibliographies clearly show that Park and Burgess were aware of Du Bois's work as a sociologist, and also that they did not recognize his work as foundational of the discipline. See Park and Burgess, *Introduction to the Science of Sociology*.

61 Lewis, *W. E. B. Du Bois, 1868–1919*, 398; Raushenbusch, *Robert E. Park*.

62 There has been a constant debate within the discipline over the relationship between history and sociology. For a contemporary restatement of these different sociological approaches, see the debate between Andreas Wimmer and Howard Winant in *Ethnic and Racial Studies*: Wimmer, "Race-centrism," and Winant, "Response to Andreas Wimmer."

63 Park, "Experience and Race Relations," 155.

64 See, for example, "Our Racial Frontier in the Pacific," "The Etiquette of Race Relations in the South," or "The Race Relations Cycle in Hawaii." All these texts are included in Park, *Race and Culture*.

65 For the analysis of sociohistorical processes as natural history in the American social sciences, see Ross, *The Origins of American Social Science*. Ross asserts

concerning Park and Burgess's model of society that "economic competition was identified as a natural process leading to a natural order of competitive cooperation. The social processes of accommodation themselves took on the necessity of a natural process" (359). Ross adds that for Park nature referred to "the realm of economic and social experience that lay beneath the level of conscious political choice and that carried with it the necessity of natural law" (360); Park and Burgess, *Introduction to the Science of Sociology*.

66 Park, *Race and Culture*, 16.

67 Robert Ezra Park, "Editor's Preface" to Anderson, *The Hobo*. *The Hobo* was the first of the Chicago monographs, and Park introduces it as a study of urban issues, a study of Hoboemia and the life of the homeless man in Chicago. In fact, *The Hobo* was not a study of the city homeless but a study of the practices and lived experience of itinerant workers. These itinerant workers had a hub in Chicago—Hoboemia—as in many other cities, and the book was a multisited ethnography of the hobo experience. *The Hobo* was in fact one of the first, if not the first, multisited ethnographies. Anderson mentions in the introduction to the 1961 Phoenix edition of *The Hobo* that he followed a participant methodology, although he did not know about it at the time. In fact, *The Hobo* is almost a work of auto-ethnography. Anderson was familiar with the lives of the itinerant workers—the hobos—because he had been an itinerant worker himself. As he points out, studying sociology was his way out of that life; when he conducted his research, he "was in the process of moving out of the hobo world" (xiii). Anderson's familiarity with the itinerant workers' lives and his ability to interview gave him access to Hoboemia, but the study goes way beyond it. Furthermore, he recalls that he did not get much guidance from either Park or Burgess. He mentions that the only guideline he ever got from Park was, "Write down only what you see, hear, and know, like a newspaper reporter" (xii). These instructions are not surprising given Park's history as a newspaper reporter. Anderson, *The Hobo*.

68 Park, "The City: Suggestions for the Investigation of Human Behavior in the Urban Environment," in Park and Burgess, *The City*, 1.

69 Burgess, "The Growth of the City," 50.

70 Abbott, "Of Time and Space," 1152.

71 Ross, *The Origins of American Social Science*, 436–37.

72 Zorbaugh, *The Gold Coast and the Slum*.

73 Zorbaugh, *The Gold Coast and the Slum*, 234.

74 Louis Wirth, *The Ghetto* (Piscataway, NJ: Transaction, 1998), 6.

75 James McKee's *Sociology and the Race Problem* shows how the concepts and disciplinary language used in the sociology of race and ethnicity—and, we would add, much of the language used in immigration studies—was established by Chicago. McKee's book points convincingly to the failure of this perspective in understanding and explaining the pervasiveness and the politics of race in the United States. Steinberg's *Race Relations* also provides a scathing critique of the scholarly paradigms that emerged from Chicago.

76 As both Andrew Abbott and Dorothy Ross point out, variable-oriented research has a long history. It starts to develop contemporarily with or even before the Chicago school. But it only becomes the dominant strand of research in sociology with Paul Lazarsfeld and the rise of what we can call the "Columbia School." See Abbott, "Of Time and Space," and Ross, *The Origins of American Social Science*.

77 Abbott, "Of Time and Space."

78 This defense of the status quo is also seen in the reluctance of sociology departments to critically examine their practices in relation to the diversity of their faculty and student bodies and in their defensive reactions to students' requests for recognition of epistemological diversity within the discipline.

79 Du Bois asserted, in describing the research program he aimed to launch in the 1940s, that "such studies to be effective must be well done and in accord with the latest scientific technique." Du Bois, *The Autobiography of W. E. B. Du Bois*, 311.

CHAPTER 4. PUBLIC SOCIOLOGY AND DU BOIS'S EVOLVING PROGRAM FOR FREEDOM

1 Du Bois, "My Evolving Program for Negro Freedom," 36.

2 Du Bois, *The Suppression of the African Slave-Trade*; Du Bois, *The Philadelphia Negro*.

3 I. A. Reed, *Interpretation and Social Knowledge*.

4 Foucault, *The Order of Things*; Du Bois, *Dusk*.

5 The W. E. B. Du Bois Center at the University of Massachusetts, *W. E. B. Du Bois's Data Portraits*; Du Bois, *The Autobiography of W. E. B. Du Bois*, 141.

6 A world's fair is an international event put on to showcase the industrial, technological, and artistic advances made by the world's nations.

7 Smith, *Photography on the Color Line*; The W. E. B. Du Bois Center at the University of Massachusetts, *W. E. B. Du Bois's Data Portraits*.

8 Du Bois, "The American Negro at Paris," 576.

9 Barthes, *Camera Lucida*; Bourdieu and Whiteside, *Photography*; Willis, *Reflections in Black*.

10 Smith, *Photography on the Color Line*, 2.

11 Smith, *Photography on the Color Line*, 22.

12 Padmore, *History of the Pan-African Congress*.

13 Pan-African Association, "To the Nations of the World."

14 Green, "W. E. B. Du Bois."

15 Du Bois, "A Proposal for a Negro Journal," 2.

16 The Niagara Movement eventually evolved into the NAACP.

17 Green, "W. E. B. Du Bois."

18 High-level for Black people, that is. The Theodore Roosevelt administration tried to ignore the color line in government appointments.

19 Du Bois, *Dusk*, 34.

20 Du Bois, *Dusk*, 28.

21 "The Atlanta Riots."

22 Du Bois, "My Evolving Program for Negro Freedom," 41.
23 The NAACP is one of the oldest civil rights organizations. It was established by a group of white liberals and members of the Niagara Movement, including Du Bois.
24 Du Bois, "My Evolving Program for Negro Freedom," 46.
25 Du Bois, "My Evolving Program for Negro Freedom," 47.
26 Du Bois, "My Evolving Program for Negro Freedom," 47.
27 Du Bois, "My Evolving Program for Negro Freedom," 47–48.
28 Gates and Jarrett, *The New Negro*, 2.
29 Locke, "The New Negro," 112.
30 Du Bois, "Criteria of Negro Art."
31 Du Bois, "Criteria of Negro Art," in Gates and Jarrett, *The New Negro*, 258.
32 For example, Percival Everett, winner of several prestigious literary awards, including the Academy Award in Literature and the PEN Center Award for Fiction, published in 2001 a satirical novel, *Erasure*, that depicts how the publishing industry pigeonholes African American writers. The book's protagonist, Thelonious Monk Ellison, is a gifted writer who has a difficult time getting his work published. His agent explains that his work is not considered "Black" enough, and therefore does not appeal to the publishing industry. Meanwhile, Ellison's fellow African American writer Juanita Mae Jenkins is reveling in national acclaim for her recently published book, *We Lives in da Ghetto*. In a moment of cathartic rage, Ellison feverishly writes a book called *My Pafology,* a book full of demeaning tropes and stereotypes about Black Americans. His agent shops the Blaxploitation book, which is immediately picked up for publication. Thus begins Ellison's rise within the elite American literati. Through this satirical novel Percival Everett depicts the dilemma of the Black artist that Du Bois, and generations of Black scholars, artists, performers, and writers, have endured and pushed against for generations.
33 Du Bois employed an apparatus to establish what Foucault calls a "discursive formation"—the set of discourses that establish the boundaries and limits of what can and cannot be said, thought, or imagined. See Foucault, *The Archaeology of Knowledge.*
34 Du Bois, "Criteria of Negro Art," 258.
35 Du Bois, "Criteria of Negro Art," 259.
36 Du Bois, "Criteria of Negro Art," 259.
37 Du Bois, "Criteria of Negro Art," 259.
38 Du Bois, "Criteria of Negro Art," 259.
39 Du Bois, *Black Reconstruction in America*, 713–14.
40 He encountered this experience in an attempt to publish an invited chapter in the fourteenth *Encyclopedia Britannica.*
41 Du Bois, "Editorial: The Crisis," 10.
42 Du Bois, "Editorial: The Crisis," 10.

43 Du Bois, "Star of Ethiopia, 1914."

44 Hewett, "'Looking at One's Self through the Eyes of Others.'"

45 W. E. B. Du Bois, "The Drama among Black Folk," 171.

46 Du Bois, "The Drama among Black Folk"; Krasner, "'The Pageant Is the Thing'"; Hewett, "'Looking at One's Self through the Eyes of Others.'"

47 Padmore, *History of the Pan-African Congress*.

48 Du Bois, "*The World and Africa*," p. 149.

49 Du Bois, "My Evolving Program for Negro Freedom," 49.

50 Du Bois, "My Evolving Program for Negro Freedom," 49.

51 Du Bois, "The True Brownies," 286.

52 To provide just one example, it was not until 1968 that the first "colored" Barbie doll appeared in stores, and not until 1980 that "Black Barbie" hit the market. Consequently, generations of little Black girls grew up playing with dolls—the quintessential object of play that transmits ideologies of gender and beauty to young children—that did not share their features. For many, this translated into the deeply held idea that beauty is reserved for white girls. The doll market is one of thousands of examples of the way racial ideologies are transmitted through visual representation and negation.

53 James Baldwin's 1965 debate against William F. Buckley in Cambridge, United Kingdom, on the issue "Is the American Dream at the Expense of the Negro," illuminates this point:

> This means, in the case of an American Negro, born in that glittering republic, and the moment you are born, since you don't know any better, every stick and stone and every face is white. And since you have not yet seen a mirror, you suppose that you are, too. It comes as a great shock around the age of 5, or 6, or 7, to discover that the flag to which you have pledged allegiance, along with everybody else, has not pledged allegiance to you. It comes as a great shock to discover that Gary Cooper killing off the Indians, when you were rooting for Gary Cooper, that the Indians were you! It comes as a great shock to discover that the country which is your birthplace and to which you owe your life and your identity, has not, in its whole system of reality, evolved any place for you.

The full transcript of Baldwin's debate can be found at Rima, "Transcript: James Baldwin Debates William F. Buckley (1965)," *Blog #42*, June 7, 2015, https://www.rimaregas.com/2015/06/07/transcript-james-baldwin-debates-william-f-buckley-1965-blog42/.

54 This speaks to the "liberation capital" conceptualized in *The Scholar Denied*. Liberation capital is the volunteer or underpaid work professionals and amateur intellectual workers contribute to amassing evidence and developing new theories and programmatic innovations. This was accomplished in spite of the absence and/or hostile resistance of the well-resourced mainstream.

55 Du Bois, "Letter from W. E. B. Du Bois to H. T. Burleigh."

56 Du Bois, "Letter from W. E. B. Du Bois to Laura Wheeler."

57 Du Bois, "The Brownies' Book," Library of Congress Digital ID http://hdl.loc.gov/loc.rbc/ser.01351.

58 Du Bois, "The Brownies' Book," Library of Congress Digital ID http://hdl.loc.gov/loc.rbc/ser.01351.

59 Du Bois, "The Brownies' Book," Library of Congress Digital ID http://hdl.loc.gov/loc.rbc/ser.01351.

60 Du Bois, "The Brownies' Book," Library of Congress Digital ID http://hdl.loc.gov/loc.rbc/ser.01351.

61 Du Bois, "The Brownies' Book," Library of Congress Digital ID http://hdl.loc.gov/loc.rbc/ser.01351.

62 Du Bois, "Krigwa Players Little Negro Theatre," 134.

63 Walker, "Krigwa," 348.

64 Du Bois, "My Evolving Program for Negro Freedom," 49.

65 Du Bois, "My Evolving Program for Negro Freedom," 49.

66 Du Bois, "My Evolving Program for Negro Freedom," 50.

67 Du Bois, "My Evolving Program for Negro Freedom," 50.

68 Du Bois, "My Evolving Program for Negro Freedom," 51.

69 Du Bois, *Dusk*, 321.

70 Du Bois, "My Evolving Program for Negro Freedom," 51.

71 Clark Atlanta University emerged out of the merger, in 1988, of Atlanta University, where Du Bois taught, with Clark College. The journal that Du Bois founded is published today as *Phylon: The Clark Atlanta University Review of Race and Culture*.

72 See chapter 13 in Du Bois, *The Autobiography of W. E. B. Du Bois*.

73 Du Bois, *The Autobiography of W. E. B. Du Bois*, 316.

74 Du Bois, "Prospect of a World without Race Conflict."

75 Du Bois, "Prospect of a World without Race Conflict," 456.

76 Du Bois, "Prospect of a World without Race Conflict," 456.

77 Du Bois, "Prospect of a World without Race Conflict," 456.

78 Du Bois, *The Autobiography of W. E. B. Du Bois*, 324.

79 Du Bois, *The Autobiography of W. E. B. Du Bois*, 326.

80 Padmore, *History of the Pan-African Congress*; Du Bois, *In Battle for Peace*.

81 Padmore, *History of the Pan-African Congress*, 1.

82 For more on Du Bois's involvement in the Peace Congresses, see chapter 4 of Du Bois, *In Battle for Peace*.

83 Lewis, *W. E. B. Du Bois, 1919–1963*.

84 Du Bois, *In Battle for Peace*, Appendix.

85 *In Battle for Peace: The Story of My 83rd Birthday*, Kindle edition (New York: Oxford University Press, 2014), Kindle locations 1082–86.

86 Du Bois, *The Autobiography of W. E. B. Du Bois*, 388.

87 Du Bois, *The Autobiography of W. E. B. Du Bois*, 395.

88 Lewis, *W. E. B. Du Bois, 1919–1963*.

89 The case is *Kent v. Dulles*, decided in June 1958.

90 The Bandung conference is considered to be the predecessor and seed for the Non-Aligned Movement. On Du Bois's invitation to the Bandung conference, see the entry "Bandung," by Kenneth Mostern, in Horne and Young, *W. E. B. Du Bois: An Encyclopedia*.

91 Du Bois, "To the Peoples of Asia and Africa Meeting at Bandung." Letter from Du Bois to the Bandung Conference, April 1955.

92 Du Bois, *The Autobiography of W. E. B. Du Bois*, 400.

93 Asia had a central role in Du Bois's anticolonial imagination. In the 1930s he saw Japan as the state leading the charge against Western colonialism, and he accepted an invitation to visit Manchukuo, a puppet state the Japanese have created in Northeastern China and Inner Mongolia. Upon return, he wrote a glowing editorial about Japanese colonialism (the editorial, titled "Japanese Colonialism," was published in the *Pittsburgh Courier* in February 13, 1937, and is included in David Levering Lewis, *W. E. B.: A Reader* (New York: Henry Holt, 1995). In the late 1950s, China took the role of Japan in Du Bois's anticolonial thought. In both cases he was blind to the violence of the ruling regimes: the violence of the Japanese rule of China, and the violence of Mao Zedong's regime (Du Bois visited China just after the "great leap forward" had caused a famine that took millions of lives). Du Bois was not immune to blindness and major political mistakes. His thinking, however, was always oriented toward finding ways to undo the color line and emancipate people of color worldwide, and he saw Asian-African cooperation as central to that goal. It would be interesting to see what he would have thought today, when China is taking the role of hegemonic power in leading a form of dependent development of sorts in parts of Africa, and reports of anti-Black racism are increasingly coming out of China.

94 Du Bois, *The Autobiography of W. E. B. Du Bois*, 407.

95 As quoted in West, *The American Evasion of Philosophy*, 142.

96 W. E. B. Du Bois, "A Statement concerning the Encyclopaedia Africana Project," April 1, 1962, http://www.endarkenment.com.

97 At least not under Du Bois's leadership. Although Du Bois pursued the project with the support of Ghanaian President Kwame Nkrumah, he did not finish the encylopedia. However, many years later an *Encyclopedia Africana* would be published under the editorship of Henry Louis Gates and Anthony Appiah.

98 King, *Honoring Dr. Du Bois*.

CHAPTER 5. A MANIFESTO FOR A CONTEMPORARY DU BOISIAN SOCIOLOGY

1 We stand on the shoulders of a long list of people who attempted this. Among the important scholars who have contributed to the rethinking of sociology are Robert Blauner, Eduardo Bonilla-Silva, Patricia Hill Collins, Joe Feagin, Julian Go, Joyce Ladner, Aldon Morris, Michael Omi, John Stanfield, Stephen Steinberg, Howard Winant, and Tukufu Zuberi. What is particular about our attempt at

expanding the boundaries of the possible in sociology is that we are building our approach on the work of one of the founders of the discipline, a towering figure who combined global historical structural analysis with community studies and the phenomenological analysis of experience. Whether we are successful in this endeavor only time will tell. Yet, as we finish the writing of this book, we are energized from the experience of organizing the Du Boisian Scholar Network. This network brings together scholars and graduate students who are looking for a different kind of sociology.

2 It is we who are describing Du Bois's analysis as phenomenology. That was not a term that he used. But we think it is an appropriate description. Furthermore, if, as Shamoon Zamir argues, Du Bois was influenced by Hegel's phenomenology, then his work was purposively phenomenological even if he did not use the term.

3 Du Bois never completely abandoned his elitist positions, though, and in *Dusk* he still has a role for the Talented Tenth, though it is an accompanying role, not a leading one.

4 At the same time, for all its problems, Du Bois's theorization of gender was more developed than that of any of the other "founding fathers" of sociology —and also better than most contemporary male social theorists!

5 Forms of colonialism include imperial expansion for the purpose of economic exploitation, settler colonialism, neocolonialism, coloniality, and sustained military occupation.

6 Du Bois made this point in *The World and Africa* and in *Color and Democracy*. Some of these points, in different ways, have been made in contemporary sociology and social theory by the decolonial school, postcolonial theorists, and dependency and world-system scholars. For a survey of these literatures, see Manuela Boatca's *Global Inequalities beyond Occidentalism*.

7 A contemporary Du Boisian sociology will enter a dialogue with postcolonial and decolonial studies around the critique of knowledge and culture, sharing a critical impulse with other interdisciplinary fields, such as Ethnic Studies and Africana Studies. It would pose questions such as, What counts as "data"? How do we orient ourselves towards it? Who does history and knowledge belong to, and what goes into its making?

8 "Analytical bifurcation" refers to the study of the social processes and histories of peoples in different parts of the world as if they were separated from each other. This is particularly problematic when studying the histories of people who have been colonized and racialized as if their predicaments were separated from the histories and actions of their colonizers. See Go, *Postcolonial Thought and Social Theory*.

9 For the idea of landscape of meaning, see Reed, *Interpretation and Social Knowledge*. This book is a must read for anyone interested in how sociological theorizing works. In terms of Reed's analysis of the different epistemic modes in sociology, a contemporary Du Boisian sociology would operate at the intersection of the realist and interpretivist epistemic modes.

10 As a point of contrast, Emirbayer's and Desmond's book, which we address in the introduction, aims to build a theory of a race field that is general and abstract enough to apply to other fields of inequality—such as gender and class. In their aim to build a theory that can apply equally to different fields of inequality, they miss the historical and contextual specificity of racism and racialization. Although their analysis is based mainly in the American experience, the links of the American experience to the history of global racism and colonialism are not part of their analysis. See Emirbayer and Desmond, *The Racial Order*.

11 While teaching the theory of double consciousness in a graduate seminar, the question arose as to whether we could talk about a veil operating in all kinds of relations between individuals characterized by a power differential. The answer to that question is that the theory cannot be applied in an abstract and general way to all relations of power imbalance. This is what mainstream sociology would be inclined to do, and then find a way to measure double consciousness and test the theory. This is not the way a contemporary Du Boisian sociology would operate. Whether the theory applies to a particular situation or not requires a specific analysis of the particular relation that is being analyzed. And this analysis is carried out through phenomenological analysis and self-reflection, not through quantitative measuring and regressions.

12 For example, can the theory of double consciousness be applied in the study of gender inequalities and gendered subjectivities? The answer cannot be given without a careful exploration of the applicability of the concept to the analysis of gender.

13 Zimmerman, *Alabama in Africa*; Steinberg, *Race Relations*; McKee, *Sociology and the Race Problem*; Zuberi and Bonilla-Silva, *White Logic, White Methods*; Zuberi, *Thicker Than Blood*.

14 Interestingly, in the introduction to the 1961 edition of *The Hobo*, the first of the Chicago ethnographies, Anderson locates the hobo in the historical context of the expansion and closure of the US frontier, as the result of the demand for labor by temporary workers as the US state expanded to the west. And while he argues that the hobo was a type of frontier worker, like the cowboy, the book focuses on the specificity of the hobo experience rather than on types of itinerant or frontier workers.

15 Michael Rodriguez-Muñiz points out that the focus of research on the poor is driven by an ontological blindness. He asks why we focus so much on the lives of the poor, rather than on the structures and actors that reproduce poverty. See Rodríguez-Muñiz, "Intellectual Inheritances."

16 Young, "White Ethnographers on the Experiences of African American Men"; Zuberi and Bonilla-Silva, *White Logic, White Methods*.

17 In its emphasis on local agency and contingency, a Du Boisian historical sociology would find elements in common with William Sewell's eventful historical sociology, which pays attention to the historical construction and micro development of historical situations. See Sewell, *Logics of History*. Yet, in its goal of put-

ting the local and the contingent in a global and relational framework, Du Boisian sociology also has complementarities with world-system analysis.

18 Itzigsohn, "Class, Race, and Emancipation."

19 Mills, *The Sociological Imagination*.

20 We can think about Steven Lukes's book, *The Curious Enlightenment of Professor Caritat*, as an example of how to use storytelling to illustrate theory. Lukes's book, however, is addressed to an academic audience cognizant of political theories, not the broad public. Lukes, *The Curious Enlightenment of Professor Caritat*.

21 There is a large literature that discusses standpoint theory. For some useful texts relevant to our discussion, see Harding, "Rethinking Standpoint Epistemology"; Harding, *Sciences from Below*; Julian Go, "Globalizing Sociology"; Collins, *Black Feminist Thought*; Connell, *Southern Theory*.

22 King, *Honoring Dr. Du Bois*.

23 We find it surprising how many sociologists who are trained to analyze how power shapes society usually present policy recommendations that are completely detached from the analysis or considerations of power relations—as if the policy making process was simply a technocratic process informed by neutral expertise.

BIBLIOGRAPHY

Abbott, Andrew. "Of Time and Space: The Contemporary Relevance of the Chicago School." *Social Forces* 75, no. 4 (1997): 1149–82.

Anderson, Elijah. "The Emerging Philadelphia African American Class Structure." *Annals of the American Academy of Political and Social Science* 568, no. 1 (2000): 54–77.

Anderson, Nels. *The Hobo: The Sociology of the Homeless Man.* Chicago: University of Chicago Press, 1961.

Appiah, Kwame Anthony. *Lines of Descent: W. E. B. Du Bois and the Emergence of Identity.* Cambridge, MA: Harvard University Press, 2014.

Barthes, Roland. *Camera Lucida: Reflections on Photography.* London: Macmillan, 1981.

Benjamin, Walter. *Illuminations.* Edited by Hannah Arendt. Translated by Zohn Harry. New York: Schocken Books, 1969.

Bhambra, Gurminder K. *Connected Sociologies.* London: Bloomsbury Publishing, 2014.

———. *Rethinking Modernity: Postcolonialism and the Sociological Imagination.* New York: Springer, 2007.

Blau, Judith R., and Eric S. Brown. "Du Bois and Diasporic Identity: The Veil and the Unveiling Project." *Sociological Theory* 19, no. 2 (2001): 219–33.

Blumer, Herbert. *Selected Works of Herbert Blumer: A Public Philosophy for Mass Society.* Champaign: University of Illinois Press, 2000.

Boatcă, Manuela. *Global Inequalities beyond Occidentalism.* Farnham, UK: Ashgate, 2015.

Bogues, Anthony. *Black Heretics, Black Prophets: Radical Political Intellectuals.* New York: Routledge, 2015.

Bonacich, Edna. "A Theory of Ethnic Antagonism: The Split Labor Market." *American Sociological Review* (1972): 547–59.

Bonilla-Silva, Eduardo, Carla Goar, and David G. Embrick. "When Whites Flock Together: The Social Psychology of White Habitus." *Critical Sociology* 32, no. 2–3 (2006): 229–53.

Bourdieu, Pierre. *Language and Symbolic Power.* Cambridge, MA: Harvard University Press, 1991.

———. *Outline of a Theory of Practice.* Stanford, CA: Stanford University Press, 1992.

———. *The Logic of Practice.* Stanford, CA: Stanford University Press, 1990.

Bourdieu, Pierre, and Shaun Whiteside. *Photography: A Middle-Brow Art.* Stanford, CA: Stanford University Press, 1996.

Bracey, Glenn. "Toward a Critical Race Theory of State." *Critical Sociology* 41, no. 3 (2015): 553–72.

Brown, Karida L. *Gone Home: Race and Roots through Appalachia*. Chapel Hill: University of North Carolina Press, 2018.

Burgess, Ernest Watson. "The Growth of the City: An Introduction to a Research Project." In *The City*, edited by Robert Ezra Park and Ernest W. Burgess, 47–62. Chicago: University of Chicago Press, 1984.

Chandler, Nahum Dimitri. "A Persistent Parallax: On the Writings of W. E. Burghardt Du Bois on Japan and China, 1936–1937." *CR: The New Centennial Review* 12, no. 1 (2012): 291–316.

———. "On Paragraph Four of 'The Conservation of Races.'" *CR: The New Centennial Review* 14, no. 3 (2014): 255–87.

———. "The Figure of W. E. B. Du Bois as a Problem for Thought." *CR: The New Centennial Review* 6, no. 3 (2007): 29–55.

———, ed. *The Problem of the Color Line at the Turn of the Twentieth Century: The Essential Early Essays*. New York: Oxford University Press, 2014.

———. "The Souls of an Ex-White Man: W. E. B. Du Bois and the Biography of John Brown." *CR: The New Centennial Review* 3, no. 1 (2003): 179–95.

———. *Toward an African Future of the Limit of the World*. Living Commons Collective, 2013.

Collins, Patricia Hill. *Black Feminist Thought: Knowledge, Consciousness, and the Politics of Empowerment*. New York: Routledge, 2002.

Connell, Raewyn. *Southern Theory: The Global Dynamics of Knowledge in Social Science*. Sydney: Allen & Unwin, 2007.

Cooley, Charles Horton. *Human Nature and the Social Order*. Glencoe, IL: Free Press, 1956.

Cooper, Anna Julia. *The Voice of Anna Julia Cooper*. Edited by Charles Lemert and Bhan Esme. Lanham, MD: Rowman & Littlefield, 1998.

Coulthard, Glen Sean. *Red Skin, White Masks: Rejecting the Colonial Politics of Recognition*. Minneapolis: Minnesota University Press, 2014.

Dennis, Rutledge M. "Continuities and Discontinuities in the Social and Political Thought of W. E. B. Du Bois." *Research in Race & Ethnic Relations* 9 (1996): 3–23.

———. "Du Bois's Concept of Double Consciousness: Myth and Reality." *Research in Race & Ethnic Relations* 9 (1996): 69–90.

Du Bois, W. E. B. "A Litany of Atlanta," 1906. W. E. B. Du Bois Papers (MS 312), Special Collections and University Archives, University of Massachusetts Amherst Libraries, http://credo.library.umass.edu.

———. "A Proposal for a Negro Journal," December 1904. W. E. B. Du Bois Papers (MS 312), Special Collections and University Archives, University of Massachusetts Amherst Libraries, http://credo.library.umass.edu.

———. *Black Folk Then and Now: An Essay in the History and Sociology of the Negro Race: The Oxford W. E. B. Du Bois*, vol. 7. New York: Oxford University Press on Demand, 2007.

———. *Black Reconstruction in America: Toward a History of the Part Which Black Folk Played in the Attempt to Reconstruct Democracy in America, 1860–1880*. Piscataway, NJ: Transaction Publishers, 2013.

———. "Criteria of Negro Art." *Crisis* 32, no. 6 (1926): 290–97.

———. *Darkwater: Voices from within the Veil.* New York: Dover, 1999.

———. *Dusk of Dawn: An Essay toward an Autobiography of a Race Concept.* Volume 8 of *The Oxford W. E. B. Du Bois.* Piscataway, NJ: Transaction Publishers, 2006.

———. "Editorial: The Crisis." *Crisis* 1, no. 1 (1910): 10.

———. *In Battle for Peace: The Story of My 83rd Birthday.* New York: Oxford University Press, 2014.

———. *John Brown.* New York: International Publishers, 2014.

———. "Krigwa Players Little Negro Theatre." *Crisis* 32, no. 3 (1926): 134.

———. "Letter from W. E. B. Du Bois to H. T. Burleigh," October 23, 1919. W. E. B. Du Bois Papers (MS 312), Special Collections and University Archives, University of Massachusetts Amherst Libraries, http://credo.library.umass.edu.

———. "Letter from W. E. B. Du Bois to Kwame Nkrumah," February 7, 1957. Special Collections and University Archives, University of Massachusetts Amherst Libraries, http://credo.library.umass.edu.

———. "Letter from W. E. B. Du Bois to Laura Wheeler," August 14, 1919. W. E. B. Du Bois Papers (MS 312), Special Collections and University Archives, University of Massachusetts Amherst Libraries, http://credo.library.umass.edu.

———. "My Evolving Program for Negro Freedom." *Clinical Sociological Review* 8, no. 1 (1944): 27–57.

———. "Prospect of a World without Race Conflict." *American Journal of Sociology* 49, no. 5 (1944): 450–56.

———. *Some Notes on Negro Crime, Particularly in Georgia: Report of a Social Study Made under the Direction of Atlanta University; Together with the Proceedings of the Ninth Conference for the Study of the Negro Problems, Held at Atlanta University, May 24, 1904.* 7–10. Atlanta, GA: Atlanta University Press, 1904.

———. "Star of Ethiopia, 1914," 1914. W. E. B. Du Bois Papers (MS 312), Special Collections and University Archives, University of Massachusetts Amherst Libraries, http://credo.library.umass.edu.

———. "The American Negro at Paris," 1900. W. E. B. Du Bois Papers (MS 312), Special Collections and University Archives, University of Massachusetts Amherst Libraries, http://credo.library.umass.edu.

———. "The Atlanta Conferences." In *W. E. B. Du Bois on Sociology and the Black Community,* edited by Dan S. Green and Edwin D. Driver, 53–60. Chicago: University of Chicago Press, 2013.

———. *The Autobiography of W. E. B. Du Bois: A Soliloquy on Viewing My Life from the Last Decade of Its First Century.* New York: Oxford University Press, 1968.

———. *The Brownies' Book.* New York: Du Bois and Dill, 1921, 1920. Library of Congress, Washington, DC, https://www.loc.gov.

———. "The Drama among Black Folk." *Crisis* 12, no. 4 (1916): 169.

———. *The Gift of Black Folk: The Negroes in the Making of America.* New Hyde Park, NY: Square One Publishers, 2009.

———. *The Health and Physique of the Negro American: Report of a Social Study Made under the Direction of Atlanta University, Together with the Proceedings of the Eleventh Conference for the Study of the Negro Problems, Held at Atlanta University, on May the 29th, 1906.* Atlanta, GA: Atlanta University Press, 1906.

———. *The Negro.* London: Forgotten Books, 2007.

———. "The Negro Race in the United States of America." In *W. E. B. Du Bois on Sociology and the Black Community*, edited by Dan S. Green and Edwin D. Driver, 85–112. Chicago: University of Chicago Press, 2013.

———. *The Philadelphia Negro: A Social Study.* University of Pennsylvania Press, 1995.

———. "The Races in Conference." *Crisis* 1, no. 2 (1910): 17–20.

———. *The Souls of Black Folk.* London: Longmans, Green, 1965.

———. "The Study of the Negro Problems." *Annals of the American Academy of Political and Social Science* (1898): 1–23.

———. "The Study of Negro Problems." In *W. E. B. Du Bois on Sociology and the Black Community*, edited by Dan S. Green and Edwin D. Driver, 70–84. Chicago: University of Chicago Press, 1980.

———. "The Study of Negro Problems." In *The Problem of the Color Line at the Turn of the Twentieth Century*, edited by Nahum D. Chandler, 77–110. New York: Fordham University Press, 2015.

———. *The Suppression of the African Slave-Trade to the United States of America.* New York: Oxford University Press, 2007.

———. "The True Brownies." *Crisis* 18, no. 6 (1919): 285.

———. "The Twelfth Census and the Negro Problems." In *W. E. B. Du Bois on Sociology and the Black Community*, edited by Dan S. Green and Edwin D. Driver, 65–69. Chicago: University of Chicago Press, 1980.

———. *"The World and Africa: An Inquiry into the Part Which Africa Has Played in World History" and "Color and Democracy."* New York: Oxford University Press, 2007.

———. "To the Peoples of Asia and Africa Meeting at Bandung," April 1955. W. E. B. Du Bois Papers (MS 312), Special Collections and University Archives, University of Massachusetts Amherst Libraries, http://credo.library.umass.edu.

———. *W. E. B. Du Bois: A Reader*, ed. David Levering Lewis. New York: Macmillan, 1995.

Emirbayer, Mustafa, and Matthew Desmond. *The Racial Order.* Chicago: University of Chicago Press, 2015.

Fanon, Frantz. *Black Skin, White Masks.* Translated by Richard Philcox. New York: Grove Press, 2008.

Foucault, Michel. *The Archaeology of Knowledge.* New York: Vintage, 2012.

———. *The Order of Things: An Archaeology of the Human Sciences.* New York: Vintage Books, 1994.

Gates, Henry Louis, Jr., and Gene Andrew Jarrett. *The New Negro: Readings on Race, Representation, and African American Culture, 1892–1938.* Princeton, NJ: Princeton University Press, 2007.

Gilkes, Cheryl Townsend. "The Margin as the Center of a Theory of History: African American Women, Social Change, and the Sociology of W. E. B. Du Bois." In *W. E. B. Du Bois on Race and Culture*, edited by Bernard W. Bell, Emily R. Grosholz, and James B. Stewart. New York: Routledge, 1996.

Gilroy, Paul. *The Black Atlantic: Modernity and Double Consciousness*. Cambridge, MA: Harvard University Press, 1993.

Go, Julian. "Globalizing Sociology, Turning South: Perspectival Realism and the Southern Standpoint." *Sociologica* 10, no. 2 (2016): 1–42.

———. *Postcolonial Thought and Social Theory*. New York: Oxford University Press, 2016.

Goffman, Erving. *Asylums: Essays on the Social Situation of Mental Patients and Other Inmates*. New York: Routledge, 2017.

———. *Stigma: Notes on the Management of Spoiled Identity*. New York: Simon and Schuster, 2009.

———. *The Presentation of Self in Everyday Life*. London: Harmondsworth London, 1978.

Gooding-Williams, Robert. *In the Shadow of Du Bois*. Cambridge, MA: Harvard University Press, 2010.

Gordon, Lewis R. *Existentia Africana: Understanding Africana Existential Thought*. New York: Routledge, 2013.

Green, Dan S. "W. E. B. Du Bois: His Journalistic Career." *Negro History Bulletin* 40, no. 2 (1977): 672–77.

Green, Dan S., and Edwin D. Driver. *W. E. B. Du Bois on Sociology and the Black Community*. Chicago: University of Chicago Press, 1980.

Harding, Sandra. "Rethinking Standpoint Epistemology: What Is 'Strong Objectivity'?" *Centennial Review* 36, no. 3 (1992): 437–70.

———. *Sciences from Below: Feminisms, Postcolonialities, and Modernities*. Durham, NC: Duke University Press, 2008.

Hewett, Rebecca. "'Looking at One's Self through the Eyes of Others': Representations of the Progressive Era Middle Class in W. E. B. Du Bois's *The Star of Ethiopia*." *Theatre History Studies* 30, no. 1 (2010): 187–201.

Horne, Gerald, and Mary Young. *W. E. B. Du Bois: An Encyclopedia*. Santa Barbara, CA: Greenwood Press, 2001.

Hunter, Marcus Anthony. "A Bridge over Troubled Urban Waters: W. E. B. Du Bois's *The Philadelphia Negro* and the Ecological Conundrum." *Du Bois Review: Social Science Research on Race* 10, no. 1 (2013): 7–27.

———. "W. E. B. Du Bois and Black Heterogeneity: How *The Philadelphia Negro* Shaped American Sociology." *American Sociologist* 46, no. 2 (2015): 219–33.

Hunter, Marcus Anthony, and Zandria F. Robinson. *Chocolate Cities: The Black Map of American Life*. Oakland: University of California Press, 2018.

Itzigsohn, José. "Class, Race, and Emancipation: The Contributions of *The Black Jacobins* and *Black Reconstruction in America* to Historical Sociology and Social Theory." *CLR James Journal* 19, no. 1/2 (2013): 177–98.

James, C. L. R. "Lectures on *The Black Jacobins*." *Small Axe* 19 (2000): 94.

James, Joy. "The Profeminist Politics of W. E. B. Du Bois with Respect to Anna Julia Cooper and Ida B. Wells Barnett." In *W. E. B. Du Bois on Race and Culture*, edited by Bernard W. Bell, Emily R. Grosholz, and James B. Stewart, 141–160. New York: Routledge, 1996.

James, William. *The Dilemma of Determinism*. Whitefish, MT: Kessinger Publishing, 1884.

———. *The Principles of Psychology*. Cambridge, MA: Harvard University Press, 1890.

Jung, Moon-Kie. *Beneath the Surface of White Supremacy: Denaturalizing US Racisms Past and Present*. Stanford, CA: Stanford University Press, 2015.

King, Martin Luther, Jr. "Honoring Dr. Du Bois." Speech delivered at Carnegie Hall, New York City, February 23, 1968. Available at http://www.ushistory.org/documents/dubois.htm.

———. "I Have a Dream," 1963. Available at National Archives, https://www.archives.gov.

Krasner, David. "'The Pageant Is the Thing': Black Nationalism and *The Star of Ethiopia*." In *A Beautiful Pageant*, 81–94. New York: Springer, 2002.

Lemert, Charles. "A Classic from the Other Side of the Veil: Du Bois's *Souls of Black Folk*." *Sociological Quarterly* 35, no. 3 (1994): 383–96.

———. *Dark Thoughts: Race and the Eclipse of Society*. New York: Routledge, 2002.

Lewis, David Levering. *W. E. B. Du Bois: Biography of a Race, 1868–1919*. New York: Henry Holt, 1993.

———. *W. E. B. Du Bois, 1919–1963: The Fight for Equality and the American Century*. New York: Macmillan, 2000.

Locke, Alaine. "The New Negro." In *The New Negro: Readings on Race, Representation, and African American Culture, 1892–1938*, edited by Henry Louis Gates (Jr.) and Gene Andrew Jarrett, 112–18. Princeton, NJ: Princeton University Press, 2007.

Loughran, Kevin. "*The Philadelphia Negro* and the Canon of Classical Urban Theory." *Du Bois Review: Social Science Research on Race* 12, no. 2 (2015): 249–67.

Lowe, Lisa. *The Intimacies of Four Continents*. Durham, NC: Duke University Press, 2015.

Lukes, Steven. *The Curious Enlightenment of Professor Caritat: A Comedy of Ideas*. Brooklyn, NY: Verso, 1995.

Luxemburg, Rosa. *The Accumulation of Capital*. New York: Routledge, 2003.

McKee, James B. *Sociology and the Race Problem: The Failure of a Perspective*. Champaign: University of Illinois Press, 1993.

Mead, George Herbert. *On Social Psychology*. Chicago: University of Chicago Press, 1964.

Memmi, Albert. *The Colonizer and the Colonized*. New York: Routledge, 2013.

Mills, C. Wright. *The Sociological Imagination*. New York: Oxford University Press, 2000.

Morris, Aldon. "Sociology of Race and W. E. B. Du Bois: The Path Not Taken." In *Sociology in America: A History*, edited by Craig Calhoun, 503–34. Chicago: University of Chicago Press, 2007.

———. *The Scholar Denied: W. E. B. Du Bois and the Birth of Modern Sociology.* Oakland: University of California Press, 2015.

Moynihan, Daniel P. "The Negro Family: The Case for National Action." Office of Policy Planning and Research, U.S. Department of Labor, 1965.

Mueller, Jennifer C. "Producing Colorblindness: Everyday Mechanisms of White Ignorance." *Social Problems* 64, no. 2 (2017): 219–38.

Mullen, Bill V., and Cathryn Watson. *W. E. B. Du Bois on Asia: Crossing the World Color Line.* Jackson: University of Mississippi Press, 2005.

Omi, Michael, and Howard Winant. *Racial Formation in the United States.* New York: Routledge, 2014.

Ortner, Sherry B. "Subjectivity and Cultural Critique." *Anthropological Theory* 5, no. 1 (2005): 31–52.

Padmore, George. *History of the Pan-African Congress.* London: Hammersmith Bookshop, 1963.

Pan-African Association. "To the Nations of the World," ca. 1900. W. E. B. Du Bois Papers (MS 312), Special Collections and University Archives, University of Massachusetts Amherst Libraries, http://credo.library.umass.edu.

Park, Robert Ezra. "Experience and Race Relations." In *Race and Culture.* Glencoe, IL: Free Press, 1964.

———. *Race and Culture: Essays in the Sociology of Contemporary Man.* Edited by Everett Hughes. New York: Free Press, 1964.

Park, Robert Ezra, and Ernest Watson Burgess. *Introduction to the Science of Sociology.* Chicago: University of Chicago Press, 1921.

———. *The City.* Edited by Roderick Duncan McKenzie. Chicago: University of Chicago Press, 1984.

Pomeranz, Kenneth. *The Great Divergence: China, Europe, and the Making of the Modern World Economy.* Princeton, NJ: Princeton University Press, 2009.

Quijano, Anibal. "Coloniality of Power and Eurocentrism in Latin America." *International Sociology* 15, no. 2 (2000): 215–32.

Quisumbing King, Katrina. "Recentering US Empire: A Structural Perspective on the Color Line." *Sociology of Race and Ethnicity* 5, no. 1 (2019): 11–25.

Rabaka, Reiland. *Against Epistemic Apartheid: W. E. B. Du Bois and the Disciplinary Decadence of Sociology.* Lanham, MD: Lexington Books, 2010.

Rampersad, Arnold. *The Art and Imagination of W. E. B. Du Bois.* Cambridge, MA: Harvard University Press, 1990.

Raushenbusch, Winifred. *Robert E. Park: Biography of a Sociologist.* Durham, NC: Duke University Press, 1979.

Rawls, Anne Warfield. "'Race' as an Interaction Order Phenomenon: W. E. B. Du Bois's 'Double Consciousness' Thesis Revisited." *Sociological Theory* 18, no. 2 (2000): 241–74.

Ray, Victor, and Louise Seamster. "Rethinking Racial Progress: A Response to Wimmer." *Ethnic and Racial Studies* 39, no. 8 (2016): 1361–69.

Reed, Adolph L., Jr., et al. *W. E. B. Du Bois and American Political Thought: Fabianism and the Color Line.* New York: Oxford University Press, 1997.

Reed, Isaac Ariail. *Interpretation and Social Knowledge: On the Use of Theory in the Human Sciences.* Chicago: University of Chicago Press, 2011.

Robinson, Cedric J. *Black Marxism: The Making of the Black Radical Tradition.* Chapel Hill: University of North Carolina Press, 1983.

Rodríguez-Muñiz, Michael. "Intellectual Inheritances: Cultural Diagnostics and the State of Poverty Knowledge." *American Journal of Cultural Sociology* 3, no. 1 (2015): 89–122.

Ross, Dorothy. *The Origins of American Social Science.* Cambridge, UK: Cambridge University Press, 1992.

Rueschemeyer, Dietrich, Evelyn Huber, and John D. Stephens. *Capitalist Development and Democracy.* Chicago: University of Chicago Press, 1992.

Schutz, Alfred. *The Phenomenology of the Social World.* Evanston, IL: Northwestern University Press, 1967.

Sewell, William H., Jr. *Logics of History: Social Theory and Social Transformation.* Chicago: University of Chicago Press, 2005.

Shaw, Stephanie Jo. *W. E. B. Du Bois and the Souls of Black Folk.* Chapel Hill: University of North Carolina Press, 2013.

Skocpol, Theda, and Margaret R. Somers. "The Uses of Comparative History in Macrosocial Inquiry." *Comparative Studies in Society and History* 22, no. 2 (1980): 174–97.

Smith, Shawn Michelle. *Photography on the Color Line: W. E. B. Du Bois, Race, and Visual Culture.* Durham, NC: Duke University Press, 2004.

Steinberg, Stephen. *Race Relations: A Critique.* Stanford, CA: Stanford University Press, 2007.

"The Atlanta Riots." *New York Times,* September 25, 1906, sec. Archives. https://www.nytimes.com.

The W. E. B. Du Bois Center at the University of Massachusetts. *W. E. B. Du Bois's Data Portraits: Visualizing Black America.* Edited by Witney Battle-Baptiste and Britt Rusert. Hudson, NY: Princeton Architectural Press, 2018.

Thompson, E. P. *The Making of the English Working Class.* New York: Vintage, 1966.

Walker, Ethel Pitts. "Krigwa, a Theatre by, for, and about Black People." *Theatre Journal* 40, no. 3 (1988): 347–56.

West, Cornel. *The American Evasion of Philosophy: A Genealogy of Pragmatism.* Madison: University of Wisconsin Press, 1989.

Wilberforce University. "Letter from Wilberforce University to W. E. B. Du Bois, August 17, 1894," August 17, 1894. W. E. B. Du Bois Papers (MS 312), Special Collections and University Archives, University of Massachusetts Amherst Libraries, http://credo.library.umass.edu.

Williams, Robert W. "The Early Social Science of W. E. B. Du Bois." *Du Bois Review* 3, no. 2 (2006): 365–94.

Willis, Deborah. *Reflections in Black: A History of Black Photographers, 1840 to the Present.* New York: Norton, 2000.

Wilson, William Julius. *The Truly Disadvantaged: The Inner City, the Underclass, and Public Policy.* Chicago: University of Chicago Press, 2012.

Wimmer, Andreas. "Race-Centrism: A Critique and a Research Agenda." *Ethnic and Racial Studies* 38, no. 13 (2015): 2187–2205.

Winant, Howard. "Response to Andreas Wimmer." *Ethnic and Racial Studies* 38, no. 13 (2015): 2206–7.

———. *The World Is a Ghetto: Race and Democracy since World War II*. New York: Basic Books, 2001.

Wirth, Louis. *The Ghetto*. Piscataway, NJ: Transaction, 1998.

Woodward, Comer Vann. *The Strange Career of Jim Crow*. New York: Oxford University Press, 1955.

Wortham, Robert A. *The Sociological Souls of Black Folk: Essays by W. E. B. Du Bois*. Lanham, MD: Lexington Books, 2011.

———. "W. E. B. Du Bois, the Black Church, and the Sociological Study of Religion." *Sociological Spectrum* 29, no. 2 (2009): 144–72.

Wright, Earl, II. *The First American School of Sociology: W. E. B. Du Bois and the Atlanta Sociological Laboratory*. New York: Routledge, 2016.

Young, Alford A., Jr. "W. E. B. Du Bois and the Sociological Canon." *Contexts* 14, no. 4 (2015): 60–61.

———. "White Ethnographers on the Experiences of African American Men." *White Logic, White Methods: Racism and Methodology*, 179–200. Lanham, MD: Rowman & Littlefield, 2008.

Zamir, Shamoon. *Dark Voices: W. E. B. Du Bois and American Thought, 1888–1903*. Chicago: University of Chicago Press, 1995.

Zimmerman, Andrew. *Alabama in Africa: Booker T. Washington, the German Empire, and the Globalization of the New South*. Princeton, NJ: Princeton University Press, 2010.

Zorbaugh, Harvey Warren. *The Gold Coast and the Slum: A Sociological Study of Chicago's Near North Side*. Chicago: University of Chicago Press, 1983.

Zuberi, Tukufu. *Thicker Than Blood: How Racial Statistics Lie*. Minneapolis: University of Minnesota Press, 2001.

———. "W. E. B. Du Bois's Sociology: *The Philadelphia Negro* and Social Science." *Annals of the American Academy of Political and Social Science* 595, no. 1 (2004): 146–56.

Zuberi, Tukufu, and Eduardo Bonilla-Silva. *White Logic, White Methods: Racism and Methodology*. Lanham, MD: Rowman & Littlefield, 2008.

INDEX

Abbot, Andrew, 123–24, 125–26
Abrahams, Peter, 173
abstract universalism, 60, 221
activism, 182; collaborations in, 12; cooperative economy advocated in, 8; dismantling color line, 3, 5; education and, 4–5; embrace of socialism, 11; Encyclopedia Africana as, 12; feud with Washington, 6; Garvey confrontation in, 8; Marxism and, 9; NAACP, 41, 46, 51; Niagara Movement, 7, 46; Pan-Africanism and, 3, 8, 10, 11; racism and, 3; radical activist, 1; of scholar activist, activist scholar, 2–13, 191; studies and publications, 5–6, 9; for world peace, 10
Addams, Jane, 12
"Address to the Nations of the World" (Du Bois), 63, 230n11
Africana diaspora, 4, 7, 8, 11, 96, 188; anticolonial movement and, 10, 25, 173; identity and, 19; in modern world history, 64
African Americans, 99; African American experience, 3, 96, 138, 182; lived experience of, 182; women, 85–86
African anticolonial movement, 10
Africanness, 68
Against Epistemic Apartheid (Rabaka), 13
agency, 106; of African American women, 85; from Black communities, 58; Black people and, 16; Black Radical Tradition and, 18; capacity for, 22; comparisons of, 53–56; defined, 217; in Du Boisian sociology, 17–19; free will and, 53, 188;

The Philadelphia Negro on, 118; pragmatism and, 56; in racialized groups, 51–52; Sewell on, 55–56; in sociology, 7; in uplift process, 191; white agency, 52, 189
All African People's Congress, 72
Allegory of the Cave (Plato), 38–39, 42
American empirical sociology, 1, 125, 189, 199
American Journal of Sociology, 170–71
American Monthly Review of Reviews, 135
American Negro Academy, 19
analytical bifurcation, 198, 245n8
Anderson, Nels, 123, 239n67, 246n14
anti-Black racism, 101–2
anticolonial movement, 10, 25, 173, 231n17
anticolonial solidarity, 11, 50
Appiah, Kwame Anthony, 20
Asylums (Goffman), 53
Atlanta Compromise Speech (Washington), 6
Atlanta Conference, 111, 172
Atlanta University: Atlanta Studies, 5, 13, 22–23, 99, 111–12, 114, 116; first position at, 5; forced retirement from, 9–10; resignation from, 141, 142, 146; return to, 8, 167–72. *See also* era of Atlanta University and cooperative economy
Atlantic magazine, 27
The Autobiography of W. E. B. Du Bois (Du Bois), 2, 52, 132; sociological understanding in, 190; on trial, 175–76
auto-ethnography, 9, 38, 114, 129, 203

ABOUT THE AUTHORS

José Itzigsohn is Professor of Sociology at Brown University. His work centers the analysis of racialized modernity, focusing both on the political economy of inequality and on processes of identity and group formation. He is the author of *Developing Poverty* and *Encountering American Faultlines: Race, Class, and Dominican Experience in Providence*. His current interest is in the development of Du Boisian sociology.

Karida L. Brown is Assistant Professor in the Departments of Sociology and African American Studies at UCLA, and a proud Du Boisian sociologist. She earned her PhD in Sociology from Brown University in 2016, and an MPA in Government Administration from the University of Pennsylvania in 2011. She is a historical and cultural sociologist whose research interests are centered on processes of racialization, subject formation, and the social construction of the self. Her book, *Gone Home: Race and Roots through Appalachia*, examines the emergence and transformation of African American subjectivity throughout the pre- and post–civil rights era.